MINORITY RELIGIONS AND FRAUD

Almost as long as organized religions have existed, some have faced charges of fraud and deception. It is valuable, then, to have a scholarly and readable collection of chapters that allow us to understand the roots of these charges, and the reasons why some systems in particular lend themselves to abuse and manipulation. Particularly intriguing is the question of when a non-provable claim veers from a matter of faith to an issue of fraud. Impressively broad in its scope, Minority Religions and Fraud *is an innovative and truly useful contribution to the literature on religious studies, as well as to criminology.*

Philip Jenkins, Baylor University, USA

Religion sometimes presents a theatre for deception and chicanery, with the high drama that can attend these. This book provides a timely correction to the media image that only several large denominations or congregations currently experience this phenomenon, and it is a welcome addition to a growing research literature on the less-than-uplifting aspects of religious practice.

Anson Shupe, Indiana University–Purdue University Fort Wayne, USA

Analysing both fraud and religion as social constructs with different functions and meanings attributed to them, this book raises issues that are central to debates about the limits of religious toleration in diverse societies, and the possible harm (as well as benefits) that religious organizations can visit upon society and individuals. There has already been a lively debate concerning the structural context in which abuse, especially sexual abuse, can be perpetrated within religion. Contributors to the volume proceed from the premise that similar arguments about ways in which structure and power may be conducive to abuse can be made about fraud and deception. Both can contribute to abuse, yet they are often less easily demonstrated and proven, hence less easily prosecuted.

With a focus on minority religions, the book offers a comparative overview of the concept of religious fraud by bringing together analyses of different types of fraud or deception (financial, bio-medical, emotional, breach of trust and consent). Contributors examine whether fraud is necessarily intentional (or whether that is in the eye of the beholder); certain structures may be more conducive to fraud; followers willingly participate in it. The volume includes some chapters focused on non-Western beliefs (Juju, Occult Economies, Dharma Lineage), which have travelled to the West and can be found in North American and European metropolitan areas.

Ashgate Inform Series on Minority Religions and Spiritual Movements

Series Editor: Eileen Barker,
London School of Economics, Chair and Honorary Director of Inform

Advisory Board:
Afe Adogame, University of Edinburgh, UK,
Madawi Al-Rasheed, King's College, London, UK,
Irena Borowik, Jagiellonian University, Krakow, Poland,
Douglas E. Cowan, University of Waterloo, Ontario, Canada,
Adam Possamai, University of Western Sydney, Australia,
James T. Richardson, University of Nevada, Reno, USA,
Fenggang Yang, Purdue University, USA

Inform is an independent charity that collects and disseminates accurate, balanced and up-to-date information about minority religious and spiritual movements. The Ashgate Inform book series addresses themes related to new religions, many of which have been the topics of Inform seminars. Books in the series will attract both an academic and interested general readership, particularly in the areas of Religious Studies, and the Sociology of Religion and Theology.

Other titles in this series:

Global Religious Movements Across Borders
Sacred Service
Edited by Stephen M. Cherry and Helen Rose Ebaugh

Revisionism and Diversification in New Religious Movements
Edited by Eileen Barker

State Responses to Minority Religions
Edited by David M. Kirkham

Minority Religions and Fraud

In Good Faith

Edited by

AMANDA VAN ECK DUYMAER VAN TWIST
Inform, London, UK

ASHGATE

Published by
Ashgate Publishing Limited
Wey Court East
Union Road
Farnham
Surrey, GU9 7PT
England

Ashgate Publishing Company
110 Cherry Street
Suite 3-1
Burlington, VT 05401-3818
USA

www.ashgate.com

British Library Cataloguing in Publication Data
A catalogue record for this book is available from the British Library

The Library of Congress has cataloged the printed edition as follows:
Minority religions and fraud : in good faith / edited by Amanda van Eck Duymaer van Twist.
    pages cm. – (Ashgate inform series on minority religions and spiritual movements)
    Includes bibliographical references and index.
    ISBN 978-1-4724-0911-9 (hardcover : alk. paper) – ISBN 978-1-4724-0912-6 (ebook) – ISBN 978-1-4724-0913-3 (epub) 1. Religions. 2. Religious minorities. 3. Cults. 4. Fraud. 5. Deception. I. Van Twist, Amanda van Eck Duymaer, editor.
    BL80.3.M56 2014
    201'.7–dc23

2014006141

ISBN 9781472409119 (hbk)
ISBN 9781472409126 (ebk – PDF)
ISBN 9781472409133 (ebk – ePUB)

Printed in the United Kingdom by Henry Ling Limited,
at the Dorset Press, Dorchester, DT1 1HD

Contents

Notes on Contributors

David G. Bromley is Professor of Religious Studies in the School of World Studies and Professor of Sociology in the L. Douglas Wilder School of Government and Public Affairs at Virginia Commonwealth University. He has written or edited over a dozen books on religious movements. Books published since 2000 include *Cults and New Religions*, with Douglas Cowan (Blackwell/Wiley, 2008); *Teaching New Religious Movements* (Oxford University Press, 2007); *Defining Religion: Critical Approaches to Drawing Boundaries Between Sacred and Secular*, with Arthur Greil (Elsevier Science/JAI Press, 2003); *Cults, Religion and Violence*, with J. Gordon Melton (Cambridge University Press, 2001) and *Toward Reflexive Ethnography: Participating, Observing, Narrating*, with Lewis Carter (Elsevier Science/JAI Press, 2001). Dr Bromley is former president of the Association for the Study of Religion, founding editor of the ASR's annual series, *Religion and the Social Order*, and former editor of the *Journal for the Scientific Study of Religion*, published by the Society for the Scientific Study of Religion. He is currently director of the Partnership for Understanding World Religions and Spirituality, and project director of the World Religions and Spirituality Project at Virginia Commonwealth University.

Michael Coffey is a London-based conjuror and mind-reader. He specializes in the deceptive practices of the fraudulent mediums of the nineteenth century, taking into account both the psychologies employed and the material ruses.

Simon Coleman is Jackman Professor at the Department for the Study of Religion, University of Toronto. He is co-editor of the journal *Religion and Society: Advances in Research* and previously was editor of the *Journal of the Royal Anthropological Institute*. His research interests include charismatic Christianity, the Faith Movement, pilgrimage, and hospital chaplaincy. He has conducted fieldwork in Sweden, England and Nigeria. Publications include *The Globalisation of Charismatic Christianity* (Cambridge University Press, 2000) and *Religion, Identity, and Change: Perspectives on Global Transformations*, editor, with Peter Collins (Ashgate, 2004). A recent piece on economics and the Faith Movement was published as 'Prosperity Unbound? Debating the "Sacrificial Economy"', _Research in Economic Anthropology_ 31: 23–45, 2011.

Marion Dapsance holds a PhD in Anthropology (Ecole Pratique des Hautes Études – Sorbonne, Paris). She works on Buddhist modernism and other forms of cultural hybridity and misunderstandings.

Amanda van Eck Duymaer van Twist is the deputy director of Inform, a non-profit information centre specializing in minority religious and fringe political movements, based at the London School of Economics and Political Science (LSE). Her research on the second generation of sectarian movements and the impact their segregated childhoods have had, is due to be published with Oxford University Press. Further publications include an article entitled 'Beliefs in Possession' in _The Devil's Children. From Spirit Possession to Witchcraft: New Allegations That Affect Children_, edited by Inform's research fellow Emeritus Professor Jean la Fontaine (2009), and 'Children in New Religions: Contested Duties of Care', _Journal of the International Society for the Study of New Religious Movements_ 1(2): 25–48 (2010).

Holly Folk is an Associate Professor in the Liberal Studies Department of Western Washington University in Bellingham, WA, where she teaches comparative religion. A cultural historian, her research focuses on 19th and 20th century dissenting social movements. She is especially interested in new religious movements, communal societies, and alternative spirituality and medicine. Folk is working on a book on chiropractic and its populist and vitalist ideological heritage.

Marion S. Goldman is Professor of Sociology and Religious Studies at the University of Oregon. Her research focuses on new religious movements and religious violence. Her books include _The American Soul Rush: Esalen and the Rise of Spiritual Privilege_ (New York University Press, 2012) and _Passionate Journeys: Why Successful Women Joined a Cult_ (University of Michigan Press, 1999). Her current work deals with new religious movements and cultural innovation.

Hermione Harris has a PhD in Social Anthropology from the School of Oriental and African Studies (SOAS) where she is a research associate. She has worked for many years with ethnic minorities in Britain, and her publications include _The Somali Community in the UK: What we know and how we know it_ (ICAR, 2004) and _Yoruba in Diaspora: An African Church in London_ (Palgrave

Macmillan, 2006). She is currently involved in preparing Expert Opinions for cases involving young Nigerian women trafficked into Europe for prostitution.

Stuart Lachs started Zen practice in 1967 and maintains it to this day. His research interests are Zen Buddhism and the sociology of religion, and he has been active in the Columbia University Buddhist Studies Workshop and the Princeton University Buddhist Studies Workshop. Later, he joined the Oslo University Buddhist Studies Forum where he has presented three times. He has presented papers at the annual conferences of the American Academy of Religion (AAR), the Association of Asian Studies (AAS) and at the International Association of Buddhist Studies (IABS).

Martin Lindhardt has a PhD in social anthropology from the University of Aarhus, Denmark, and is an associate professor in cultural sociology at the University of Southern Denmark. His research and writing focus on Pentecostalism in Chile and on Charismatic Christianity and witchcraft in Tanzania. He is the author of *Power in Powerlessness, A Study of Pentecostal Life Worlds in Urban Chile* (Brill, 2012) and the editor of *Practicing the Faith. The Ritual Life of Pentecostal Charismatic Christians* (Berghahn, 2011).

Stuart McClean has a PhD in social anthropology and is a senior lecturer at the University of the West of England. Stuart is a fellow of the Royal Anthropological Institute and book review editor for the international journal *Health*. Primarily he is interested in complementary and alternative health practices, the people who practice them, the ideas and principles underpinning them, and the individuals who use them. He is co-author (with E. Frost) of *Thinking About the Lifecourse: a Psychosocial Introduction* (Palgrave, 2014).

Ronnie Moore has a D.Phil in Social Anthropology and works in Public Health Medicine at University College Dublin, Ireland. His interests are in folk and alternative medicines, ethnicity, identity, conflict theory and health. Ronnie is a fellow of the Royal Anthropological Institute. He is currently PI on a large European FP7 research project looking at social, cultural and behaviour aspects of research on pandemics. Ronnie and Stuart McClean are co-editors of *Folk Healing and Health Care Practices in Britain and Ireland* (Berghahn, 2010).

Acknowledgements

There are several individuals who should be thanked for having a part in the creation of this volume. Professor James Beckford raised the question of a potential link between affinity fraud and religion, especially when religion appears in unexpected places – or when it involves endeavours that normally are not self-evidently religious.[1] Professor Eileen Barker, the series editor, fully supported, as always, the further investigation of this issue and the publication of new ideas. Both Professors Beckford and Barker have long been exemplary, and a great influence in the work of Inform, and of its staff. The feedback on the book proposal received from readers on the series' editorial board has been gratefully received and incorporated.

I also thank all staff at Inform for their support, for taking on some extra work in order to help make this volume happen, and for listening to and commenting on the ideas and efforts involved: Adviya Khan, Sibyl Macfarlane and Silke Steidinger. In particular, I thank Sarah Harvey and Suzanne Newcombe for helping with the editorial red pen, and for feedback on my contributions – for which I thank Nick Parke as well. I am also indebted to the contributors of this volume, who I thank for their insights and dedication, and to the editorial team at Ashgate, Sarah Lloyd and David Shervington.

Finally, but essentially, a large thank you to those who have communicated to me their frustrations, thoughts, feelings and insights after having been defrauded by a trusted religious teacher. These include the individuals who bravely allowed me to use communications in my contribution to this volume, and those who have contacted Inform and told their stories in an effort to bring fraudulent behaviour to light and to inform others.

---

[1] Beckford, J. (2010). 'Constructing Religion in Unexpected Places: Phishers of Men and Women', *Implicit Religion*, 13(1): 71–83.

Introduction

Amanda van Eck Duymaer van Twist

Toleration of religious diversity has become an important pillar of contemporary society, but as religions become more innovative and diverse, more questions are raised. What are the lines between legitimate faith and illegitimate exploitation of an individual's credulity? For example, how can we distinguish between spiritual encouragement and emotional manipulation, between charging for religious services and extortion, between a sage and a charlatan? How, when dealing with religion in contemporary society, can we identify religious fraud? Can we be certain that we are not persecuting misunderstood conventions? Finally, is it possible to find the right balance between regulation and freedom of religion?

Over the years, Inform has been involved in a couple of court cases where a religious leader was charged on criminal charges.[1] In those cases, professionals involved in the case would speak in disparaging terms about the associated beliefs and ask us questions along the lines of 'Do you think the leader believes this himself?', and occasionally make incredulous statements along the lines of 'I cannot believe the followers fell for this.' Invariably, the religious leaders in question were seen as fraudsters who did not believe themselves the message they were 'peddling', and the followers as victims who should have known better. This is a simplistic binary representation that may fit a minority of scenarios. Perhaps these assumptions are a better 'fit' for those groups where the weight of evidence against them is such that allegations do eventually go to court.

But of course things are never simple. In most cases, 'fraudsters' and 'victims' in the contemporary religious scene cannot be unambiguously categorized. When fraud and religion come together, there are inevitably questions about

---

[1]   Inform is an independent charity that was founded in 1988 by Professor Eileen Barker with the support of the British Home Office and the mainstream Churches. It is based at the London School of Economics. The primary aim of Inform is to help people by providing them with information that is as accurate, balanced, and up-to-date as possible about alternative religious, spiritual and esoteric movements. See http://inform.ac/ (accessed 14 March 2014).

causality. Is a particular religion inherently fraudulent, a cover for fraud, a motivator in fraud, invoked in fraud, or simply incidental context? Issues of right and wrong become muddled when alleged supernatural forces and subjective hopes and expectations enter the equation, along with novel and unfamiliar religious beliefs, practices, and forms of association. This volume will examine these problems by focusing on the concept of fraud.

Mechanisms used to facilitate fraud can be found ubiquitously in religious contexts, for example, power differences, hierarchical structures, access to fellow believers, and a context of faith, affinity and trust. Despite this, none of the UK main fraud information sources mentions religion in conjunction with fraud (although the Serious Fraud Office does, in their fraud taxonomy, mention 'abuse of position of trust' under 'fraud against the individual'). The UK Fraud Advisory Panel, in conjunction with the Metropolitan Police, published a booklet to alert people to fraud, which includes a page about psychic and clairvoyant scams.[2] But the emphasis here is on 'scammers', rather than on the beliefs and the larger group and/or context. Yet beliefs can be used for exploitative purposes (van Eck Duymaer van Twist 2010: 4). Furthermore, religions and the organizational forms they take can form a smokescreen for authorities (the victim chose to get involved, the deception was not intentional, this is about race, gender, nationality, culture, or other issues).

The issues raised in this volume are central to vibrant academic debates on the limits of religious toleration in diverse societies, and contemporary debates about the possible harm (as well as benefits) that religious organizations can inflict upon society and individuals. Anson Shupe, a leading criminologist, has written several books on abuse in religion, focusing mainly on clergy malfeasance and child abuse within churches (1995, 1998, 2007a, 2007b). He has done much to analyse the structural context in which abuse can be perpetrated within religion. This volume will proceed from the premise that similar arguments about ways in which structure and power may be conducive to abuse can also be made for fraud. It will offer a comparative overview of the concept of religious fraud by combining papers about different types of fraud (financial, biomedical, emotional, breach of trust and consent). And it will focus on minority religions, beliefs and/or practices, that is, lifestyles that are considered outside of the mainstream. In doing so, specific questions are addressed, including whether such social structures, cultures and/or fringe religious beliefs particular to minority and/or marginal communities may be more likely to enable fraud.

---

[2]   http://www.met.police.uk/docs/little_book_scam.pdf (accessed 14 March 2014).

promising big returns on investments. As a preacher's son, he knew the language to reach the congregations to which he was introduced.[13] Taylor is accused of a variety of violations, including operating a pyramid scheme involving $11 million, primarily aimed at socially conscious investors within African-American congregations.[14] But some victims are suing their bishop, Eddie Long, as well, arguing that he abused his position and 'coerced' his parishioners into investing in Taylor's fund.[15] The feel-good factor involved in Taylor's ruse, investing in socially conscious projects, was attractive to his particular congregations. This is reminiscent of the Foundation for New Era Philanthropy, a pyramid scheme that initially focused on non-profit organizations and Christian charities, but later expanded to include some public organizations.[16]

Beliefs that people hold can be harnessed for good purposes, but also for exploitative purposes (van Eck Duymaer van Twist 2010: 4). The Greater Ministries International Church (GMI) took in a reported half-billion dollars from tens of thousands of believers over several congregations throughout the US. Many of the investors were fundamentalist Christians, including Mennonites in rural Pennsylvania, Ohio and Virginia. They were told their money would double; investors were quoted Luke 6:38: 'Give, and it shall be

---

[13] See, for example, http://www.economist.com/node/21543526 (accessed 14 March 2014).

[14] See, for example, http://www.sec.gov/news/press/2012/2012-62.htm and http://www.huffingtonpost.com/2011/12/02/ephren-taylor-youngest-ceo-faces-lawsuits-over-ponzi-schemes_n_1125187.html (accessed 9 April 2013).Pyramid schemes, sometimes called 'Ponzi schemes' are frauds based on an unsustainable business model that involves promising participants payment or services, primarily for enrolling other people into the scheme, rather than supplying any real investment or sale of products or s ervices to the public (http://www.fbi.gov/scams-safety/fraud/fraud#pyramid) (accessed 1 November 2013).

[15] See http://www.huffingtonpost.com/2011/12/02/ephren-taylor-youngest-ceo-faces-lawsuits-over-ponzi-schemes_n_1125187.html (accessed 9 April 2013).

[16] It operated in the area around Philadelphia, Pennsylvania, USA, affecting 1,100 individuals and charities, including more than 180 evangelical groups, colleges, and seminaries. John G. Bennett, a Christian businessman, invited his friends to become beneficiary donors, promising that secret donors would match any contribution paid, which would double their contributions. Bennett had some famous philanthropists as friends, and people assumed these were the secret donors. Bennett was charged in 1996 in an 82 count indictment, found guilty, and sentenced to 12 years in prison. See http://www.fbi.gov/philadelphia/about-us/history/famous-cases/famous-cases-foundation-for-new-era-philanthropy (accessed 9 April 2013).

given unto you.'[17] GMI's leaders, Gerald and Betty Payne, insisted in court that their actions were guided by the Holy Spirit. They were sentenced to 27 (Gerald) and 12 (Betty) years.

The notion that your money will double by God's will is a powerful motivation for those who believe. Faith, after all, is the main force behind both placebos and nocebos. This may explain some issues for the victims of fraud or deception; there are ways in which they can be manipulated. But what do we know about the perpetrators? Are they always swindlers? When fraud or deception happens within the context of religious beliefs, among the faithful, the distinction between 'good faith' and 'bad faith' is not always easy to establish.

What if the perpetrator believes in something that turns out to be a scam? The religious group may be 'genuine' (whatever that means), but suffer from a negative public image, because of how they are perceived rather than the nature of their beliefs/practices. There may be situations, as Beckford has argued (1985: 293), where religious groups insist they are spiritually authentic while their opponents cry 'charlatan'. Also, a leader may use small deceptions in order to lead people to the 'truth' in the spirit of 'the ends justify the means.' Are the actions then really motivated by 'ill will' alone?

One of the original religious movements founded on teachings of the Ascended Masters, I AM Activity, founded in the early 1930s by Guy Ballard (1878–1939) and his wife Edna (1886–1971), brought us a seminal fraud case within a small religious movement. The movement, influenced by Theosophy, had up to a million followers in 1938 (Barrett 1996: 191). Having reportedly encountered Saint Germain, the Ascended Master, while hiking on Mount Shasta, Guy Ballard began publishing the messages of Saint Germain and other Ascended Masters, and trained others to spread the messages across the USA. I AM became a predecessor of several New Age movements, and is itself still active on a smaller scale.

In 1942, Mrs Ballard and her son were charged with 18 counts of mail fraud – namely the 'false and fraudulent representations, pretences and promises' contained in the material sent through the mail, through which they were charged to have fraudulently collected over $43 million from their followers. The materials contained the messages from Ascended Masters as reportedly given to the Ballards, the divine messengers, which included claims of healing otherwise incurable illnesses. The indictment in essence charged Mrs Ballard

---

[17]   See http://www.crimes-of-persuasion.com/Crimes/InPerson/MajorPerson/affinity. htm and http://www.christianitytoday.com/ct/2001/october1/15.21.html (accessed 9 April 2013).

and her son with *knowingly* offering false representations through the US Mail for fraudulent purposes.

The presiding judge advised the jury that some of the teachings may seem improbable, but that whether these statements are true or not is neither the concern of the court, nor the jury. The cardinal question, he argued, is whether the defendants 'honestly and in good faith believe those things':

> The question of the defendants' good faith is the cardinal question in this case. You are not to be concerned with the religious belief of the defendants, or any of them. The jury will be called upon to pass on the question of whether or not the defendants honestly and in good faith believed the representations which are set forth in the indictment, and honestly and in good faith believed that the benefits which they represented would flow from their belief to those who embraced and followed their teachings, or whether these representations were mere pretenses without honest belief on the part of the defendants or any of them, and, were the representations made for the purpose of procuring money, and were the mails used for this purpose.[18]

The jury found them guilty, but later the conviction was overturned on the grounds that the judge should not have excluded the credibility of the beliefs from consideration. Yet later again, the decision and conviction were affirmed (and later again overturned after it was found that women had been wrongfully excluded from the jury).[19] In the end, the court ruled that the teachings of the I AM movement were immaterial, because content of religious convictions cannot be judged as either correct or incorrect. It also ruled that it was proper for the jury to base its decision on the sincerity of the Ballard's beliefs – hence they could believe whatever they wanted as long as they believed it in good faith.

Some judges dissented from the legal strategy. Justice Jackson argued that the judiciary should not be examining people's faith. Hence he disagreed with the judge ruling that on the one hand the court should not try whether the statements were untrue, but that, on the other hand, it could inquire whether the defendants knew them to be untrue. He asked, 'How can the Government

---

[18]   http://caselaw.lp.findlaw.com/cgi-bin/getcase.pl?court=us&vol=322&invol=78 (accessed 1 November 2013).
[19]   http://supreme.justia.com/cases/federal/us/329/187/case.html (accessed 1 November 2013).

prove these persons knew something to be false which it cannot prove to be false?'[20]

There have been, without a doubt, clear cases of intentional fraud – and religious groups can on occasion form evocatively enabling frames for this. But there have also been accusations of fraud where the intentions were ambiguous, where the perpetrator may have been a believer, or both a believer and a fraud. Whether someone genuinely believes something is difficult to establish. Furthermore, in some interactions, any results cannot be easily proven to be the result of the methods/means involved. Take, for example, what some people refer to as pseudo-medicine, or alternative healing: how can a healer prove, taking placebo effects and other correlations into consideration, that the client was healed because of the healer's interventions? And, how can the client prove that they were not healed due to the healer's lack of skills and/or metaphysical contacts? The healer may just argue that the client was not healed because they didn't believe enough in the metaphysical elements involved in the prescribed cure.[21]

Deliberate deception is not necessarily straightforward, as one cannot always prove that the deception was deliberate. And not all deception is inevitably completely deceptive; deception, beguilement, mystification and subterfuge are ambiguous acts that may involve truths as well as half-truths, omissions, or other sleights of hand. This is especially the case when faith, beliefs and/or alleged supernatural elements are involved, all of which can be quite unpredictable, inconsistent and temperamental. The final goal on offer is always a very desirable one, such as good health, riches, happiness or even salvation – hence the means are often seen to justify the ends. This is easily justified and rationalized (perhaps with a bit of subterfuge).

Deceptive or even fraudulent acts involve violations of expectations, but expectations can always be miscommunicated and/or misunderstood. Furthermore, expectations are personal, and subjective. As Beckford has argued, ' ... it is our expectations that define what counts as unexpected' (2010: 72). In some cases we also suffer from self-deception – perhaps a wilful blindness in the building of our expectations. This, in turn, can also be exploited, as grifters rely on human characteristics (such as greed, (dis)honesty, vanity, compassion, credulity) as part of their act. Hence it is rarely a one-way act, rather a game of give-and-take, a two-way street.

---

[20]   http://caselaw.lp.findlaw.com/cgi-bin/getcase.pl?court=us&vol=322&invol=78 (accessed 14 March 2014).

[21]   As religions in general tend to emphasize the importance of faith over proof, legal arguments around religious beliefs are bound to be problematic.

This Volume

In this volume, there are, naturally, descriptive analyses of cases of fraud. However, many of the chapters also question the concept of fraud itself – its use and its function highlighting the often subjective nature. Quite a few chapters question the motivations behind accusations of fraud and the contexts in which accusations have been made. The analysis hasn't ended there, several chapters also provide introspective reflections on the process of research. Throughout the chapters in this volume, some themes have emerged.

The Social Status of Minority Religions

Many of the chapters comment on the social status of the religious movements involved in issues of fraud; often they are seen as significantly different to the 'majority' culture. This makes for an increased likelihood of them being misunderstood, as well as an increased likelihood of them being faulted – they are visible and different. Bromley, who analyses the characteristics of both religious movements and society that may lead to attributions of fraud, emphasizes that new religious groups by their very nature challenge existing cultural and social logic, and as a result create more discord as they mobilize. Hence they make themselves vulnerable to allegations that they make false representations – and their social status makes them more likely to be accused. This sentiment is also discussed by Coffey (in a chapter about the role of trickery and deception in magic and religion), who argues that targeting the fake psychics and spiritualists seems to be more than a little like shooting fish in a barrel, and we should perhaps be asking ourselves some deeper questions about why their trade has persisted throughout history. Coleman, who discusses Prosperity Christianity, argues that fraud engenders epistemological as well as motivational questions, hence we should be aware of the function of accusations of fraud in our society. He argues that the label of 'fraud' on a religion can be considered as the witchcraft accusations of our time, revealing how moral frameworks are frequently constructed around and in protection of local systems of authority and law, but also how believers and their opponents, 'cults' and 'anti-cults' (Beckford 1985: 7), co-create religious controversy – and themselves – through their interactions (this volume, p. 77).

McClean and Moore, in their chapter about folk healing, question on what basis things are defined as either trustworthy or fraudulent. They ask whether ideas of authenticity and credibility are perhaps not more subjective than we, as a society, perceive them to be. In comparison to the global dominance of bio-medicine, folk healing is stigmatized and consequently questions about fraud are never far. This idea becomes more pertinent when considered in conjunction with Lindhardt's chapter entitled 'Miracle Makers and Money Takers', where he describes how complex changes in social circumstances (such as commercialization of religion) have contributed to the emergence of a culture of distrust of providers of spiritual products and services. With increasing diversification, the moral reputation of some providers has been put into question.

The marginal status of groups and communities interacts with the legitimacy they are given. New and alternative groups are least likely to be part of accepted safety and regulation structures, and more likely to be operating outside of these structures or as part of a self-regulating network. Folk, in mapping out an approach in analysing and understanding what she refers to as 'ritual fakery', argues that ritual fakery happens throughout the world religions as well as in new religions, but that sectarian patterns of leadership can certainly provide an edge to ritual deception.

Personal Commitment

Several chapters comment on the significance of personal perspective and the importance of feeling part of a community and the narrative of meaning and purpose to life. How they come to define the process has an important role to play. In these chapters, cries of 'fraud' come from those who have been disappointed in their expectations, and have come to redefine their experiences in light of their disappointment. Both Goldman and Van Eck Duymaer van Twist discuss that such a so-called 'change of heart' may very well depend on the social structure. Goldman, who presents different perspectives on fraud in minority religions, suggests that as members redefine their histories, some question whether what seemed like a good idea, but later appeared to have led to undesirable consequences, was really freely chosen. From this perspective, what later seems like fraud, may actually not be the result of manipulation or purposeful exploitation perpetrated by leadership. Previous acquiescence may have been based on the suspension of disbelief, or wishful thinking. Goldman's research suggests that those who leave are likely to interpret their past more negatively. Those who remain with the group are more likely to continue to see it in a positive light, as a necessary stage, any problematic aspects justified by positive results. As Goldman writes, faith may negate dissent, while scepticism may encourage it (this volume, p. 149).

Van Eck Duymaer van Twist describes that interpretations of 'what happened' may suffer from their own forms of sleight of hand, as history is stylized, and personal or social narratives of denial infiltrate. The social environment around an individual influences what conclusions participants make with the benefit of hindsight. Perhaps it is not only our expectations that define what counts as unexpected, as Beckford wrote, but also the defining and contextualizing of the experiences that follow these expectations (2010: 72). In Marion Dapsance's chapter, a case study analysing the spiritual path of some devotees in Rigpa, a Tibetan Buddhist group, this issue comes to light as she describes women who have found difficulty in defining the nature of their relationship with their guru. From her ethnographic research, she has found that although unusual 'crazy wisdom' teachings were contextualized, ritualized and explained in group-contexts, the more intimate and private relationships some former members have reported with the leader were not ritualized and contextualized in this way – hence they became more complicated to define and understand within the overall experience of the spiritual life in Rigpa.

But is it really fraud?

Harris raises the question of whether the perpetrators believe in what they are doing, and whether it can be considered fraud if they are acting in 'good faith'. In her research, juju and curses were used in criminal cases of human trafficking. For the victims, beliefs that they were affected by juju and curses helped to control them. But what did these rituals represent to the perpetrators? Are the threats used cynically to control the victims, did the traffickers themselves fully believe in the power of juju (perhaps being afflicted by a curse themselves), or were the curses commissioned to bring the traffickers better luck and fortune? The wider question here is: does the definition of fraud depend on purposeful or conscious deception? This question is raised by many of the contributors, including Folk, McClean and Moore, and Van Eck Duymaer van Twist. For example, in the context of healing practices, McClean and Moore describe how medicine men may 'add on' to their ritual specialties. This is also discussed by Folk in her chapter. Both chapters raise the point that this in itself is not evidence that they do not believe in what they are doing; this does not make it a conscious or wilful deception. Or does it?

Lachs, in his chapter about Dharma transmission in Zen Buddhism, also considers deception to be a complex issue – he analyses this issue as both an insider and a scholar. He argues that deception implies intentionality, which cannot always be clearly established. For example, one could see Zen's history as mythology established over a thousand years. If a leader relies on the reification of such a mythologized lineage for authority, is this an intentional misrepresentation to mislead for personal gain? Furthermore, if this is half of a *pas de deux* where the other half is filled with particular expectations, should these not also be investigated? The issue of how exactly the weight of responsibility is distributed in a *pas de deux* is also raised in the chapters by Folk, Goldman, Van Eck Duymaer van Twist, and Coffey, among others. As Coffey, a conjurer, writes, 'The majority of people who attend a mind reading show already have pre-existing notions about hypnosis, influence, suggestion, which they wish to have confirmed. Their expectations colour and shape their belief, which in turn determines what they perceive' (this volume, p. 193).

He discusses the work of magicians (as well as, in passing, psychics and spiritualists), and observes that, in cases of accusations of fraud, it appears to him that the small fish are accused of acts that the large fish in the pond manage to get away with unquestioned. If conscious manipulation of beliefs amounts to fraud, should we not hold advertising and marketing agencies more to account? Coffey suggests we should ascertain why we, as humans, so readily put our faith, freedom and material rewards in the hands of individuals and/ or groups without thorough checking, testing and investigation. Folk reminds us of the long history of anthropologists grappling with the problem of ritual fakery, who have detected stagecraft in the rituals of many cultures. In her words, 'Anthropology problematizes the axis of belief and non-belief, by presenting a cascade of evidence of audiences aware of ritual fabrications, and of performing perpetrators who seem to believe in their misrepresentations' (this volume, p. 38). As Coleman argues, patterns of religious commitment, engagement and practice are complex, contradictory, situationally-based and ambiguous (this volume, p. 87). The authors grapple with these complex, ambiguous and often controversial issues from their own perspectives, and in their own way, combine to produce a volume that I hope will challenge assumptions, shed some new light, raise many new questions, and draw attention to patterns and trends in a field where there are no straightforward answers.

This volume is one within a series with Ashgate and Inform. The Ashgate-Inform book series addresses themes related to new religions, many of which have been the topics of seminars, or planned future seminars, organized by Inform.

References

Barrett, D.V. (1996). *Sects, Cults and Alternative Religions: A World Survey and Sourcebook*. London: Blandford.

Beckford, J.A. (1985). *Cult Controversies. Societal Responses to New Religious Movements*. London: Tavistock.

— (2010). 'Constructing Religion in Unexpected Places: Phishers of Men and Women', *Implicit Religion* 13(1): 71–83.

Cohen, M.H. (2002). 'Healing at the Borderland of Medicine and Religion: Regulating Potential Abuse of Authority by Spiritual Healers', *Journal of Law and Religion*, 18(2) (2002–03): 373–426.

Iadicola, P. (1998). 'Criminology's Contributions to the Study of Religious Crime', in *Wolves Within the Fold: Religious Leadership and Abuses of Power*, ed. Anson Shupe. New Brunswick, NJ: Rutgers University Press.

Oppenheimer, M. (2013).'The Zen Buddhist Who Preyed on His Upper East Side Students', *New Republic*, 15 November http://www.newrepublic.com/article/115613/zen-buddhist-sex-controversies-america-excerpt (accessed 14 March 2014).

Shupe, A. (1995). *In the Name of All That's Holy: A Theory of Clergy Malfeasance*. Westport, CT: Praeger.

—, ed. (1998). *Wolves within the Fold: Religious Leadership and Abuses of Power*. New Brunswick, NJ: Rutgers University Press.

— (2007a). *Rogue Clerics: The Social Problem of Clergy Deviance*. New Brunswick, NJ: Transaction.

— (2007b). *Spoils of the Kingdom: Clergy Misconduct and Religious Community*. Champaign: University of Illinois Press.

— and Janelle M. Eliasson-Nannini (2012). *Pastoral Misconduct: The American Black Church Examined*. New Brunswick, NJ: Transaction.

Van Eck Dumymaer van Twist, A. (2010). 'Children in New Religions: Contested Duties of Care', *International Journal for the Study of New Religions*, 1(2): 183–206.

Chapter 1

New Religions and Fraud: A Double Constructionist Approach

David G. Bromley

Allegations of fraud by religious groups and leaders are commonplace throughout history. Such allegations are more likely to be directed at new religious traditions and developing groups. Since new groups by their very nature challenge existing cultural and social logic and since religion offers a foundational meaning system in human groups, it is not surprising that charges of fraudulent belief or conduct occur frequently as these groups mobilize. Allegations of fraud clearly are not unique to religious groups and leaders, of course. Where new economic or political groups, for example, offer radical challenges to the existing social order, the charges rendered against them are remarkably similar. None the less, new religious groups offer particularly fertile ground for investigating the religion-fraud relationship both because they often are contested and because the controversy is contemporary and therefore can be investigated as it is occurring.

In this chapter, I address one specific, but foundational, issue: what are the characteristics of new religions, on the one hand, and conventional society, on the other hand, that lead to attributions of fraud? The premise of the argument to be developed here is that both 'religion' and 'fraud' ultimately are status claims, most broadly to legitimacy and illegitimacy, respectively. The substance of the argument to be pursued here is that (1) new religious groups by their very nature mobilize in such a way as to challenge the established social order and in a way that leaves them vulnerable to fraud allegations, and (2) established institutions by their very nature defend the logic and boundaries of that order, which often makes new religious group claims appear inauthentic and problematic from their perspective. Put another way, new religious groups challenge the existing social order because they arise in response to that order, and they are vulnerable to fraud claims because established institutions are structured so as to defend that order. As new religious groups emerge, these two sets of claims often are occurring simultaneously and stand in opposition to one another. It is this dynamic that underpins the claims-making process, and the outcome of the interactive claims-making process defines the social locations of the group and its opponents at that historical moment (Bromley and Melton 2012).

On the Concepts of Religion and Fraud

Conventional definitions of religion and fraud typically specify what are regarded as the essential characteristics of each. So, for example, definitions of religion often incorporate characteristics, such as beliefs concerning supernatural entities or powers; rituals through which adherents solemnize, enact and validate the mythic system; religious functionaries who mediate between adherents and the supernatural, and moral codes that are binding upon adherents (Wilson 1982). Definitions of fraud refer to false factual representations, knowledge of that falsity by the representer, ignorance of the falsity by the representation receiver, reliance on the representation by the receiver, and damage suffered by the receiver as a result of accepting the false representation.

While essentialist definitions may be useful for certain purposes, I propose an alternative approach that emphasizes the socially constructed qualities of both religion and fraud. From this perspective, both 'religion' and 'fraud' can be productively understood as knowledge and status claims, religion a claim about self and fraud a claim about other. Religion is one subcategory of knowledge claims. Specifically, religion is a claim to the possession of knowledge from a transcendent, sacred power source that reveals the true nature and meaning of the everyday world. This claim, if accepted, legitimates a privileged moral status for the group, since it would putatively benefit those who accept it, and reduce moral status for opponents who would denigrate or deny access to the knowledge. Fraud is a subcategory of deviance claims. Specifically, fraud is a claim of discovery of knowledge that transcends the apparent patterning of another's actions and offers insight into their essential qualities (intentionality). This claim, if accepted, supports a privileged moral status for the accuser, since it presumably offers protection and safety to others who accept the allegation, and reduces the moral status for the perpetrator, who is putatively engaged in a project of secrecy and manipulation.

It is important to emphasize that the social constructionist approach does not in any way deny that both religion and fraud possess *social* reality. Claims-making is not a free-floating process; there is a material base for social claims. There are 'cultural formations' – traditions, conventions, cultural norms, popular culture, media depictions, institutional regulations, and civil and criminal laws – that constitute historically grounded, socially actionable prescriptions and proscriptions of what constitutes religion and fraud, even if these are subject to ongoing amendment. Likewise, there are 'social formations' – religious, governmental, economic, occupational organizations – that represent the legitimate institutionalization in those arenas of social life, possess a stake in existing social arrangements, and operate with independent sanctioning power. These social and cultural formations create and sustain the boundary markers between religion and secular and between legitimate and illegitimate activity. Therefore, while the focus of this chapter is on contextual factors producing attributions of legitimate and illegitimate religion rather than applications of existing definitions to specific cases, both issues are equally important.

The Social Construction of Religion and Fraud

It is virtually axiomatic in social science theory on religion that religion is 'invented', or 'socially constructed' (Smith 1962, Hobsbawn and Ranger 1983, Berger 1990, Cusack 2010). The work of major theorists from Karl Marx and Sigmund Freud to Emile Durkheim and Peter Berger all proceed from the premise that humans create the gods rather than the reverse, even if the theories founded on this common premise move in dramatically different directions. Whether we take William James's 'unseen order', Joseph Campbell's 'invisible plane behind the visible one', or Peter Berger's socially constructed 'sacred cosmos' as the starting point, these formulations share in common what I term a transcendent, sacred power source (hereafter, the transcendent) as the essential feature of what scholars term 'religion'. The social construction of the transcendent usually involves four components:

- symbolic representations of the transcendent and its relationship to the everyday world (mythic narratives);
- symbolic representations of the human source of discovery/knowledge about the transcendent (hagiographies);
- dramatic representations of the independent power of the transcendent and its connection to the everyday world (rituals); and
- social representations of the appropriate relationship to the transcendent (associational collectivities).

The social construction of religion is complicated, however, by the fact that if humans create the transcendent to ensure meaning, order and control in social life, then it must be independent of the creators. That is, the project of social construction must be 'mystified', so that the participation of human actors in the construction process is masked. Mainstream religions in the contemporary world that operate as denominations in an increasingly secular/rational environment manage this issue in a variety of ways, for example, by distancing the past, in which transcendent power was more active, from the present, in which it remains accessible but less deterministic of contemporary events. The composition of the sacred texts is settled and solidified, and mythic texts may come to be viewed in metaphorical rather than literal terms. Hagiographic narratives about the founders are enshrined, but as accounts of enduring wisdom and guiding principles rather than actual historical events. Ritual encounters with the transcendent are moderated and regulated, taking on the form of an aesthetic drama. Associational collectivities move away from covenantally oriented communities toward contractually oriented voluntary networks.

The need to demonstrate the reality, power and accessibility of the transcendent is an historical element common to all the world's major religious traditions, but that need is more immediate for new religious groups. Established religious traditions through history have used a variety of means to make the gods real. Early Greek history offers an instructive example of the active involvement of the priesthood in orchestrating miraculous events:

> The ancients not only formulated the laws of mechanics and put them to practical use but also devised ingenious machines whose only purpose was to serve as marvels ... During the Hellenistic period, mechanical marvels proliferated. We read of temple doors operated by warm air that opened automatically when a fire was lit on the altar and closed again as the flames died down. Philo of Byzantium (third century B.C.) describes in his *Pneumatics* siphons that allow vessels to empty and refill themselves automatically, or pour wine and water alternately. There are also washbasins worked by counterweights and pulleys, which make a bronze hand extend a pumice stone to the user, disappear when he takes it, and reappear to receive it again after enough water has flowed out of a spout to allow him to wash his hands. A major part of a treatise on mechanics by Hero of Alexandria (ca. 100 A.D.) is devoted to similar gadgets. ('Pontus Hulten ...' n.d.)

One of the best documented cases involves Hero of Alexandria, an extraordinary creator of advanced technologies that only centuries later did scientists begin to understand (Boas 1949). Priests in Alexandria were engaged in intense competition for adherents and paid Hero well to develop 'machines of the gods'. He invented a variety of devices that used the heat of the temple fire and steam produced from it to create moving statues, a device that dispensed holy water upon the insertion of coins, temple gates that appeared to open and close automatically, hidden metal balls that fell and produced a sound resembling thunder, and weeping statues (Fylaktou n.d). It seems clear that the priesthood used these extraordinary demonstrations to enhance their own authority and the belief by adherents in the presence and power of the gods. However, the fact that what were perceived by adherents as miraculous events are now recognized as simple, if impressive, technological feats has no impact on contemporary religious faith. Nor do active debates of the actual authorship of sacred texts or accounts of miraculous events in ancient times. The partitioning of the 'sacred times', the social and cultural legitimacy accorded to established religion, and the accommodation of established religion to other institutional arenas substantially insulates these religions from fraud claims.

Such is not the case for new religious groups. These groups are progressively constructing their mythic and hagiographic narratives in the moment; they are devising ritual observances and experimenting with different forms of collective associations. To connect these observations to the central argument, then, new religious groups are likely to be the target of fraud allegations both because they are challenging movements and because they are visibly constructing what is understood to possess an independence from human control. Their contestive stance and vulnerability to disconfirmation yield a steady flow of fraud allegations. Correspondingly, established institutions have formal and informal definitions of legitimate/fraudulent principles, practices and procedures for countering illegitimate conduct. The challenging nature of new religious groups renders them attractive targets for social control measures.

Endogenous Factors in Fraud Allegations

A variety of endogenous characteristics that are elemental to challenging movements, particularly during their initial period of mobilization, have the effect of predisposing movements to activities that are socially defined as fraud. Put another way, these very characteristics, which are central to movements' identity and cohesiveness, are likely to be externally assessed as demonstrating that the group and/or its leadership are fraudulent. They also are constructed in such a way as to increase movements' vulnerabilities to fraud allegations. The characteristics of new religious groups that trigger fraud allegations include claims of sole possession of new knowledge that is transformative in its implications, claims of extraordinary charismatic authority, ritual demonstrations of access to the transcendent, and inappropriate collective associational forms.

Mythologies

The mythic systems of new religious groups predispose them to fraud allegations in four ways:

- they directly challenge established cultural understandings;
- they are vulnerable to charges of not being original, unique discoveries but rather borrowed or stolen ideas;
- they are also vulnerable to questions of authenticity of authorship; and
- the visibility of the construction undermines claims of a transcendent source.

While such common features, ambiguities, and discrepancies are not damaging to established religions, they are to new religious groups.

Since the mythic systems of new movements are formulated in response to the established institutional order of the host society, the challenge they proffer is quite specific and direct. One of the most common claims by new movements is that established religious organizations have been compromised and corrupted beyond redemption. For example, Moses David Berg, founder of the Children of God movement, now known as The Family International, routinely referred to established churches derisively as 'churchianity' (Berg 1984). Claims by religious movements that they alone possess new revelations from the transcendent power source, if taken seriously, destabilize the theologies of established religions, which typically are careful to place the period of revelation in the past. Similarly, prophesies of an impending apocalypse can diminish the viability of the everyday world, thereby undermining the ability of established churches to create a stable meaning system for adherents and preserve their own spiritual authority. New religions may also use their extraordinary revelations and the lofty moral status that derives from those to place themselves above the regulation of a flawed, corrupted social order. For example, both Unificationists and Hare Krishna devotees engaged in deceptive fundraising practices that they justified on the basis that the group was engaged in a morally privileged purpose and the funds collected brought spiritual benefits to the donor, irrespective of the 'donor's' intent. In some cases, broader normative non-compliance is legitimated. Moses David Berg taught followers that the only law to which they were held was the 'Law of Love', which supplanted all other biblical laws. Jehovah's Witnesses have condemned Christianity as a tool of Satan and rejected loyalty to the state, symbolically by refusing to salute the flag and substantively by refusing military service. Rejection of the established normative order moves groups in the direction of being labelled as illegitimate religion. Established religious groups are therefore likely to assert that novel relations are 'heresies', that is, fraudulent doctrines.

A second issue is that the mythic systems of new religious groups that are announced as unique revelations or discoveries are never entirely new; they always draw on contemporary and historical knowledge to some degree, just as established religions have done. Indeed, a number of central components of Christian mythology, such as the virgin birth, a global flood, and a god who dies and then is reborn, pre-date the emergence of Christianity and can be found in other traditions, such as Hinduism. There is ongoing debate over the actual authorship of the sacred Christian texts that became the 'New Testament'. Sun Myung Moon, for example, has been accused of appropriating some basic ideas from another Korean group, the Pure Water Church led by Kim Baekmoon, because some ideas were similar and Moon was in fact a member of that congregation for a time prior to establishing the Holy World Association for the Unification of World Christianity (Chryssides 2007). To the extent that common themes or 'borrowing' can be discerned, the claim to unique knowledge and to a special relationship with the transcendent is undermined, opening up the group to fraud claims.

Third, since sacred texts are typically assembled over an extended period of time and a number of parties contribute to the process, actual authorship is frequently contested. Hammer and Lewis (2007: 7) note that 'The Bible is studded with historically untenable references to its own legendary origins.' And Thomassen (2007: 141) observes that 'Of the twenty-seven writings added to the Jewish Scriptures by the Christians in antiquity as a "New Testament," only seven are unambiguously accepted by modern scholars as genuinely carrying the name of their original author.' The Church of Scientology asserts that all of its teachings are the product of L. Ron Hubbard as he is understood to have discovered and recorded an infallible technology. For Scientologists, the teachings are and must be based on Hubbard's original texts; there can be no changes or additions. However, Rothstein (2007: 35) finds this claim highly questionable. He concludes that 'Texts not written by Hubbard are presented as if they were, because doctrine demands it. Those who actually are behind the Post-Hubbard texts simply cannot appear as authors or editors. Their only possible role is that of caretakers.'

Finally, new religious groups face the problem that myths are being constructed as the movement mobilizes, and so the construction process is simply too visible and therefore more vulnerable to fraud claims. As Palmer and Bromley note with respect to the mythic systems of these groups:

> The two most prominent characteristics of NRM myths and rituals are that they are in the process of being born and they are oppositional in nature. NRM myths express an oppositional stance towards the myths legitimating the institutions of the larger society – churches, state, nuclear family, government, science – or social conventions governing other types of social relationships – race and gender. A survey of case studies reveals that the myth-makers in new religions (usually the charismatic leaders) are deliberately and self-consciously heretical ... The original myth imparted by the charismatic leader also typically undergoes surprising revisions over the course of time, often in response to or at least in synchronicity with, changes of circumstances, censure, or pressure. Because NRM myths are in the process of being constructed and undergo frequent change, they seem to outsiders to have an artificial carefully crafted, self-consciously concocted, expedient quality about them. They appear to be unlike myths found in tribal societies or established religious traditions whose origin is hidden in the mists of time or in the mystery of inadequately documented exotic or ancient cultures whose sacred narratives must be accepted by contemporary scholars as a 'given' that just 'happened'. (Palmer and Bromley 2007: 136)

Leadership

As Max Weber (1964) observed, new religious groups often are founded and led, at least for the first generation, by charismatic individuals. The charismatic founder/leader typically claims some kind discovery (revelation, mystical experience, unearthing of sacred texts) that transcends existing knowledge and that becomes the foundational element of the mythic structure, as discussed above. These leaders, implicitly and often explicitly, also claim elevated moral authority based on their connection to the transcendent sacred power source. In some cases, these claims rise to the level of the charismatic leader claiming prophetic status, as Moses David Berg did, messianic status, as Sun Myung Moon did, or even godly status, as Sai Baba did. It is commonplace for leaders of new groups to initially claim limited charismatic authority but subsequently expand those claims as movement development proceeds. For example, Moses David Berg initially presented himself to followers as 'Uncle Dave', but within a short time had elevated his claims to being 'God's Endtime Prophet.' The leader of the Branch Davidians first joined the Branch Davidians as a handyman under his birth name, Vernon Howell, and subsequently claimed messianic status as David Koresh.

Charismatic leaders do not necessarily confine their charismatic authority claims to their followers, however. They also may attempt to extend their influence by offering their discoveries to leaders of established institutions, as the founder of Transcendental Meditation, Maharishi Mahesh Yogi, had with the United Nations, and Scientology founder, L. Ron Hubbard, did with the psychiatric and psychotherapeutic communities. The leaders of some groups have gone even further and have sought to formally combine secular and religious authority through holding governmental positions. Aum Shinrikyo founder, Shoko Asahara, ran for public office, as did Westboro Baptist Church founder, Fred Phelps. Soka Gakkai formed the Clean Government Party through which its supporters could seek political office, and Rajneeshpuram sought to assume control of the local government, thereby effectively merging the commune and municipality.

These patterns of elevated and expanding moral authority claims by movement leaders function to increase both leader authority and the solidarity and significance of the movement, at least from the perspective of members. However, rhetorical inferences that movement leaders should enjoy enhanced status outside of the movement at least theoretically challenge the legitimate authority of established institution leaders and are immediately rebuffed. Attempts to appropriate actual formal authority outside of the movement usually meet more determined and organized resistance from established interest groups.

The various claims to elevated moral authority are incorporated into hagiographies, spiritual biographies that are filled with elements such as accounts of precocious childhoods, early signs of spiritual qualities, amazing accomplishments, a devotion to the well-being of humanity, and evidence of dramatic moments of connection between the charismatic leader and the transcendent. Hagiography, of course, is a staple of many religious traditions. As Rothstein (2007: 20) observed in assessing L. Ron Hubbard's hagiography, 'The fact that his life is mythologized is as obvious as in the cases of Jesus, Muhammad or Siddhartha Gotama.' Hagiographies are carefully constructed within movements as they legitimate leaders' calls for loyalty and sacrifice and provide followers with justification for answering those calls.

In some cases, movement leaders build and solidify hagiographies. Scientology has gone to great lengths to attempt to corroborate details of L. Ron Hubbard's life and at the same time to embellish actual events and accomplishments so as to validate his standing as a truly extraordinary individual in human history. In the Scientology case, Hubbard is presented as a world traveller, navigator, sailor, pilot, blood brother of the Native Americans, and explorer. He could have completed an advanced education in engineering at George Washington University but withdrew as he became disenchanted with existing human knowledge. It was his enormous range of abilities and lifetime of searching that led to the extraordinary discovery of a technology that could liberate humanity. By contrast, Anton La Vey, founder of the Church of Satan, was the primary source of numerous claims about remarkable achievements in his own life, such as having been a circus lion-tamer, stage hypnotist, nightclub organist, police department photographer, and romantic partner of Marilyn Monroe and Jayne Mansfield. In some cases, grassroots followers add informal elements to hagiographies. Unificationists tell stories of Sun Myung Moon, an avid tuna fisherman, catching large tuna that jumped on his baitless hook in order to be caught by the messiah. While extending claims of extraordinary accomplishments beyond the spiritual realm bolsters charismatic standing, such claims are much more vulnerable to disconfirmation. Investigative journalists, scholars and former members have been instrumental in undermining the embellishments added to claims of Hubbard's accomplishments and La Vey's claims in their entirety.

Rituals

As challenging movements, NRMs have a stronger proclivity than established religious organizations to orchestrate dramatic confirmation of their extraordinary discoveries. Myth and charisma claims are likely to be incorporated into ritual displays in which transcendent power is made real and active. Both leaders and followers have an interest in these ritual displays. As with hagiography, ritual displays validate charismatic leader pronouncements and moral authority claims for leaders; for followers the displays justify and validate their commitment to the group and the leader. This need for validation is likely to provide an impetus for ritual events in which the operation of transcendent power in the everyday world is visible. Violation of what is understood as natural laws of the universe, of course, constitute the most impressive case. A broad range of new religious groups engage in ritual displays that appear to violate physical laws. Psychic surgeons appear to remove diseased organs without making incisions, spiritual leaders look as if they are physically levitating during ritual events, gurus magically produce material objects apparently out of thin air at the behest of followers, firewalkers remove their shoes and traverse beds of red hot coals that apparently should result in devastating burn injuries, serpent handlers pick up venomous snakes with apparent impunity, solid statues of the Virgin Mary seem to suddenly begin to weep tears of water or even blood, and demonic entities appear to speak as they are exorcized from suffering victims.

Leaders and/or followers may take the lead in creating active transcendent power. In the case of the Solar Temple, for example, movement leaders orchestrated holographic demonstrations of the presence of Ascended Masters. In the Brownsville Revival and Toronto Blessing, leaders initially set the stage for dramatic displays of transcendent power in the form of 'being filled with the Holy Spirit', as manifested through glossolalia and holy laughter. They set expectations for visitation by the Holy Spirit, visited other religious venues where such visitation had occurred, brought in visiting evangelists who were expected to raise the level of spiritual intensity, and interpreted actually occurring events as signs of the presence of the Holy Spirit. Followers were equally important. When confirming experiences did begin to occur, extraordinary numbers of pilgrims appeared very rapidly, yielding two of the largest revival movements of the twentieth century. It was the dramatic displays of connecting with the Holy Spirit by revival participants that provided direct confirmation of the presence of transcendent power. In the Catholic tradition, Marian apparition movements reveal a similar pattern (Bromley and Bobbit 2011). In many cases, once a woman or child has claimed a visitation from the Virgin, thousands of pilgrims began congregating at the site within a matter of days or weeks. Further, followers independently begin reporting phenomena such as miraculous healings, extraordinary movements of the sun, and the powerful scent of roses. In the case of weeping statues in the Catholic tradition, it appears that both clergy and parishioner may initiate such displays through some rather simple alterations of statues.

Associational Collectivities

New religious groups innovate not only with respect to myth, hagiography and ritual, but also with new associational forms. There is no template for these developing associational forms; rather, movements become 'laboratories of experimentation' (Robbins and Bromley 1992, 1993). Because new religious groups challenge the established social order, they construct alternative associational forms that seek to resolve tensions in the lives of adherents, create high-demand environments that move adherents outside conventional social networks, and fashion organizational forms that inappropriately mix activities that are partitioned in established institutions.

New groups address certain life-problems that their membership encounters in conventional society. Some of these issues are longer term in nature. Marian apparition movements, for example, tend to be responses to the continuing liberalization of the Roman Catholic Church over several centuries that erodes the traditional female role. Women have responded by envisioning divine intercession by the most powerful female figure in the Roman Catholic tradition, the Virgin Mary. New Age movements are in part responses to the contemporary felt need to empower and defend the self against the increasing regimentation of the public sphere in ever more rational/secular modern societies. They envision a much more powerful, even god-like self capable of sustaining a strong individual identity in a repressive social environment. In some cases, movements may emphasize specific aspects of behaviour and components of identity. A number of contemporary movements have addressed gender and sexuality issues, for instance. Movements such as Rajneesh/Osho and the Raelians have attracted female members partly on the basis of legitimating sexual freedom for them in a way that allows them to be both liberated and female. Both groups adopted a 'free love' style of organization during their early histories. By contrast, other groups have sought to counter the sexual pressures on young adults by mandating celibacy and assigning female members traditional roles such as 'sister' (Unificationism) or 'mother' (Hare Krishna).

One major issue in establishing a new religious group is assembling the various resources necessary for movement growth and development. Movements need some base of operations, members, leadership, financial resources, myth and ritual development. Lacking existing resources, new movements are likely to rely on converts to provide the labour to establish their communities. Some of these community-building efforts have indeed been impressive; complete, fully functioning communities have been erected, as in the case of the network of Twelve Tribes communities, Hare Krishna's New Vrindaban community in West Virginia, and Rajneeshpuram in Oregon. In addition, there typically is a high level of member commitment to the movement's unique role in history, as described in movement mythology, and allegiance to the charismatic leader. The combination of community building and intense individual commitment leads to at least some degree of separation from conventional society. In the more extreme cases, groups may withdraw from conventional society, organize as communes, and condemn established institutions. Early in their histories, The Family International, Unificationism and Hare Krishna adopted this posture. The totalistic environment created by oppositional, communal organization places movements in the position of hostile 'outsiders'. Even groups that do not organize communally often have a tightly organized inner core of leadership that approaches a communal/oppositional model, as in the case of Sea Org in Scientology. This kind of organization yields both suspicion and, in many cases, organized opposition.

In their organizational experimentation, new religious groups create social forms that mix types of activity that conventionally are partitioned. In creating these hybrid forms, new religious groups create an organizational profile that does not match conventional understandings of religion and may violate established boundaries with other institutional arenas. In some cases, the mixing of different forms of organization is limited in scope. The Twelve Tribes/Messianic Communities, for example, have established businesses as key elements of their communally organized religious communities. This kind of structure offers a competitive economic advantage over conventional business that must pay their employees. Amway has combined religion, family and corporate organization by making the family a business and the business a family, while overlaying both with a larger religious mission. A number of religious movements, such as The Family International and the International Churches of Christ, have combined religion and family by creating 'spiritual families' to which adherents owe their primary loyalty. Synanon began as a respected, secular therapy group that sought to treat serious drug-addiction problems. However, Synanon subsequently transformed itself into a communally organized church, which placed it outside the reach of government regulatory agencies and moved it in the direction of encapsulating drug users rather than returning them to conventional social lives. Transcendental Meditation sought to detach its meditation techniques from their Hindu roots as part of its programme to introduce those methods into publicly funded schools and prisons. In some cases, the mixing of organizational forms has been even more extensive. Unificationism created spiritual families, paired religious and corporate organization, and at least envisioned a theocratic type of governmental structure. The Church of Scientology has claimed religious status while organizing its primary rituals in a way that closely resembles therapy, asserting that these practices have a scientific base, and organizing them in a fee-for-service form. The more there is of this kind of institutional arena-mixing, the less the group conforms to conventional understandings of what it means to be a 'church', and the more potential opponents it generates.

Exogenous Factors

Established institutions have a vested interest in sustaining and defending symbolic and organizational boundaries that protect their own authority and legitimacy. To the extent that they are successful in this project, each becomes the legitimate representation of one arena of social life. Each supplies appropriate answers to such questions as what social processes constitute justice, how should children be raised, or how may economic exchanges be structured. The organizationally embedded answers to these kinds of questions constitute the society's normative structure and ultimately establish the boundary between insiders and outsiders. In their strongest form, institutionalized rules and procedures come to be recognized as the only reasonable way of ordering social life or the way most consistent with the natural order of things. Challenging groups serve as particularly useful representations of otherness as solidarity around conventional norms can be bolstered and problems can be displaced on external parties. Both for individual movements and for sets of groups that are deemed similar, the social control process in its most extreme form involves constructing a vision of transcendent evil as well as methods for combating it.

As I have already noted, new religious groups assume a challenging posture that in one way or another contests the legitimacy and authority of established institutions. They are therefore likely to violate established normative boundaries. There is no shortage of examples of serious, criminal violations by new religious movements. David Koresh certainly would have been charged with child sexual abuse had he lived, and several Davidians served long prison terms for their armed resistance to federal agents. Many members of the Peoples Temple fed their children a poisonous cocktail as part of the mass suicides/murders at Jonestown. Rajneesh was charged with immigration violations and deported; his followers planned assassinations and placed toxic substances in local residents' food to disable them. The leader of the Church of the Lamb of God declared war on competing polygamous Mormon leaders; the death toll from these assassinations exceeded the number of people killed by the Manson Family. Sun Myung Moon served time in federal prison for tax evasion. Scientology leaders burglarized federal offices, and several received prison terms. The inner circle of Aum Shinrikyo killed defectors and placed deadly sarin gas in Tokyo subways. In addition, new religious groups are relatively powerless and possess few allies. With the exception of their membership, civil libertarian organizations, and sometimes a small coterie of celebrity supporters, these movements have few defenders in the event of a 'dramatic denouement' with conventional society (Bromley 2002). Established institutions have shown themselves relatively effective in handling these kinds of offences as they are covered under existing criminal law, and groups that have engaged in criminal acts have diminished grounds for claiming religious legitimacy.

The problem with new religions from an established institutional perspective is much more with behaviours that are not formally regulated, or that are difficult to enforce, and practices that do not conform to conventional institutional boundaries. There are numerous kinds of behaviours, such as the faked healings by Jim Jones at Jonestown and the orchestrated healing events by Benny Hinn; the sleight-of-hand materializations by Sai Baba; the sexual manipulation of adherents by a large and growing list of gurus; reliance on faith healing practices that put children at risk of death that is not uncommon in conservative Christian groups; deceptive fundraising and witnessing practices for which Unificationism and Hare Krishna became well known, and the establishment of armed survivalist communities like The Covenant, the Sword, and the Arm of the Lord. Mixed forms of organization that do not comport with institutional normative guidelines and boundaries are also problematic to control. Such forms would include the assertion of the priority of spiritual over birth family by The Family International as a means of creating a faithful remnant that rule at the hand of God in the Endtime; the combination of family and business by Amway as a means of offering financial freedom to families by replacing wage labour with business ownership; the organization of religious ritual as therapy in order to eliminate the effects of debilitating life traumas and allow the expression of full individual potential. In these and other cases, new religions have created hybrid forms that circumvent and problematize normal social control mechanisms by the impacted institutions. In these kinds of cases, formal controls are difficult to exercise, but the practices involved are widely regarded as involving fraudulent intent or behaviour. The result is ongoing tensions and conflict that is difficult to resolve, particularly when the religious movements vigorously proclaim their moral superiority over established institutions.

While established institutions clearly possess greater legitimacy and power than new religious groups, they often face social control implementation issues. The privileging of religion in western, democratic societies places constraints on external regulation where groups claim religious status. Each institution also has a clearly defined mandate and span of control. The usual result, therefore, is that institutions confront new religions on a specific set of issues related to their mandate and issues that do not violate religious protections. Various religious denominations published materials designed to educate adherents about the theological deviations of certain new religions. Investigative journalists have run exposé series on groups in their locales, as the *Point Reyes Light* did for Synanon and the *Oregonian* did for Rajneesh/Osho. Labour departments in several US states have penalized the Messianic Communities for illegal use of child labour in cases where minors worked in family businesses. American federal courts have ruled against religious groups attempting to inject religiously based experiences into public schools, as the courts did in forbidding the practice of Transcendental

Meditation in schools, given its roots in Hinduism. The US Internal Revenue Service has revoked tax-exempt status of new religious groups, as it did with the Church of Scientology in California in 1967, in part because the church's activities were deemed to be commercial in nature. Higher education institutions have banned some new religious groups, such as the International Churches of Christ, from their campuses as a result of the aggressive proselytizing tactics.

In instances where conflicts with several institutions arise simultaneously, coalitions of control agencies begin to form and claims-making by oppositional coalitions becomes a mirror image of religious movements' claims-making. That is, the oppositional coalition begins to elevate its claims to moral superiority and undermine the moral standing of the target groups. This is exactly what occurred in the 'cult wars' of the 1960s and 1970s. An anti-cult ideology emerged that asserted the existence of a set of pseudo-religious movements, referred to as 'cults', that posed an imminent danger to established social order and possessed the extraordinary ability to undermine the individual authority of individuals in those groups through a subversive process referred to as 'brainwashing'. Therefore, the claims to religious status by these groups were fraudulent, and affiliations with them did not constitute authentic religious conversion and should not receive the protections afforded to legitimate religious groups.

Given the lower moral status accorded to cults, institutions were able to extend their mandates and exercise stronger social control over their members. Families of movement members lacked formal authority to control the young adults who affiliated with new religious groups. However, they expanded their authority by forming anti-cults associations that for a time sponsored the physical extraction and 'deprogramming' of members of Unificationism, Hare Krishna and The Family International. Journalists freely labelled controversial groups as 'cults' and reported apostate accounts of group life uncritically. Police raids were launched against movements such as the Messianic Communities and the Branch Davidians under questionable legal authority. Some governmental units in Europe and the United States passed laws restricting group rights.

Conclusions

At its core, the argument presented here is that no group is inherently religious and no action is inherently fraudulent. Both religion and fraud are status and knowledge claims. As challenging movements, new religious groups develop in ways that contest the established social order and hence are conducive to fraud allegations. As representations of appropriate social order, established institutions seek to preserve, protect and defend their legitimacy and authority, and are predisposed toward enforcement targets that externalize social problems. Therefore, from a sociological standpoint at least, studying the religion-fraud connection involves examining the factors that lead movements in the direction of challenging action that draw fraud allegations and that lead established institutions to target these movements. All analyses of the relationship between religion and fraud must, of course, be historically situated. In the current, western context, this means societies that, formally at least, privilege voluntaristic relationships between autonomous, rationally oriented individuals. Therefore, many new religious group innovations concern individual-group relationships and established institutions are in the process of redefining individual-group boundaries. Religion-fraud analyses, therefore, are likely to cluster around this issue. I have suggested the kinds of factors relevant to a constructionist analysis of these and other issues. What emerges from case studies following this approach is a more complex, nuanced analysis that contributes to a broader understanding of how social reality is created and recreated.

References

Berg, M.D. (1984). 'To Win Some, Be Winsome', *DO* (Disciples Only), 1855 (October) http://www.exfamily.org/pubs/ml/b5/ml1855.shtml (accessed 17 March 2014).

Berger, P. (1990). *The Sacred Canopy*. Garden City, NY: Anchor Books.

Boas, M. (1949). 'Hero's Pneumatica: A Study of its Transmission and Influence', *Isis*, 40(1): 38–48.

Bromley, D.G. (2002). 'Dramatic Denouements', in *Cults, Religion, and Violence*, eds D.G. Bromley and J.G. Melton. Cambridge: Cambridge University Press, pp. 11–41.

— and R. Bobbitt (2011). 'Visions of the Virgin Mary: The Organizational Development of Marian Apparition Movements', *Nova Religio* 14: 5–41.

— and J.G. Melton (2012). 'On Reconceptualizing Types of Religious Organization: Churches, Sects, Ethnic Churches, and New Religious Movements', *Nova Religio*, 15: 4–28.

Chryssides, G. (2007). 'Heavenly Deception: Sun Myung Moon and Divine Principle', in *The Invention of Sacred Tradition*, eds J. Lewis and O. Hammer. New York: Cambridge University Press, pp. 118–40.

Cusack, C. (2010). *Invented Religions: Imagination, Fiction and Faith*. Farnham, England: Ashgate.

Fylaktou, E. (n.d.). 'The Ancient Science in Service: The 12 Theistikou Priesthood', *Free Inquiry* http://www.freeinquiry.gr/pro.php?id=1565 http://www.freeinquiry.gr/pro.php?id=1565 (accessed 25 June 2012).

Hammer, O. and J. Lewis (2007). 'Introduction', in *The Invention of Sacred Tradition*, eds J. Lewis and O. Hammer. New York: Cambridge University Press, pp. 1–17.

Hobsbawn, E. and T. Ranger (1983). *The Invention of Tradition*. Cambridge: Cambridge University Press.

Hulten, K.G.P. (1968). *The Machine: As Seen at the End of the Mechanical Age*. New York: Museum of Modern Art.

Palmer, S.J. and D.G. Bromley (2007). 'Deliberate Heresies: New Religious Myths and Rituals as Critiques', in *Teaching New Religious Movements*, ed. D.G. Bromley. New York: Oxford University Press, pp. 135–58.

'Pontus Hulten: The Machine as seen at the End of the Mechanical Age' (n.d.). Available at http://swiki.hfbk-hamburg.de:8888/seminare/uploads/132/THE_MACH.DOC (accessed 5 July 2012).

Refslund, C.D. (2005). 'Inventing L. Ron Hubbard: On the Construction and Maintenance of the Hagiographic Mythology of Scientology's Founder', in *Controversial New Religions*, eds J. Lewis and J.A. Petersen. New York: Oxford University Press, pp. 227–58.

Robbins, T. and D.G. Bromley (1992). 'Social Experimentation and the Significance of American New Religions: A Focused Review Essay', in *Research in the Social Scientific Study of Religion*, eds M. Lynn and D. Moberg. Greenwich: JAI Press, pp. 1–28.

— (1993). 'What Have We Learned About New Religions: New Religious Movements as Experiments', *Religious Studies Review* 19: 209–16.

Rothstein, M. (2007). 'Scientology, Scripture, and Sacred Tradition', in *The Invention of Sacred Tradition*, eds J. Lewis and O. Hammer. New York: Cambridge University Press, pp. 18–37.

Smith, W.C. (1962). *The Meaning and End of Religion*. Minneapolis, MN: Fortress Press.

Thomassen, E. (2007). '"Forgery" in the New Testament', in *The Invention of Sacred Tradition*, eds J. Lewis and O. Hammer. New York: Cambridge University Press, pp. 141–57.

Weber, M. (1964). *The Theory of Social and Economic Organization*, trans. A.M. Henderson and T. Parsons. New York: The Free Press.

Wilson, B. (1982). *Religion in Sociological Perspective*. New York: Oxford University Press.

Chapter 2

Minority Religions and Fraud: Preliminary Theories on Ritual Deception

Holly Folk

Introduction

In this chapter, I define ritual deception as the 'intentional fabrication of supernatural phenomena in a ritual setting'. Compared to other forms of fraud such as embezzlement, deception transpiring within rituals holds special importance in both scholarly and public views of new and established religions. Almost invariably, ritual deception presents alongside innovative truth claims about the supernatural. Thinking the acts that they see or take part in are 'real', followers believe their leaders have special powers. This means that until exposed, ritual deceptions can serve as primary means of religious legitimation. Once the truth is known, disconfirmation of ritual events pushes equally powerfully against interpreting the perpetrators as practising 'real' religion. The debunking of a leader can result in the complete invalidation of a religious ministry, as seen in the falls from grace of faith healers such as Peter Popoff, whose clairvoyance was exposed on national television as transmissions sent through a miniature radio system (Nickell 2007: 94–102).

The vocabulary of my argument is holistic, because ritual deception is a multi-dimensional issue, and because instances of religious deception are almost always contested sites. I understand instances of ritual deception as situations experienced and interpreted differently by individual participants. The perspectives of different stakeholders are amenable to description variously as 'deception', 'trickery', 'symbolism', or many other word choices, with different implications. I hope my work shows the open borders across these categories and the metaphysical realities they uphold or deny. In rituals, the double meanings of the world coexist and are in tension. For these reasons, it is impossible to reduce case studies to one explanatory theory. Thus my goal here is to make several observations potentially applicable to various parts of this topic, but perhaps disparate against each other. Through all its ambiguities, one point seems clear: that the distribution of knowledge and its social production mediate individual experience of ritual deception. A lot can be gained from considering several variables, including the distribution of knowledge and social power; the intent and justifications of deceiving performers; and the perceptions among non-performing participant-observers.

Falling on the lines of loyalists and apostates, sources about ritual deception nearly always contradict each other. In these disputes, it is right to question the reliability of both sides. What is needed is a framework capable of handling the multiplicity of perspectives inevitably found in disambiguating situations. Because it highlights the diversity of subjective experiences, 'Lived Religion' is an optimal heuristic for considering religious trickery, where unequal access to knowledge generates sharply different understandings of events. The ritual's leader, the participants who are aware of the deception, and those who are not (yet) aware that trickery is involved all have fundamentally different understandings. For a sense of how this might be applied to a ritual setting, one might borrow a metaphor proposed by Wendy Doniger (2000). To think of a ritual setting as 'pointillist' is to see it constituted by subjective religious encounters which retain their individuality but come together to form a collective image, as in a painting by Seurat. This image helps me balance the subjectivity of individual experience and the aggregate observations that form the basis of comparative religion.

Obstacles to Discussion

Because establishing ritual as deception so often delivers a referendum on the group in question, the right interpretation of religious disambiguation is critical for properly understanding any group practising it. Yet the study of religious deception faces distinct obstacles.

The public hostility against new religious movements (NRMs) and minority religions leads to them often being suspected or accused of crimes. One of the core charges advanced by anti-cult activists has been that NRMs deceive their members, and even resort to conjure tricks to do so. Accusations of fraud have been launched against NRMs by at least three types of opponents, with complicated sets of motives. Having left the group, former members often remember their participation very negatively, and possibly overstate deceit. Anti-cult organizations led by Evangelical Christians are hostile to alternative religions, but often interested in maintaining the possibilities of supernatural reality. The 'Skeptics' network of science writers is interested in debunking the miraculous where it is claimed to be found, and seems to bear no special animus against NRMs, but the felt effect on the public of their well-documented investigations has been great (Nolen 1975, Randi 1989, Nickell 1998, 2007). None the less, all three groups have contributed to popular understandings of 'cult' leaders as manipulative individuals, who have the unique ability to control followers. Religious 'fakery' becomes the strongest evidence of a leader's predatory nature. Scholars do not want to collude with anti-cultists, but using the category of fakery invites comparison to them.

Equally important, the scholarly commitments within religious studies direct against this line of inquiry. The perspective known as 'structured empathy' asks for restraint in making value judgements, but much of the vocabulary of ritual deception – including words like 'fake', 'fraud' and 'trickery' – carry overwhelmingly negative connotations which make them evaluative even more than descriptive. In addition, it is customary to recognize the altered terrain of belief as characteristic of religious systems. Religions constantly make appeals to things about which there can be no objective knowledge. For scholars, religious 'truth claims' are widely understood to be subjectively real, though acceptance is not demanded of the outside observer. Allowing 'false' and 'deceptive' labels exposes the scepticism hidden in the second half of this orientation. It goes against our instincts to say that religious people are 'duped', for this undercuts the agency religious studies tries to ascribe to religious actors. 'Trickery' raises the possibility that religious participation is not voluntary. Furthermore, 'ritual deception' poses questions about the metaphysical claims one can make, and many more about the social construction of reality. It ignites the border between substantive and functional definitions of religion. As David Bromley has pointed out in Chapter 1 of this volume, identifying religious content as 'fake' implies its misrepresentation of something that could or should be 'real' in a literal sense.

Misrepresentation in the Study of Religion

The concept of 'fraudulent' rituals thus rubs against many of the founding principles of religious studies, but both actual disambiguation and its theological justifications have historically been part of many world religions. Greco-Roman and Egyptian religions used 'dissimulative technologies', such as trapdoors, cranes and statues with speaking tubes (Horace 1989). The Mahayana Buddhist concept of *upaya* ('skilful means' – the preaching of the dharma in the form a person can understand) could be said to endorse tricking the ignorant for their own spiritual benefit. Tantrism, especially, has certain ideas that facilitate ambiguity, such as *mahasiddi* (spiritual adept), or *Kshobana* (testing chelas by confusing them). Even those that officially shun magic and wonder-working, like Judaism and Islam, have sub-traditions where these are present. The figures of the Sufi Shekh and the Hasidic Rebbe are both credited with supernatural abilities, and by trade, the Baal Shem Tov was a magician (Idel 1995).

Furthermore, throughout history, human beings have been open to the supernatural – imagined or staged – and despite hypotheses about secularization, this tendency has not eroded in the modern world. Recent years have offered spectacular instances of false miracles – proving their existence as a living aspect of world religion, and not something that died out in the Middle Ages. The Catholic Church has issued formal statements concerning revelations and visions declared by laypeople around the world, and has challenged the authenticity of many reporters. One noteworthy incident occurred in Florence, Italy, in 2008. At the House of the Sainted Archangels, Father Francesco Saverio Bazzoffi conducted fake exorcisms, with the help of accomplices who pretended to be victims of demonic possession (Moore 2008).

Certain family traditions in North American Protestantism have long been linked to both miracles and fraud. Faith healers Peter Popoff and Benny Hinn are prominent examples in the US. Since their exposure in the 1990s, the growth and spread of Pentecostalism has made fraudulent healing a global issue. The 'Miracle Babies' of Gilbert Deya Ministries is among the most remarkable episodes of healing deception (see Van Eck Duymaer van Twist, in this volume). From 1997 to 2007, Kenyan evangelist Gilbert Deya and his wife ran an illegal adoption scheme that involved convincing infertile British women they had miraculously become pregnant. The women would travel to Africa to give birth under heavy sedation, in clinics often immediately adjacent to orphanages. Several of the 'Miracle Babies' were later identified as victims of child trafficking. It is unclear how deeply the women knew their real medical conditions. Some women and couples may have been complicit, but a judge in Britain found them unable to provide definitive information about the 'birth experiences' (Boggam 2006).

Interpreting the enduring presence of ritual fakery in religion is a problem long grappled with by anthropologists, who detect stagecraft in the rituals of many cultures. Anthropology problematizes the axis of belief and non-belief by presenting a cascade of evidence of audiences aware of ritual fabrications, and of performing perpetrators who appear convinced of their misrepresentations. Lévi-Strauss (1963) was puzzled by practitioners of religious stagecraft who seemed to believe their own rhetoric. He called this 'self-deception', and admitted he could find no psychopathology to explain this delusion. Simultaneously and in contrast, other anthropologists discovered that in cultures with disambiguating rituals, many people can be 'in on the joke'.

Ritual deception is an activity associated with animist and shamanic traditions, which are prevalent in much of the non-western world. Shamans often palm small objects, for example, to draw disease out of the body in the form of a tooth or stone. Victor Turner (1967) found that in these traditional settings, only the performing practitioner might truly have known the specific location of a palmed stone or extracted 'tooth', but the witnessing community was often aware of the stagecraft, teasing the practitioner about where the object was hidden.

At the same time, stagecraft can have a great influence on affective spiritual reality. A well-known example is provided in the case of the Kwakiutul Winter Ceremonies of British Columbia. These theatrical productions involved the use of speaking tubes to throw voices, and the disappearance and reappearance of people through tunnels and trapdoors to create the illusion of rebirth from an incendiary death. Tellingly, their indigenous name, *Tsitsika*, means 'Everything is Not Real'. As reported by Tlingit commentator George Hunt, emotional identification with the myth caused the relatives of the girl playing the 'burned' role to weep: 'Although they know it is not real, it looks so real they can't help it. It was all a trick' (Ford 1941: 110, 120).

Anthropology holds a key to understanding the production of belief: fakery and knowledge of it, the two categories constitutive of religious deception, are intertwined and interdependent. Victor Turner and Edward Evans-Pritchard both noticed that it was common for African patrons of witchdoctors to believe most of them fraudulent, with their chosen practitioner being the exception. Evans-Pritchard wrote, 'Indeed, skepticism is included in the pattern of belief in witchdoctors. Faith and skepticism are alike traditional. Skepticism explains failures of witchdoctors, and being directed towards particular witchdoctors even tends to support faith in others' (Evans-Pritchard 1937: 193). Their observations summon an assertion very often made by nineteenth-century converts to Spiritualism: that most mediums were charlatans but that some were real. In these cases, the possibility of deception is made less troubling to believers by their developing channels for their own scepticism or that of their peers. With most practitioners acknowledged as frauds, the 'hermeneutic of suspicion' is reversed.

Belief and scepticism are entangled in more than one way. Like Turner, Michael Taussig (2003) has noticed that not only do patrons of shamans know healing rituals typically include stagecraft, they can delight in exposing the sleight of hand by pointing out, for example, where a palmed object has gone to. Taussig asserts that the 'skilled revelation of skilled concealment' undergirds shamanic ritual. By calling out the shaman, witnesses to the ritual become participants, and implicitly uphold its message. The revelation of concealment thus strengthens belief in the effectiveness of the ceremony. Taussig finds a pattern of believers becoming enchanted in the sacred drama of rich symbolic behaviour. Renaming stagecraft 'mimesis', he joins other theorists who have turned to dramatic models, including Antoine Artaud (1994), Clifford Geertz (1973), and Erving Goffman (1959). Their interpretations frame acts of deception in light of spiritual transformation, invoking realities greater than their material components. In successful religious rituals, what Geertz calls the 'really real' replaces the worldview generated by mundane experience. He illustrates this insight with the description of a Balinese re-enactment of a mythic battle, which ends with the audience 'rushing' the stage to drive the witch demon away. What all these anthropologists seem to be detecting is the oscillation between regular living and transformation that undergirds human religious experience, not just between ritual and non-ritual settings, but within the setting of ritual itself.

Clearly, the drama in religion is central to its appeal. Recognition of the presence of stagecraft in world religion should influence how one interprets its appearance in new religious movements. That many instances appear consistent with broader patterns of human religious behaviour should lead to a primary consideration: disambiguating religious performances are not in themselves sinister. Perpetrators of ritual deception hold many intentions. Of secondary importance is to seek what is distinctive for NRMs, that would speak to them as a social type. I hope my discussion shows that sectarian patterns of leadership are critically important.

Varieties of Ritual Deception

There are several prominent types of ritual deception, cutting across religious traditions. Healing rituals encompass a variety of techniques lending to the appearance of bodily cure. Communication includes the channelling of spirits or aliens, claiming to speak in tongues, and revelations from divine figures like Jesus and Mary. Apparitions involve the production of supernatural beings in ghostly or human form, such as Katie King in Spiritualism (Owen 2004: 45–75, 223–35). Materialization refers to the creation of physical evidence of the supernatural world. For example, in India, the 'God Men' are known for their abilities to summon small objects like coins and pieces of candy. Detecting the motives behind ritual deception with certainty is almost impossible, but some possibilities come out through multiple case studies. Two of the best-documented instances of ritual deception in New Religions are Jim Jones's healings in People's Temple and the miracles of the Indian guru Sathya Sai Baba. In addition to academic literature, questions have generated extensive online debates. While each case delivers multiple accounts, the available sources about People's Temple and Sathya Sai Baba are grouped differently on the Internet.

The Alternative Considerations of Jonestown website seeks to represent the broad spectrum of views of survivors, who have a range of views about Jones' miracles (Jonestown Institute: http://jonestown.sdsu.edu/). The ends of the spectrum are seen in two long posts that address Jones's miracles. In 'The Healings of Jim Jones', Don Beck describes the evidence of Jones's supernatural beneficence in his own life (Beck 2005). This leads him to believe in Jones's metaphysical power. Beck's conclusion: 'I know some healings were faked, just as I know some were not', is in marked contrast to Mike Cartmell, author of 'Temple Healings: Magical Thinking'. Because he was asked to help in some of the audience manipulation, Cartmell had first-hand knowledge about Jones' healings: 'It's obvious, even to a blind horse, the healings were utterly and preposterously fake!'(Cartmell 2006). That these items appear on the same website is a reflection of the commitment among Jonestown survivors to respect one another's opinions.

The adherents to and disaffected former followers of Sathya Sai Baba are much more factionalized. Attacks and rebuttals between defenders and ex-members appear on separate websites and publications. One of the most extensive collections on Sai Baba's deception is in *The Findings*, a site compiled by an English ex-member named David Bailey (Bailey n.d.). It is significant that, even after rejecting Sai Baba, Bailey asserts his belief in spiritual phenomena. In contrast, supportive websites like *The Sai Critic* (http://www.saibabacontroversy.com/) defend Sai Baba. Video footage both proving the reality of Sai Baba's miracles and debunking them is widely available on the Internet. Despite their differences in online presentation, the Jonestown and Sai Baba case studies have certain commonalities that allow one to venture a rough 'typology of perspectives' for ritual deception.

Sathya Sai Baba

Miracles legitimate both the message and behaviour of the performer, by demonstrating his or her divine status. In this way, they frame the conduct of the leader, in and outside the ritual, as spiritually legitimate. Sathya Sai Baba was the best-known Indian wonder worker (Gogineni 1999). He stands atop a cadre of 'God Men' that includes Minu Bhowmick and Gyatri Swami, and Swami Vishwananda (Visham). Sai Baba performed healings, and even claimed to have raised people from the dead, but he is best known for his ability to materialize small objects like candy, jewellery and *Vibhuti* (sacred ashes). He also was credited with changing water into petrol – a useful skill in the industrialized world, though one reminiscent of the Wedding at Cana. In statements about the miracles, Sai Baba asserted that his gifts were only used for generosity. At the same time, they proved his status as an avatar. Sai Baba rejected a magical framework for his deeds, but he reinforced their supernaturalism by citing them as proof of heightened spirituality. In a speech given on his forty-third birthday, Sai Baba (1968) advised:

> You must have heard people say that mine [divine power] is all magic. But the manifestation of divine power must not be interpreted in terms of magic. Magicians play their tricks for earning their maintenance, worldly fame and wealth. They are based on falsehood and they thrive on deceit, but this body could never stoop to such a level. This body has come through the Lord's resolve to come.

Even while the performer comes to believe the message, confederates and members can come to doubt. Later in his life, some of Baba's faithful did discover that the materializations were sleight of hand. This brought a variety of responses and created factions among the followers. Some identified all his actions as teachings, and aligned his spiritual pedagogy with that of Tantric adepts, long associated with trickery and deception. One long-time devotee, Isaac Tigrett, confessed to not knowing how to regard Sai Baba's miracles: 'I know that he materialises things, because I've seen him do it. And I know he fakes materializations, because I've him seen him do that too. I don't know why. Maybe it's just a game' (Brown 2000).

People's Temple

Even more than for Sai Baba, miraculous healings were a central feature of Jim Jones' ministry in Indiana and California. The healings in People's Temple required the elaborate cooperation of many people. Most often, Jim Jones's secretaries wore disguises to church services, where Jones cured them of devastating illnesses and conditions. Rose Shelton was one of the members most involved in the staging of healings. A People's Temple newsletter reported that:

A most outstanding miracle occurred when Mrs. Rose Shelton, former instructor of cosmetology at the Regina beauty College in San Francisco, was called out by Pastor Jones and told to immediately stop work or she would have a stroke. She did not heed this warning and one week later as she was conducting her theory class, her right side became very, very weak and she could not use her right hand at all. The next morning her right side was totally paralyzed and she could not walk. However, the very next day Pastor Jones contacted her and meditated for her and all ability to use her right side was totally restored and she is perfectly healed to this day. She writes us that 'I owe it all to the mighty power of God that works through this modern-day prophet Jim Jones.' (Peoples Temple Newsletter 1971)

Perceptions of Jones's healings illustrate Doniger's pointillism. Some members doubted the veracity of Jones's miracles, or saw little meaning in them. This was especially true of adolescent children of 'joiners', and for the college-age members attracted by social justice. But many of Jones's followers were converts from Pentecostalism, and were disproportionately elderly, African American and female. For this group, the healings were a wondrous sign of Jones's 'power' that they apprehended as subjectively "real."

I cannot defend the harm suffered by members of a disturbing number of religions. The healings in Peoples Temple show how deception can be perpetrated on a participant without their knowledge or consent. The 'cancer' healings often involved a high-ranking member forcing a piece of rotting meat into the mouth of a subject: the gag reflex prompting the 'tumor's' expulsion. One elderly woman was drugged and woke to find her leg set in a cast; days later, Jones healed the 'fracture' in a church meeting (Hall 1987: 20, 35–37). These graphic examples show how in some contexts, participants are truly deceived. In large ritual settings, especially, audience members often are too physically distant to recognize what is happening.

The Order of the Solar Temple

Truth be told, it can be very difficult to pull apart the categories of believers. This can be seen in a third case study, the Order of the Solar Temple (OST). Though many questions remain unanswered, the leaders Josef Di Mambro and Luc Jouret were known to have staged ritual materializations of the 'Ascended Masters' in ceremonies with considerable special effects (Palmer 1996). When the Ascended Masters would appear and give orders to the group, it is unclear the extent to which participants knew these figures were actors playing parts.

Jean-Francois Mayer found members' understandings of the apparitions to be highly ambiguous:

> Probably a large number of people in the group believed the phenomena were real – or at least could be real in some instances ... It seems obvious that some people in the core group were more or less aware that a number of supernatural phenomena were faked – anyway, it would not have been possible for a single person to stage everything alone. But I met even somebody who had been in the core group and remained convinced, years after the end of the OST, that the phenomena he witnessed, and supernatural music he heard, were real. (Personal communication)

If the expression of fakery is varied, so are the consequences of its appearance within different NRMs. The Solar Temple was a rare instance where leaders acted proactively to suppress the secret. In the OST, while a core group knew about the stagecraft behind spiritual apparitions, the leaders seem to have felt great pressure to maintain the social reality of the Ascended Masters. On two occasions, though, the reality of the spiritual phenomena was challenged. In the early 1990s, Elie, the son of Joseph Di Mambro, learned his father had staged the miracles witnessed in the group's esoteric ceremonies, such as the materializations of the Ascended Masters. Elie discussed this with several members, and around 15 quit the group. Others chose to stay, however, out of commitment to the greater message – which the OST leaders also seem to have believed quite strongly. Jean-Francois Mayer found Di Mambro enmeshed in 'his own virtual reality. His was a world with secret masters, miraculous phenomena during impressively staged nightly ceremonies, an elite of Knight Templars gathered around him in order [to] fulfill a cosmic mission' (Mayer 1998).

The second moment of disconfirmation in the OST happened immediately before the first set of suicides, in 1993. At the time, the OST was subject to many social pressures, with ritual deception growing more important as other concerns mounted. A mixture of accusations runs through a letter from an OST member, written late in 1993:

> Rumours about embezzlement and various [forms] of skulduggery are propagated by influential ex-members. Many members ... have left or are leaving. They feel their ideals have been betrayed ... It is even said that you have fallen because of money and women, and you're no longer credible. This is very serious for the Order's mission. There are even more serious grumblings, and you know them. Here they are: everything we saw and heard in certain places has been a trick.

> I have known this for some time. Tony [Dutoit] has been talking about this for
> years already ... I have always refused to pay attention to these rumours, but the
> evidence is growing, and questions are being asked. This calls into question many
> things I've seen, and messages. I would be really upset if I had to conclude that I'd
> sincerely prostrated myself in front on an illusion!!! (Walliss 2004: 142).

When the technician Tony Dutoit announced he planned to reveal the secrets
to the light shows, he and his wife and son were murdered, their bodies found in
the blazing condominium in Morin Heights, Quebec. His impending disclosure
may have been an accelerant to the suicide ritual:

> What does this mean? Even at the higher levels, and certainly more so at lower
> levels of the group, people were convinced that the phenomena were authentic.
> This means that the threat by Dutoit to tell it all was not something to be taken
> lightly: it could have just shattered the support basis for the movement ... We know,
> however, that some people who had believed sincerely were really upset when
> discovering that Di Mambro had lied to them. (Mayer, personal communication)

Theorizing Ritual Deception in New Religious Movements

Borrowing a metaphor proposed by William James, we might think of 'Once
Born Believers' as those witnessing an event who are unaware of the deception,
and who respond to the message as if the performance is 'real' in the sense of
supporting a supernatural interpretation. 'Doubt' in the miraculous does not
stand as a major problem in this group, but thinking about them asks for special
care. Instances of abusive fraud are most likely to involve these supernaturally
oriented victims. One should remember that for Weber, charismatic authority
is a type of *domination*. It is no small point that ritual deception can be directly
connected to social control. For example, Jim Jones used members' belief in
his 'power' and threatened some of them with 'metaphysical destruction'. As a
result, 'the superstitious and the fearful didn't want to leave' (Mills 1979: 310).

Yet in some religious settings participants may suspect stagecraft is not
literally 'real', but it might fit quite well with what they know to be spiritually
'true'. To the extent that ritual deceptions 'work', it appears to be most strongly
in their generating of affective truth. This implies that substantive categories like
the supernatural, sacred and miraculous are sustained by relational webs and
personal apprehensions. The 'will to believe' thus seems to have a great influence
in the plausibility of religious deception for all participants in ritual deception.

Like shamans who trust the efficacy of their magic, deceptive performers in new religions also may come to believe in their own supernatural powers. This belief is often supported by group dynamics, in which a leader's ideas are reconfirmed by obedient members. Archie Smith has identified 'audience corruption' as a major factor in Jim Jones's unbalancing. In his work, the adoration of followers created a 'feedback loop' in which Jones came to believe in his own supernatural powers: 'When he announces he is God, the followers feed back the supporting behavior, and the leader soon comes to believe unquestionably in his own deification. In turn, his unquestioned assent to divinity is believed by the followers' (Smith 2004: 48).

Smith's perspective comports with observations made by other Peoples Temple members. Jeannie Mills felt, 'Jim was starting to behave as if he were totally convinced he was divine' (Mills 1979: 296). His findings also comport with other investigators of ritual deception. Joe Nickell's (1993) interactions with fake mediums, spiritual healers and other paranormal practitioners alerted him of the high proportion for whom the boundary between fantasy and reality was deeply blurred. He and other Skeptics seeking to understand the beliefs of claimants to spiritual powers have turned to the theory of 'fantasy-prone personalities' developed by psychologists Sheryl Wilson and Theodore Barber (1983). Their research helped establish the capacity to conflate illusion and reality as a naturally occurring trait.

Both the feedback loop and the practical execution of ritual fakery depend on an 'inner circle' of cooperating disciples. It is important, therefore, to consider how this group understands what they are doing, and to look, especially, for their justifications, theological or otherwise. 'Confederates' who know and perpetrate are a group with considerable complexity. One should be open to the possibility that they can be transformed through mimetic ritual, like the participants in shamanic ceremonies. The social dynamics are different, however, in traditional societies and many NRMs. Tribal healing rituals might call on the participation of many family members of the ill person. In charismatic NRMs, members' primary commitment is more likely to be the leader, unless the person taken ill is an actual family member. In both contexts, participants in deception 'know' and 'help', but in NRMs, participation may have special importance, as a way to bond with one's leader. That is to say, helping may help build personal commitment. Ironically, this may happen simultaneously with the disillusionment knowledge of fraud can bring.

Though people might doubt things long before they are disproved, the 'disenchanted' emerge as information about ritual deception is made known. The potential for defection makes their responses critical for group survival.

As it turns out, both defections from a group and a cognitively dissonant intensification of belief tend to occur in the wake of detection. For believers with strong investment, it can be advantageous to accommodate the discovery. However they respond, discovery entails a certain measure of 'moral work'. Believers are tasked with psychically managing a new understanding of a figure who is tremendously important to them. In NRMs, where many converts participate for only a limited time, it is likely that ritual settings can contain people in varying stages of commitment and disconfirmation. In contexts of high turnover, one is likely to find a vivid spectrum of enchantment and its undoing.

Whether confederate or knowing spectator, participants who are aware of deception must decide whether to 'go along' with the presentation. Their reluctance to challenge their leaders reflects the atmosphere of 'enforced misrepresentation'. Social pressure seems to be the common thread connecting instances of religious deception.

Many members find ways to maintain partial, 'Twice Born' belief after learning of deception. Like those whose faith is renewed after religious despair, they reinterpret disambiguation to support its social reality and meaning, though not always its literal truth claims. It is possible their faith finds routes similar to those of the deceiving practitioner convinced of his own magic. We know that when confronted with evidence, some members find theological explanations, which might include 'lying to support the cause'. In the Solar Temple, fakery was justified as 'an unfortunate but necessary way to keep weaker souls within the fold' (Introvigne 2000: 151). Similarly, after watching Jim Jones stage the resurrection of a boy he had ordered sedated with drugs, Jeannie Mills was conflicted, but told herself the deception served a greater good: 'I justified Jim's actions when I realized Anthony's whole life had been changed that night' (Mills 1979: 206).

Some members thus confronted quietly re-evaluate the power they once accorded their leaders. The end result often is a more discerning faith, poignantly mature in its evaluation. Former follower Tim Conway eloquently expresses his disillusionment in a piece called, 'My Concerns About Sathya Sai Baba':

> For a growing number of the rest of us who've closely studied the extraordinary phenomenon of Sathya Sai, the reality about him is somewhere in between – a very gifted yet also deeply flawed human being. Perhaps he is just a highly adept but fallen yogi or an inter-dimensionally powerful but contaminated 'channel' for the former Sai Baba of Shirdi (d.1918). Perhaps he is some unknown other type of being altogether! Whatever the reality, Sathya Sai, it would appear, is perhaps the most enigmatic case of 'Jekyll and Hyde' split-personality in the

entire known history of religion ... Between the two opposing camps of those
who, on the one hand, continue to try to deny, cover-up and rationalize Baba's
sexual behavior as 'Divine activity,' and those who, on the other hand, think that
Baba is an incarnation of evil, 'the imposter God,' there is a growing third camp
of those of us who feel that, yes, much good has come through Baba's form and
world mission, and yes, there are some paranormal and beautiful things that
happen around him and in Sai Centers worldwide ... But it also seems very likely
that the human personality of Sathya Narayana Raju [Sathya Sai's name in early
childhood] is NOT fully enlightened and has a considerable shadow side of lust
and trickery that is interfering with the transmission of the Divine through his
form. (Conway 2007)

The disparate reactions among believers makes public exposure the likely
eventual outcome for many or most deceiving performers. Undermining
religious drama requires only a few people, while religious belief is best
maintained with communal support. Even so, there seems to be no direct
line from discovery to disconfirmation. Exposures of ritual fakery can lead
to defections, but do not necessarily cause the break-up of a group. Typically,
public knowledge of disconfirmation is managed or suppressed until another
precipitating event. At this point, private doubt becomes public scandal, and
members' responses become factionalized. The Sai Baba case shows that for
many followers, disconfirmation of the miracles was managed until a far more
serious issue prompted them to break with their guru. A devotee of Sai Baba
told Richard Wiseman (1997: 192) that if his guru had used 'a mild deception
to give the semblance of supernatural power', it was of minimal harm. What
prompted several families to finally expose the materializations were revelations
that Sai Baba had sexually abused many teenage boys (Brown 2000).

Disconfirmation built gradually in Peoples Temple. Jones did not perform
miracles in Guyana, but as his health and mental condition declined there, some
members questioned the fakery of the healings that had been done in California
and reported in newspapers. At one meeting in April 1978, a few members raised
the issue, with great hesitancy. Jones dismissed their questions about 'chicken
guts' with streams of profanity, but the transcript shows the conversation clearly
unsettled the group (Jonestown Institute 1978). At the time of the suicide-
murders, though, questions about the healings still were unresolved. Privately,
however, members had begun to worry whether Jones was losing his powers. As
Hyacinth Thrash explained:

Somehow he got off on the wrong track ... He changed! I saw him change before my very eyes. He got mad, for power and riches. You know, there's an Evil Spirit as well as a Good Spirit. The Devil will do anything to get a man. Jim just got the wrong Spirit. It's a gift, the Spirit, and it can be used for good or evil. Jim got out so far he couldn't go back. He tried to heal people, but he didn't have the power anymore. God just took the gift away from him. (Thrash 1995: 54–7)

Across movements, participants can and do recognize fakery, but they often stay silent, not challenging the spoken consensus. A mixture of emotions, including adulation, a desire to please, and fear of supernatural powers might keep members from speaking out. Sociologist Rodney Stark reports having visited a UFO cult in the 1960s where most contactees 'were aware that they were making it all up', but also thought 'they were the only ones who were shamming' (Stark and Bainbridge 1985: 272).

Conclusions

With lines of intersection between belief and scepticism, and faith and doubt, ritual disambiguation offers rich food for thought about the study of religion. The potency of a religious message is partly expressed as the ability to transform the affective reality of the believer. This may involve inverted logic and the embrace of ideas at odds with evidence from the physical world, but it does not need to. The impact of rituals also is felt on affective bonds, personal empowerment, and in some cases, negative emotions like fear.

The distribution of knowledge and its social production mediate individual experience of ritual deception. Such sites are cathectic arenas, containing many motives and potential interpretations. The deceptive milieu holds the potential for transformation, ambivalence, ambiguity and doubt. In these ways, it expresses the ambiguities and uncertainties of everyday religious life. Reframing stagecraft as the potentially efficacious, ritual enactment of symbolic elements works well as an explanatory theory for people who are 'immersed' in the religious encounter, but the subjectivity of human religious experience shows their limits. If the topic of ritual deception poses some questions about the nature of belief, it asks many more about the social construction of reality.

Acknowledgements

My interest in ritual deception grew out of an online conversation on the NRM listserv (NRM@listproc.cc.ku.edu). In addition, a number of scholars contributed greatly to my understanding of this topic, and many provided critical research materials, including David Bromley, Gordon Melton, Ralph Hood, Fielding McGehee, Jean-Francois Mayer, Joe Nickell, Candy Brown, Anson Shupe, Larry Foster, Robert Stoops and Stephen Stein. Special thanks to Inform, for allowing me access to their fascinating archive.

References

Alternative Considerations of Jonestown and Peoples Temple (n.d.). Department of Religious Studies. San Diego State University http://jonestown.sdsu.edu/ (accessed 3 December 2013).

Artaud, A. (1994). *The Theater and Its Double*. New York: Grove Press.

Bailey, D. (n.d.). *The Findings* http://www.npi-news.dk/page152.htm (accessed 3 December 2013).

Beck, D. (2005). 'The Healings of Jim Jones', *The Jonestown Report* 7 (November) http://jonestown.sdsu.edu/AboutJonestown/JonestownReport/Volume7/reflbeck3.htm (accessed 3 December 2013).

Boggam, S. (2006). 'Gilbert Deya & Missing Babies: God Knows', *Guardian*, 5 June.

Brown, M. (2000). 'Divine Downfall', *Telegraph* (UK), 28 October.

Cartmell, M. (2006). 'Temple Healings: Magical Thinking' http://jonestown.sdsu.edu/AboutJonestown/PersonalReflections/v8/Cartmell.htm (accessed 3 December 2013).

Conway, T. (2007). 'My Concerns About Sathya Sai Baba' http://www.enlightened-spirituality.org/Sathya_Sai_Baba_my_concerns.html (accessed 3 December 2013).

Doniger, W. (2000). 'Post-modern and -colonial -structural Comparisons', in *A Magic Still Dwells: Comparative Religion in the Postmodern Age*, eds K.C. Patton and B.C. Ray. Berkeley: University of California Press, pp. 63–74.

Evans-Pritchard, E.E. (1937). *Witchcraft, Oracles, and Magic among the Azande*. Oxford: Oxford University Press.

Ford., C.S. (1941). *Smoke from Their Fires: the Life of a Kwakiutl Chief*. New Haven, CT: Yale University Press.

Foreman, E. (2005). 'World of Yaad', in *The Encyclopedia of New Religious Movements*, ed. P.B. Clarke. London: Routledge, pp. 694–5.

Geertz, C. (1973). *The Interpretation of Cultures: Selected Essays*. New York: Basic Books.

Goffman, E. (1959). *The Presentation of Self in Everyday Life*. New York: Anchor.

Gogineni, B. (1999). 'The Godmen of India', *Skeptic*, 7(3): 56–9.

Hall, J.R. (1987). *Gone from the Promised Land: Jonestown in American Cultural History*. Edison, NJ: Transaction Publishers.

Horace (1989). 'Ars Poetica', in *Epistles Book II and Ars Poetica*, ed. N. Rudd. Cambridge: Cambridge University Press, lines 182–8, note p. 179.

Idel, M. (1995). *Hasidism: Between Ecstasy and Magic*. Albany: State University of New York Press.

Introvigne, M. (2000). 'The Magic of Death: The Suicides of the Solar Temple', in *Millennialism, Persecution, and Violence: Historical Cases*, ed. C. Wessinger. Syracuse, NY: Syracuse University Press, pp. 138–57.

Jonestown Institute (1978). 'Tape Number: Q 591 (April 13, 1978)' http://jonestown.sdsu.edu/?page_id=27476 (accessed 23 February 2014).

Lévi-Strauss, C. (1963). 'The Sorcerer and His Magic', in *Structural Anthropology*. New York: Basicbooks, pp. 167–85.

Mayer, J.F. (1998). 'Apocalyptic Millennialism in the West: The Case of the Solar Temple', lecture at the University of Virginia, sponsored by the Critical Incident Analysis Group, 13 November.

Mills, J. (1979). *Six Years with God*. New York: A&W Publishers.

Moore, M. (2008). 'Priest "made £3m from fake exorcisms"', *Telegraph* (UK), 3 April.

Nickell, J. (1998 [1993]). *Looking for a Miracle: Weeping Icons, Relics, Stigmata, Visions and Healing Cures*. Amherst, NY: Prometheus Books.

— (2007). *Adventures in Paranormal Investigation*. Lexington: University Press of Kentucky.

Nolen, W.A. (1975). *Healing: A Doctor in Search of a Miracle*. New York: Random House.

Owen. A. (2004). *The Darkened Room: Women, Power, and Spiritualism in Late Victorian England*. Chicago, IL: University of Chicago Press, 2004.

Palmer, S.J. (1996). 'Purity and Danger in the Solar Temple', *Journal of Contemporary Religion* 11(3) (October): 303–18.

Peoples Temple Newsletter (July 1971), available at the Jonestown Project Website http://jonestown.sdsu.edu/wp-content/uploads/2013/10/Newsletter 3.pdf (accessed 23 February 2014).

Randi, J. (1989). *The Faith Healers*. Amherst, NY: Prometheus Books.

Sai Baba, S. (1968). 'Why I Incarnate' (23 November). This speech has been reprinted in many sources, and also is available at http://www.saidarshan. org/baba/docs/d681123.html (accessed 8 October 2013).

Smith, A. (2004). 'An Interpretation of Peoples Temple and Jonestown: Implications for the Black Church', in *Peoples Temple and Black Religion in America*, eds R. Moore, A.B. Pinn, and M.R. Sawyer. Bloomington: Indiana University Press, pp. 47–56.

Stark, R. and Bainbridge, W.S. (1985). *The Future of Religion: Secularization, Revival and Cult Formation*. Berkeley: University of California Press.

Taussig, M. (2003). 'Viscerality, Faith, and Skepticism: Another Theory of Magic', in *Magic and Modernity: Interfaces of Revelation and Concealment*, eds B. Meyer and P. Pels. Palo Alto, CA: Stanford University Press, pp. 272–306.

Thrash, C.H. (1995). *The Onliest One Alive: Surviving Jonestown, Guyana*. Indianapolis, IN: M.K. Towne.

Turner, V. (1967). *The Forest of Symbols: Aspects of Ndembu Ritual*. Ithaca, NY: Cornell University Press, pp. 358–93.

Walliss, J. (2004). *Apocalyptic Trajectories: Millenarianism and Violence in the Contemporary World*. Bern: Peter Lang.

Wilson, S.C. and Barber, T.X. (1983). 'The Fantasy-prone Personality: Implications for Understanding Imagery, Hypnosis, and Parapsychological Phenomena', in *Imagery, Current Theory, Research and Application*, ed. A.A. Sheikh. New York: Wiley, pp. 340–90.

Wiseman, R. (1997). *Deception and Self-deception: Investigating Psychics*. Amherst, NY: Prometheus Press.

Chapter 3

Bona Fide?

Amanda van Eck Duymaer van Twist

From Quacks to Cults – They're Just in it for the Money!

> When I had faith in [him], particularly in my late teens and twenties, it was an absolute honour to contribute financially ... I would give monthly sums and also annual lump sums. Also every time we would go for a meal, I would insist in treating him. Every time we went on holidays abroad I would pay for most or all his expenses. My only regret at the time was that I could not spend more for him. To financially give to what I considered to be the closest thing to god on earth was an amazing feeling.[1]

In my research and work I have often encountered total incredulity in regards to some minority religions, such as: 'This seems strange, it must be a scam', 'Yogic flying is physically impossible, hence the other teachings must also be lies', 'They claim to be spiritual but charge a lot of money, that can't be right', 'Quacks are praying on the vulnerable', 'It may claim to be a religion, but it is really a money-making scam.' Arguing that the unfamiliar is not necessarily problematic appears counter-intuitive to most, and many people will know of an anecdote where someone was deceived by a 'cult'. Yet, at the same time, we're living in diverse societies where many are seeking for new spiritual experiences. How can we safely distinguish 'quacks' and 'cults' from healers and religions? Equally important, how may we identify fraud, deception, deceit and/or breach of confidence in some religions without tainting all minority religions?[2]

Donald Capps in his presidential address at the annual meeting of the Society for the Scientific Study of Religion in November 1991, stated: 'The title of my address, "Religion and Child Abuse: Perfect Together," might offend, but this does not mean it isn't so' (Capps 1992). Similarly, in the case of fraud and deception in minority religions, the thought might offend some sensibilities, but

---

[1] Former student of a fraudulent teacher, from personal communication with the author, 2012. This case is discussed in more depth later in this chapter.

[2] In this chapter, I will approach the concept of fraud defined in its simplest form, as intentional deception made for personal gain at the expense of another or others, in light of minority religions, beliefs and practices.

this doesn't mean it isn't so. There is a coming together of people who are already willing to look for religious compensators (a belief in a future reward and/or justice) outside mainstream frames of reference, thought and understanding. They can be relatively easy targets to those who proclaim to offer better, bigger, or faster compensators. Especially in new and non-institutionalized groups, the teachings (and supernatural offerings) can be adjusted, changed and reinterpreted at will, and there are less likely to be checks and balances.

Fraud can also be adjusted to many circumstances; it can be found anywhere, including minority religions. And although some may say it also raises questions about the nature of new and minority religions, one could equally argue that in reality it raises questions about the social position of new and minority religions – their minority status rendering them more vulnerable to accusations (Bromley, in Chapter 1 of this volume). The nature of fraud can be unclear, and when belief and trust are involved, it can become very ambiguous indeed. There are cases of demonstrable and verifiable fraud, yet there are also cases where motivations are not clear and an intention to defraud cannot be established. Could the fraudster be a believer, too, in what they were 'peddling'? Or did the victim perhaps have unrealistic expectations beyond what was promised and offered? Can we always tell the difference between situations where individuals have been wilfully defrauded and cases where once enthusiastic believers later become disenchanted and angry after their expectations have not been met?

In this chapter, I will analyse some cases that went to court, thus where some form of deception was agreed upon and proven to have occurred, in order to highlight ambiguities that were glossed over, or not discussed – often because it would have impeded a conviction. I will also discuss cases from Inform's files that did not go to court, or went to court on limited charges, and highlight the aspects that would make the cases difficult to convict in a court of law. But first I will go through an analysis of fraud in light of new, minority, and other forms of relatively non-institutionalized religion.[3]

Cult Malfeasance?

Unjust power relations can arise in many milieus, especially where an ideology can be used to justify the dominance of some over others. Shupe defines the abuse of authority by a religious leader as 'excessive monitoring and controlling

---

[3]   See the Introduction to this volume for a brief discussion of fraud in institutionalized religions, referred to there as 'clergy malfeasance'.

of members' livelihoods, resources, and lifestyles to enrich that leader, either in money or power' (1998: 7). However, such a dynamic can be interpreted in different ways, as Shupe also states: 'The category of authoritative malfeasance is the most sensitive and difficult to examine ... because what to an outsider looks grossly exploitive may to an insider represent a voluntary trade-off of "outside" goods and comforts for "inside" privileges and promises of spiritual reward' (1998: 7).

Authority, power dynamics and unequal hierarchies do not need to be institutionalized to be effective. Religious beliefs do not need to be established to be able to provide a frame for fraud. Indeed, there have been some well-publicized cases of fraud within new religions (for example, the case of the I AM movement, described in the Introduction of this volume), and 'cults' have often been accused of being more likely to be fraudulent, destructive, or involved in criminal activity. This does however raise some questions. Could deceptive practices be more visible in religions that are already stigmatized? Are outsiders more likely to notice fraud in unorthodox religions because they expect it? Are the minority of cases of fraud perhaps more visible and known because they are disproportionately discussed in the media – because they make for attention-grabbing headlines – and hence are more likely to sell newspapers (Beckford 1985)?

Some Examples

Below I will focus on religious practices that are not institutionalized. They are not necessarily new, and may in some cases be connected to established traditions (such as new developments within old traditions), but the reason for including them in this discussion as examples is to highlight how beliefs and practices can be used or even manipulated to enrich or otherwise benefit the perpetrator.

In the UK, Niem Mohammed, a faith healer and spiritualist, claimed his skills had been passed down through generations. Among numerous clients, he charged one couple £9,650 to break a black-magic spell he said had been placed on the woman by her jealous sister, which was keeping her from getting pregnant. Another woman was charged £1,300 to help mend a broken relationship, but when nothing changed, he asked for another £1,300, before allegedly threatening to send a Jinn (a spirit) to her home. Local trading standards officers had become involved in 2008 after a client approached them with a complaint. It probably didn't help that Niem Mohammed used an alias, Peer Sayed Sahib ('Peer', or 'Pir', is a title used for a Muslim or Sufi Master or Saint), used a picture on his website of this Peer who appeared older, and lived in a large house with designer cars on the driveway. In his defence, Mohammed denied being a 'conman' and argued that having one or two complaints does not necessarily devalue his work of 15 years. His grandfather, who had inherited his gift from earlier ancestors, had started a clairvoyance, palmistry and faith-healing business that had been in the family for nearly fifty years by 2010, and passed on these gifts to Mohammed. He argued that he prayed for the former client, but that in the end everything is in the hands of God, and the latter client, he said, should not receive her money back as she had benefited of his work for two years (Bourke 2010a, 2010c).

In this case, fraud was operationalized within the terminology of the Consumer Protection from Unfair Trading Regulations 2008, alleging that Mohammed had been 'falsely claiming that a product is able to cure illnesses, dysfunction or malformations' (Ballard 2010: 5).[4] Hence the charge was wilful deception – that he was fully aware that his claims were false. Mohammed was in Wolverhampton Crown Court on 14 charges, involving deception, blackmail and fraud. He was found guilty on 11 charges of fraud and jailed for 18 months (Bourke 2010b).

The expert witness in that case, Professor Roger Ballard, commented that the Pir's practice was not out of the ordinary in the context of spiritual masters of his cultural background – be they Pirs, Sheikhs, Babas, Yogis, or Naths. Also, in South Asia, there is a widespread belief that such figures may be able to harness occult forces. However, Ballard argued, not all such figures have good reputations, and it is relatively common for people to compare Pirs and shop around for a Pir with a good reputation. Ballard, in conclusion, stated that although he conceded that some financial contributions were excessive, he could not answer whether the Pir was a conman and a charlatan, but suggested it may be interesting to see a balance of the Pir's satisfied and unsatisfied customers in order to establish an empirically grounded measure of his success rate.

Another interesting case was that of Archbishop Gilbert Deya (ordained by the United Evangelical Church of Kenya), and the so-called 'miracle babies'. Deya came to the UK from Kenya, Africa, in the mid-1990s. Gilbert Deya Ministries became a fast-growing church with congregations in over eight cities. Deya's ministry included teachings of spiritual warfare, and he was known for casting out demons and performing exorcisms (Waite 2004). But more serious allegations were claims that Deya could produce 'miracle babies' – his power, he claimed, could enable women to fall pregnant and give birth. A UK investigative report alleged that British women, after Deya's blessings, travelled to Nairobi

---

4   These regulations serve to replace the provisions of the Fraudulent Mediums Act of 1951, which itself replaced a series of Witchcraft Acts.

to 'give birth' in a clinic that was situated next to an orphanage (Waite 2004). Despite Deya being adamant that the births were miracles, there were naturally fears of child trafficking and illegal adoptions. By 2004, over thirty couples had come forward to claim they had 'miracle babies' (Mwaniki 2004, Anon. 2004).[5]

One case involving three miracle babies was tried in a London family court, and the judge felt it was important for his judgment to be known and gave leave for it to be reported, to prevent a repetition of 'this deception' (Ryder 2004). He directed in the introduction to his Judgment:

> Let me emphasise what this case is not about. It is not about a court's approval or disapproval of anyone's beliefs. It is not about the truth or otherwise of a particular religious belief. I do not presume to have that knowledge. Likewise, and despite some of the evidence that I have heard, this is not a case about the relative merits on the one hand of rational scientific theories of creation and life and on the other of charismatic belief i.e. divinely inspired power and revealed truth. (Ibid.: para. 4)

In summary, Mrs E claimed to have given birth to three miracle children between 4 September 2003 and 2 June 2004; the gestation times for all three children would have been over twelve months for the first, no more than 27 days for the second, and just over seven months for the third child. Mrs Deya had prayed for Mrs E in front of the congregation – prayers for 'barren women' to receive the 'fruit of the womb'. Two months later, Mrs E felt what she thought were signs of pregnancy. She went to see two doctors; in both cases, all tests were negative. Mrs Deya told Mrs E she had experienced the same with doctors in this country, and had subsequently given birth in Kenya; Mrs Deya informed the court in a written statement that she had given birth to three miracle children.

Mrs and Mr E told the court they thought the miracle had already occurred during the first 'pregnancy', the physical symptoms were there. Mrs E travelled to a clinic in Kenya recommended by Mrs Deya, where she was told that she was well over twelve months' pregnant and could give birth any time. The second child was born soon after in the same clinic and the third child in another clinic. The clinics involved, according to Kenyan authorities, have never been registered

---

5   In one reported case, Eddah Odera, a 56-year-old woman in Nairobi, claimed to have given birth to 13 miracle babies in five years. She was taken into custody for questioning and the children were placed in protective custody. The medical records for the children could not be traced. DNA tests confirmed that Mrs Odera and her husband had no biological link to the children, and they were charged with baby theft and abduction – alongside two British nationals of Ugandan descent (Mwaniki 2004).

with the Ministry of Health. Mrs E reported pain before each birth. In each case, she was told the baby was in breech position, and received injections before an alleged medical intervention, followed by a birth along traditional methods. She never saw the moment of birth, but in each case, the child was held up for her to see, wrapped up, and then removed – and seen again, along with Mrs Deya, after Mrs E had gotten up and washed herself.

The judge was clear that he considered the Deyas' practices deceptive. But many testimonies were not so easily categorized. Members of the congregation with medical training who had examined Mrs E seemed to both believe and not believe. Dr O said he felt movement, yet accepted that the doctor's scan was negative. Dr E accepted that the births could not be medically explained, and added that the only explanation was divine intervention. Both suggested it may also have been pseudocyesis (phantom pregnancy), yet Mrs E had declined any assessments, as to do so would be to doubt what God had done. The judge concluded that Mrs E may have lied to herself, and to the court, and may have had some wilful blindness; she perhaps relied on what others had told her, was at least inconsistent, and perhaps disingenuous on occasion. Mr E appeared to the judge to be a true believer, yet he had not been present with any of the births, and perhaps had nothing to question. Mr E did argue that any questions raised about the births were actually politically motivated acts by Kenyan authorities to undermine Deya. The judge concluded that Mrs E was deceived into thinking she had given birth, and that Mr Deya is a corrupt man who has financially benefited from this deception that involved the trafficking of children.[6]

In June 2006, Gilbert Deya was arrested in Scotland, detained for ten days, and released. Mrs Deya had already been taken into custody in 2004, and in June 2007, she was sentenced to two years in prison in Nairobi, Kenya, for stealing a child (Cramb 2004). In December 2006, Gilbert Deya went to court to fight extradition to Kenya, and in October 2007, a district judge ruled that Deya should be extradited to Kenya. The following year, two High Court judges ruled that Deya could not appeal to the House of Lords to have extradition quashed, and in September 2011, Home Secretary Theresa May decided that Deya will be extradited.[7] However, at the time of writing, he is still in the UK, and has since

---

[6]   Not through direct payment from the 'expecting parents', rather through the effect his miracles had on the rest of the congregation and his ministry.

[7]   Gilbert Deya Ministries is a registered charity and relies on the donations of members, and it has continued to operate. In 2012 the Ministry had an income of £1.67 million http://www.charity-commission.gov.uk/Showcharity/RegisterOfCharities/CharityWithPartB.aspx?RegisteredCharityNumber=1051722&SubsidiaryNumber=0. But in 2012 Ofcom, revoked the licence of Praise TV, the religious channel linked to Gilbert Deya. Praise TV

faced new charges, three counts of rape and attempted rape. He was remanded in custody, and this new case is also ongoing.[8]

A fascinating yet difficult aspect of these cases mentioned above is the lack of a clear distinction between deceptions and frauds on the one hand, and possible acts of God or miracles on the other. The Pir may have had some satisfied clients, as well as some who felt deceived. Ballard argued that it is common for consumers of spells to shop around and ask trusted friends for suggestions for 'good Pirs', which reveals an assumption that there are also 'bad Pirs'. Similarly, members of Deya's congregation believed enough to be witnesses in family court on behalf of the parents of 'miracle babies', and there are undoubtedly members of Deya's congregation who believe that denial of these miracles is all a smear campaign orchestrated by Kenyan authorities, who do not like Deya's alleged ties with the former president. In both cases, the fraudsters benefited from a trusted network in conjunction with distrust towards other options. The Pir and Deya offered something the local doctors could not – magic and miracle babies – and they were trusted over and above the local medical system. Ballard argues that migrants, within their own cultural networks, often hold more fast to their beliefs and practices precisely because they are derided and stigmatized in their new environment (Ballard 2011: 28).

It is also important to note here, however, that affinity bonds are not essential to fraud. As migration increases, the market for alternative forms of magic, miracles and folk healers becomes more diverse and complicated. Secularization has perhaps also come with a new romanticism of ancient and/or foreign practices, considered to be holistic and beneficial in comparison to the current post-industrial world considered by many to be dualistic and detrimental. Hence healers, Pirs and shamans may find that they can find clients well beyond their ethnic or cultural community. But the search for more 'genuine' practices, and perhaps the desire of some to work holistically and globally and introduce indigenous practices to other parts of the world, can be problematic. Aside from the concern that it can provide more cultural and religious frames for affinity fraud, it can also provide more fuel for accusations of the appropriation of other cultures, beliefs and/or practices. These accusations often also carry the charge that this is for financial gain, as is often the case with stories of 'plastic shamans

---

was broadcast under a licence issued to Destiny Broadcasting Network Europe by the media regulator. But Ofcom was concerned that the licensee was not in fact 'the person with general control over which programmes are comprised in the service' http://www.guardian.co.uk/media/2012/aug/28/ofcom-revoke-licence-praise-tv.

[8] See http://www.theguardian.com/uk-news/2013/oct/28/miracle-babies-preacher-gilbert-deya-sex-offences-rape (accessed 6 March 2014).

and New Age frauds' (Mumm 2002).[9] Fraud and deception appear throughout society – yet it does appear that religious beliefs can create good plausibility frames for fraud, and that when the beliefs intersect with culture, ethnicity, or other aspects of identity, then the bonds of affinity may work to enable the frame to be carried further.

Fraud and Minority Religions: Perfect Together?

Inform Cases

Below I summarize some contemporary cases that have come to Inform, and a particular case at length. But let me begin with some methodological notes. When searching Inform's database of cases over the last few decades, I have had to look beyond 'fraud', as people have not always used that term when describing their discontent and complaining about religious groups they had encountered. This is an exploratory effort; I cannot search the database with a combination of keywords and produce a number of cases that represent the level of fraud occurring in minority religions by any means. There are too many independent variables, including the range of terminology used, reasons for calling (or not calling) Inform, and ways in which case notes have been recorded in the past. Furthermore, Inform's dataset cannot be exhaustive. However, what I have found in our database and archive is a number of case studies, small and large, which raised questions and out of which certain patterns emerged which can illustrate what we may already know about fraud and religion, and perhaps raise some new issues. They are the motivation behind this volume.

Notable were the cases where enquirers alleged fraud, yet there were no specific examples or reports of deception, confidence tricks, or scams – the allegations were generalized. In many cases, people had left a religious group that did not meet their expectations, and they had felt deceived in a general sense. These were, however, not always cases where one could easily argue that any deception was calculated and purposeful. In many cases, there was a compelling argument that the group had not been entirely upfront to potential converts about the reality of day-to-day existence as a rank-and-file member. Yet there were also cases where terms such as fraud, scam, or deception were used in an effort to discredit the religious group for other, often more personal, reasons. This is also,

---

9   A good source for such stories and warnings is http://www.newagefraud.org/ (accessed 15 October 2013).

of course, an integral part of the so-called cult scene, where unfamiliar minority groups with unpopular practices are easily demonized. Inform has received, over the years, countless reports of 'cult leaders' abusing their authority, healing scams in churches and New Age circles, overzealous tithing demands, breaches of trust, and more. In many cases, groups were accused of fraud or deception when particular business practices or decisions were out of line with what some followers believed *should* have been their religious values. In almost all cases, the charges would probably not stand up in a secular court. However, they were very significant to individuals who felt that certain practices were not correct within the context of the religious teachings.

There were over thirty cases where people accused another or others of using curses, spells, witchcraft, black magic, vodun (although usually referred to as voodoo), or other supernatural powers or entities to negatively interfere on their behalf. In contrast, two enquirers asked for help in finding 'voodoo cures' for ailments. However, the latter says much about the former cases, where some had in fact sought out practitioners for spells in order to change something in their life (also see Ballard, discussed above). This had led to negative spells or curses, which reportedly could only be removed after more money was paid.

In a little more detail, Ms X contacted an 'occult organization' through an advertisement and paid them £80 to do rituals on her for good luck, but has had bad luck since. Another occult practitioner then told Ms X she was under a black spell, and offered to lift the curse for £100. Ms X couldn't afford this and felt she was doomed to a life of bad luck as a result. Mr L contacted a magician who advertised in a Pakistani paper. The magician claimed that he combines black and white magic to solve all your problems – and offered a free consultation. After the consultation, the magician demanded £140 and upon payment by Mr L, the magician informed him that he had put a spell on him and that 'no one can save him now'. Mr. L believed this – he was distraught and his health and career suffered. Mr L contacted the magician again, who demanded more money. In another case, a woman asked for money she had loaned to an acquaintance to be returned, only for the acquaintance to tell her she had put a spell on her and bad things would happen if she ever asked for the money back.

These cases appear to be quite clearly manipulative with the aim to gain financially, or, in case of the latter, to not have to repay a debt. However, if considered in light of secular fraud, they may only be a drop in the proverbial bucket. Furthermore, the victims are unlikely to see it as a simple case of fraud. Hence, they are unlikely to go to the police, and they are unlikely to add to the fraud statistics.

Personal Vulnerabilities?

Fraud agencies and other institutions are constantly telling us about those who are vulnerable to scams (the 'super victims', the emotionally weak and the elderly) and ways in which we may have made ourselves vulnerable to varieties of fraud such as identity theft, online fraud and confidence scams. Yet it is not only the weak and gullible who are defrauded; New Era (mentioned above) had high-end and successful investors, including Ivy League colleges, wealthy donors and endowment funds, all of which could donate millions at a time. Any social institutions and networks can be used and abused for fraud. It is helpful to be aware that there are individual vulnerabilities that can make one more susceptible, while being aware that this applies to all individuals – we are all vulnerable in some ways at some time.

In one case, several dozen people felt victimized by a certain teacher they had known for a long time, some of them over the span of two decades. They were generally all educated and successful professionals. Yet, over a long period of time, they found themselves deceived and defrauded. (I have summarized this case here based on communication with 25 former students and quoted from further communication with five of them.) The teacher had developed a particular style of martial arts that attracted boys and young men from a particular community of immigrants to which he belonged. Over time, he introduced after-practice meetings where politics and philosophy would be discussed, along with religious messages and concepts – he also hinted at mystical experiences and supernatural powers. He became a teacher on several levels, and students were in awe of his martial arts skills and assumed he had supernatural powers.

Over time, the young men were joined by their girlfriends and other friends they had introduced to the teacher and his teachings. The young students enjoyed the lessons, the connection with their roots, and the friendships they forged with the other students. The teacher, meanwhile, became more preoccupied with the politics of his homeland as well as his mystical experiences and writings. Talks now focused on the unity of monotheistic religions, and politics, as well as healing demonstration and miracles. Another new development was that messages were now relayed to him by angels. He had Divine inspiration. The students, by then, were young men and women who felt politically, socially and spiritually alive and were looking forward to the changes their teacher was telling them about. These were changes that he would lead and in which they would have active roles, that would change the future of the world.

As the teacher began to attract a more diverse following, he syncretized his teachings and messages. Other pantheons became involved, and he introduced purification practices for his students. He also began to synthesize his writings. The leader evolved from being a messenger of divine messages to becoming, eventually, a creator himself. This culminated in his 'awakening', after which he claimed he was the personification of the divine and had the keys to humanity's salvation. In this time, he also progressed from living in city council housing to a large free-standing house in a leafy suburb:

> When I joined [the martial arts] class, I paid a monthly fee for the class. However gradually [the teacher] began to create convincing story plots and a collective goal for which he rallied everyone around, encouraging them to sacrifice as much of their time or finances as they could. Thinking back, every time I was requested to help financially, I felt I had to help as a sense of duty, loyalty, group pressure and the fact that you felt in competition with others to show more commitment to the cause and therefore become closer to [him] as a student / follower. Being sensible with my finances, the amount I contributed was always limited to my means and income. But unfortunately this was not the case [with] other followers, some of whom went into huge debts to provide [the teacher] the fund he asked for … However, there were never any signs of transparency of how the money was spent. It was one of these unwritten rules where no one ever dared to ask how the money was used by their Master, Prophet, Manifestation of Divine on Earth … etc. If one questioned [his] actions, it was considered a sign of miss trust [*sic*] towards Him (i.e. disloyalty towards him was the ultimate sin), and depending on how threatened [he] felt, you were sure to be punished in the form of him ignoring you, character assassination, group isolation, physical intimidation and threat … .

At the height of the group's popularity, there were 70–80 core members and up to 120–50 followers who would regularly attend teachings. Most of the core members were married or in a relationship with one another. Former students, many of whom were first- or second-generation immigrants, reported a family atmosphere with a close network of friends, eating and spending much time together. Many would spend all their free time at the teacher's house, often until the early hours of the morning. The students were vibrant and intelligent young people and professionals, with a mission to do something positive and useful – they were idealistic. Furthermore, they had by then created a strong network of friendships, and had a strong sense of community, and loyalty, towards each other as well as towards the teacher.

The teacher formalized his teachings – both martial arts and religious texts – in order to communicate his wisdom to the public. Students aimed to complete the courses in order to acquire superhuman powers and control their destiny.

Despite being young professionals at the start of their careers, their free time was spent at the teacher's house. There, they would study, work on their progress and purity, and do chores in order to help any projects along – help him with writing, publishing, do works on the house, and so forth: '"We over the years became more and more dependent to him and our decision making in life [r] evolved around him looking upon him as the closest thing to god on earth'

Although the students spent much time in each other's company, they actually did not know much about each other's day-to-day lives. They had been ritually purified in each other's presence, which involved intimate and intense practices, and felt close. But most students felt closest to the teacher who would guide them in their lives. They did not actually confide in each other, and most of what they knew of each other they had heard from the teacher.

Approximately twenty years after the first students joined the martial-arts class, some began sharing some knowledge, questions and doubts about their teacher, and particular details of their own lives that they had so far kept to themselves. In a matter of a couple of months, this led to all but a few students leaving the group:

> There were many factors that contributed to my decision to leave, which was by far the biggest decision I have ever made in my life. For days I felt like a zombie; I could not even read a newspaper, because I doubted my own ability to understand information ... Ultimately, the doses of truth accumulate and reach a critical level and one cannot simply brush them away or make excuses.

The idea of 'accumulating truth', mentioned by the former member above, is something that came up regularly. Students were aware of 'little deceptions' and let them slide, as they may not interfere with the final goal – they may even help it along. But then, for some, there was an accumulation that at some point amounted to too much deception to be able to ignore:

> Throughout my ten years with him, on many occasions, I had to deal with issues that caused cognitive dissonance. However, on every occasion (until the last few days), these doubts were brushed aside because doubting just ONE thing meant doubting EVERYTHING and I was not mentally prepared to accept that. [The teacher] was either god or a fraud; he could not be something in between, and I, like many others, was not ready to accept he was a fraud.

Since leaving, many have felt betrayed and deceived by their teacher. Students had felt they had a personal relationship with their teacher; they received special attention and gave special favours. Many men had given significantly in terms of their time, resources and money. Many women also gave significantly in terms of their time; furthermore, a significant number of the women had had a physical relationship with their teacher – often as a part of the spiritual teachings, healing, or purification rites. (This was also within a context of an unequal power relation.) In the words of one former member:

> ... he had the power to make people around him compete for his attention and favour. The women gave all they could which was themselves and the men tried to give all they could which was either in the form of time, money or blind dedication. This made you feel part of the group and gave you a personal anchor to him.

There has been much soul-searching since the members left, and in hindsight, some aspects of the teacher's leadership and their following has been analysed in a different light:

> Over the years, there were incidents which in my mind raised question marks about his behaviour, particularly with the so-called miracles he was performing, his relationship with his female followers and his general treatment of his followers. These incidents became more frequent and his behaviour towards us more bullish and at times intolerable. However my faith in him being a chosen soul on earth to help mankind, made me turn a blind eye to those problems.

Another former member later realized that the small deceptions and the innocent gossip relayed to the teacher may have had a purpose:

> I thought that sometimes his actions were sly but for a better purpose which was to bring the party involved 'to the light'. 'Sly' meaning he may have asked a devotee about something personal about some other devotee, [he] would then try and pass off that he knew that personal snippet of info about that person from the 'Universe' or by the fact that he was the memory of God.

Many also realized they themselves had had some part to play in the events. Being part of this group, and being close to the teacher, made them feel special: '[M]aybe it was just the appeal of being chosen: the ones that found the true "religion", what [the teacher] called "the souls of fire". This feeling of being special could of course also add to a dynamic that could be manipulated by the teacher:

> [The teacher] used us in a clever way. Educated people in the group would be
> pointed out by him, subtly, when needed. And we would think 'Surely if Dr
> [name of student] believes, then there must be something genuine to all of this.'
> And he would also get us to compete with each other; if person X has done [the
> teacher] a favour, then I better do something bigger and better.

In the words of another former student:

> I could almost compare this to an addicted person with the sole aim in life of
> getting his or her fix. The fix in this case being to receive the Love and attention
> from [teacher]. This could be as little as a smile or a simple kind gesture or
> affection from him. [The teacher] was very much aware of this need from his
> followers and used it extremely effectively in order to take advantage of them in
> anyway that pleased him financially or otherwise!

The teacher was eventually arrested, charged and convicted for a crime, along
with some of his closest followers – they all spent time in prison. However,
many of the issues mentioned above were not part of the court case. The court
case focused on one particular event where violence was involved, and where
police had been called to the scene and found the evidence. Yet the court case
didn't debate the teachings in much depth, or the extent to which he may
have believed that he was God. Although frustrating to many of the former
members, this perhaps also made the case more straightforward and, perhaps, a
conviction more likely. The teacher was absolutely deceptive, but was he always
deceptive? Some still struggled after they had left to state whether the teacher
himself believed he was divine or not. Furthermore, some followers admitted
they had been complicit in some of the deceptions, or at least knew of them.
They rationalized at the time that small deceptions were acceptable, as long as it
brought people to the truth. Finally, many had serious doubts, but stayed in the
fold for their friends and the sense of community. In a sense, the fraudster had
been enabled for quite some time.

Cults or Bad Apples?

Part of the ambiguity of many cases of fraud within minority religion is due to
the difficulty in locating exactly who is to blame. In some cases, one may speak
of institutionalized fraud; the deception is enabled by existing structures that
allow for it. Power and authority, in conjunction with faith and trust, form the

elements of opportunity structures for fraud. These are found in abundance in religious communities. Richard Sipes, in discussing Anson Shupe's book (for which he wrote the introduction), explains this in light of clergy malfeasance:

> Clerical elites, not only in the Catholic Church, consistently try to reduce problems to the psychological motives of greedy, weak, or sick personalities. Clergy malfeasance occurs in a systematic, or structured, context and is not merely the result of a 'few bad apples in the barrel,' however discomforting that thought is to any religious apologists or believers.[10]

Many minority religions may have less institutionalized structures, yet they still rely on institutionalized concepts of hierarchies and authority structures found within the religious traditions within which they operate. Shupe argues that clergy malfeasance is probably as old as practiced religion itself – because of the power differentials between leaders and followers – which, of course, is ubiquitous in all human organizations (Shupe 1995: 59). Religious language in general is filled with concepts of spiritual hierarchy – shepherds and lambs, teachers and students, gurus and chelas – the list goes on. There are of course cases where fingers can be pointed at one or several 'bad apples' who seized upon a rare opportunity, but they often do so within an enabling structure – be it real or symbolic.

Another enabling structure is a historical acceptance of misrepresentation that can be invoked for positive as well as nefarious purposes; we have all come across white lies in a spirit of 'the end justifies the means.' The Jesuits taught a moral doctrine of Mental Reservation, which meant that one did not have the responsibility to tell the truth to one who does not have the right to it. Although not widely accepted within the Roman Catholic Church, it was justified by some as a justified deception that was not an outright lie. Similarly, Mahayana Buddhism allows for 'skilful means', which can be interpreted as occasionally prioritizing expedient ways over correct or true means in order to get (someone) on the 'right path'. 'Moonies' were controversial for their teaching of 'heavenly deception', where deception was acceptable as long as it was for a higher purpose (which was defined by the Unification Church). There have been, and still are, many different ways to rationalize that the end may justify the means.

However, we cannot always blame enabling structures only. The culpability of one side does not necessarily preclude culpability on the other side of the

---

[10] Available on his website, http://www.awrsipe.com/RecommendedReading/spoils_of_the_kingdom.htm (accessed 18 October 2013).

exchange. Groups or recruiters may have offered an unrealistic image of things to come, yet the 'marks' may have enabled the situation in some way – be it wittingly or unwittingly. Perhaps their expectations were unrealistic (a fast path to enlightenment), or they may even have been greedy (unrealistic returns on investment).[11] The relationship between fraudster and victim is interactive, and that dynamic can muddy the waters significantly.

It is often this relationship that is important, as much of the interaction relies on trust, faith and belief. If one believes in a cause, and happily and voluntarily donates money, time and effort towards that cause, no one bats an eyelid. But if suddenly the premises underlying this cause change, and the whole effort is subsequently framed as a fraud, then the belief changes to disbelief. Yet if one cannot establish that the initiator of the cause lied and deceived from the outset, and actually does not believe in the cause, then a case may be difficult to build. Trusting that the perpetrator of the cause is a believer makes it all an unfortunate mistake. But realizing that the perpetrator orchestrated a pre-meditated deception turns the whole endeavour into a fraud.

Finally, interpretations of 'what happened' change. In hindsight, the culpable become more blameworthy, and history more black and white. After fraud, victims often become underdogs, fighting against a structure (be it real or symbolic) that enabled the deceptions from which they suffered. Yet at the same time, as stories are retold and the event becomes stylized for ease of representation, the victims often lose a certain agency they had before. The fraudster becomes the scapegoat. In interpreting 'what happened', other forms of sleight of hand may enter the equation. Denial, the negating of one's responsibility or complicity, is also a misrepresentation of what really happened. Institutions are likely to blame the bad apples, fraudsters often deny ('I didn't do it', 'I didn't mean to do it', 'It wasn't as bad as they say it was'), and victims deny any agency they may have had.[12]

---

[11]   In researching and writing a book about magic, Siegel came to realize that there is an ambivalent relationship between magic (entertainment) and miracles (supernatural acts), which leaves the door open for the possibility of tricks (deception) to lead to magic. Hence, the central theme of his book is about deception, and a kind of human longing to be deceived. The street magicians he joins make a living on people believing in the possibility of miracles (Siegel 1991).

[12]   Stanley Cohen's book *States of Denial* provides an insightful analysis of the different kinds of denial and their implications (2002).

Conclusions

Most of the cases and examples above did go to court, fraud was established, and perpetrators charged and convicted. But I have also discussed some cases, in brief, that did not go to court. In some cases, the relation between fraudster and victim was more complicated, and culpability not entirely straightforward, which may have posed difficulties in a court of law. But in many cases, the victims simply do not go to the police. There can be a variety of reasons, including fears that the claims are not strong enough, a lack of witnesses, a realization that secular courts need a higher threshold of evidence than a believer, and fears that the beliefs will be considered marginal at best, if not cultic, and may be ridiculed.

If victims do go to police, this does not mean that this will lead to a prosecution. Police may dissuade victims from pursuing a claim if they feel that a case will be difficult to make. Furthermore, a fraudulent religious leader may have the means to hire good legal representation to fight the allegations. There is, of course, also the chance that victims and/or witnesses will be harassed and/ or threatened in order to dissuade them from making formal complaints and/or reports. Online forums of ex-members and critics of minority religious groups are rife with allegations and reports of fraud and deception. These discussions are an important force in alerting others to aspects of the internal life of some religious groups, yet the claims made often do not reach the court – for the reasons listed above. Another important point to keep in mind here is that some claims in anonymous forums may be made partially in light of other, non-criminal, grievances, and may be embellished, and lack evidence – hence they may again muddy the waters.

Consequently, the discussion of fraud and minority religion not only revolves around the question of whether there is more or less of it – fraud can occur whenever there is a hierarchy of unequal power. Then, access to believable conceptual frameworks and affinity groups can greatly help any scams along. However, it is the marginal and often stigmatized status of some communities and groups that make the conceptual frameworks more outrageous to most (for example, 'miracle babies', voodoo curses, black magic). Furthermore, the social status of the victims means that they are less likely to have faith in the authorities, or confidence that they will be taken seriously – hence they are less likely to report. The already slippery nature of fraud and deception, in light of frequently institutionalized (and/or doctrinally justified) unequal relationships and adjustable religious frames, becomes more complicated. Awareness of the often interactive relationship between deceivers and believers, and ways in which particular contexts can affect these dynamics, is an essential tool.

References

Anon. (2004). '"Miracle Babies" Couple in Court Today', *East African Standard*, 30 August.

Austin, D.E. (2004). '"In God We Trust": The Cultural and Social Impact of Affinity Fraud In The African American Church', *Race, Religion, Gender & Class*, 4: 365.

Ballard, R. (2010). 'The Practice and Underlying Premises of "Faith Healing" in South Asian Contexts', in the Crown Court at Wolverhampton, Case No. T09/0395 *Regina* v *Niem Mohammed*, FRAI, 15 March.

— (2011). 'The Re-establishment of Meaning and Purpose: Madri and Padre Muzhub in the Punjabi Diaspora', in *Mobile Bodies, Mobile Souls: Family, Religion and Migration in a Global World*, eds M. Rytter and K.F. Olwig. Aarhus, Denmark: University of Aarhus Press.

Beckford, J. (1985). *Cult Controversies: Societal Responses to New Religious Movements*. London and New York: Tavistock Publications.

Bourke, F. (2010a). 'Bogus Birmingham Love Doctor Connned People out of Thousands Court Hears', *Birmingham Mail*, 24 March.

— (2010b). 'Bogus Love Guru Jailed for 18 Months for Swindling Vulnerable Midlanders', *Birmingham Mail*, 1 April.

— (2010c). 'Midland Love Guru Tells Jury He Didn't Force People to Hand Over Money', *Birmingham Mail*, 31 March.

Capps, D. (1992). 'Religion and Child Abuse: Perfect Together', *Journal for the Scientific Study of Religion*, 31(1): 1–14.

Cohen, M.H. (2002) 'Healing at the Borderland of Medicine and Religion: Regulating Potential Abuse of Authority by Spiritual Healers', *Journal of Law and Religion*, 18(2) (2002–03): 373–426.

Cohen, S. (2002). *States of Denial: Knowing About Atrocities and Suffering*. London: Polity.

Cramb, A. (2004). 'Preacher Denies Child trafficking', *Telegraph* (UK), 30 September.

Mumm, S. (2002). 'Aspirational Indians: North American Indigenous Religion and the New Age', in *Belief Beyond Boundaries: Wicca, Celtic Spirituality and the New Age*, ed. J. Pearson. Aldershot: Ashgate Press, pp. 103–31.

Mwaniki, M. (2004). '13 "Miracle Babies" Seized By Police', *The Nation*, 18 August.

Ryder, The Honourable Mr Justice (2004). Neutral Citation Number: [2004] EWHC 2580 (Fam) Case No: FD03C00814 in The High Court of Justice Family Division.

Shupe, A. (1995). *In the Name of All That's Holy: A Theory of Clergy Malfeasance.* Westport, CT: Praeger Publishers.

— (1998). *Wolves Within the Fold: Religious Leadership and Abuses of Power.* New Brunswick, NJ: Rutgers University Press.

— (2007). *Spoils of the Kingdom: Social Exchange and Clergy Misconduct in American Religion.* Champaign: University of Illinois Press.

— (2012). *Pastoral Misconduct: The American Black Church Examined.* (with J.M. Elliasson-Nannini). Edison, NJ: Transaction Publishers.

Siegel, L. (1991). *Net Of Magic: Wonders And Deceptions In India.* Chicago, IL: University of Chicago Press.

Waite, J. (2004). 'Miracle Babies', *Face The Facts*, 13 August, BBC Radio 4.

Chapter 4

Between Faith and Fraudulence?
Sincerity and Sacrifice in
Prosperity Christianity

Simon Coleman

Introduction: Fraud as a Lens of Analysis?

It is fair to say that Prosperity Christianity has not only acquired a bad name in some intellectual and cultural circles, but has also acquired *many* names. Some commentators refer to the 'Faith Movement', or the 'Word of Faith' Movement; others talk of adherents to the 'Health and Wealth' Gospel; for still others, such self-ascribed names as the 'PTL Club' (the early title of a television show run by American preachers Jim and Tammy Bakker in the 1970s and 1980s) could cynically be taken to refer not to 'Praise the Lord' or 'People that Love' but rather to 'Pass the Loot'. The variety and the moral charge of such names tell us much about a movement – or perhaps a religious orientation – that has gained a high if not always enviable profile in religious and academic circles, but which has been hard to pin down in terms of its actual institutional spread or ideological influence.

Perhaps more predictable have been the kinds of questions I have been asked about such Christians in the quarter-century or so that I have been studying them. 'Why on earth do you want to study those nuts?' was the immediate and unguarded response from one anthropologist in Sweden, when I told him in a casual conversation that I wanted to do my PhD research on a new Prosperity ministry in Uppsala (see also Coleman 2002: 79). I remember another question, this time posed at an academic seminar, which boiled down to 'Why are you studying such crap?' This latter inquiry was notable because it came from a distinguished scholar of popular religion, though not of Christianity. I was therefore given the impression that materially oriented practices, 'tasteless' to many anthropologists, were inherently interesting in other, non-Western religious contexts, but not in the one that I had chosen to research.

In fact, I would divide up the most common questions I have been asked about Prosperity Christians into three basic kinds. First, there have been variations on 'Yes, you've told us about what they *say* they believe, but what are their *real* motivations?' Usually, the implication here is that Prosperity Christianity is ultimately about siphoning money away from the pockets of gullible followers towards the bank accounts of rapacious preachers, and that it does so by making outrageous and fraudulent claims about the possibility of acquiring wealth or health through tithing or giving donations. This is hardly a surprising attitude to encounter. But note some of the further assumptions implied in the question: that a religious orientation is really about some *other*, separate, more real reality; that such an orientation can plausibly be reduced to a single, fundamental meaning or explanation, and that followers form a single, unthinking, uncritical mass.

Secondly, there is the 'Are they really *Christian*?' question (see Coleman 2002). Here, the implication is that there are authentic and inauthentic versions of Christianity, and that Prosperity practices and ideologies clearly fall on the wrong side of the divide. This is a query that has been posed by both social scientists and believers, and also points to what Garriott and O'Neill (2008) in a general, theoretical article see as an issue fundamental to dialogical, politically sensitive approaches to the faith; namely 'Who is a Christian?' In more specialized circles, I have also been asked whether Prosperity Christians are 'really' Pentecostals. In such cases, an obvious concern revolves around how seemingly brash, well-resourced neo-Pentecostals relate to classical (that is, long-established, often more conventionally pious) congregations, but in some instances it leads to the further suggestion that the Christians I study are not what they seem, but are *really* Gnostics, or New Agers, or both.

Finally, I receive variants of the question of how it is possible to study such an evidently distasteful religious expression objectively, while avoiding what is assumed to be the almost irresistible temptation to be hyper-critical of its politics, or its deceptive and/or foolish tactics. That kind of approach contains shades of the kinds of queries posed to Susan Harding (1991) in her well-known study of fundamentalists – queries that characterized such Christians as a 'repugnant cultural other' that confounded rationales for either joining or studying its activities. In distinction from Harding's experience, as far as I know, my interrogators do not assume that I am a religious supporter, and therefore by definition a suspect researcher, but they have wondered about my subject-position as an observer in the face of 'self-evidently' objectionable religion.

Identifying Fraud

Of course, sociologists have a long history of studying controversial religious activities such as sects, cults and New Religious Movements, but I think one dimension of the questioning posed to me and Harding refers to the fact that we are both anthropologists, and so it is often assumed that we are – or at least should be – studying people less powerful than ourselves and (in post-colonial morality) need of some sort of advocacy. In response, it is not too difficult to argue for the value of an anthropology of elites or of those aspiring to be powerful (for example, Abbink and Salverda 2013); but thornier questions are raised as to the wider purpose, effects and character of what we write as scholars. We can hardly argue that what we say as ethnographers is so insignificant that it does not matter what position we take. Nor should we assume that we can avoid the political implications of our academic work, no matter how 'neutral' we attempt to be. When I published a report (Coleman 1991) in Swedish about my fieldwork among Prosperity Christians, I found that some local theologians were critical of my approach because I had not exposed such Christians for what they 'really' were (deceptive, politically reprehensible, heretical, fraudulent, and so on), but also because I had made the assumption that the comments and actions of these theologians were an inherent part of the local ethnographic context, rather than somehow inhabiting an autonomous sphere of analytical activity.

One of the most significant points to make about these questions and responses is that they show how many researchers and lay (that is, non-academic) people, including Christians, tend to converge on their intense dislike of Prosperity Christianity. Such dislike takes on various forms, but notice how the assumption of gullibility sometimes shades into assertions of the presence of deception. The former implies a lack of sense or rationality, whereas the latter implies *too much* rationality and self-serving strategy in effecting religious practice.

But such questions also reveal some of the complexities of what might be meant by referring to a religious organization as fraudulent. Who is defrauding whom, for instance? What proportion of defrauders is required before we declare a religious phenomenon inherently or systematically fraudulent? And who decides what is to be considered fraudulent anyway, using which authoritative set of criteria? Do we invoke so-called commonsensical principles to determine what is acceptable? That latter approach is surely problematic, not least because invocations of common sense tend to bypass reflection and self-awareness. In addition, as someone who has carried out fieldwork among Prosperity Christians in Sweden, the UK and Nigeria, whose version of common sense should I draw upon?

An alternative approach might simply be to invoke local legal frameworks, to indicate that fraud has occurred if a preacher or some other adherent has patently committed a crime in the eyes of the relevant state apparatus; but that again is a decidedly meagre approach if we are trying to develop a sophisticated understanding of the cultural, political and social dimensions of religious action. The problem with the law – at least that of the courts – is that it is orientated towards decision making rather than opening up morally complex ambiguities. And after all, religious groups might rebel against what are considered to be harsh laws precisely in the name of superior morality and probity.

There are further epistemological as well as motivational questions to consider. As noted, fraud normally implies deception, for instance – a sense that all is not as it seems, or is made to seem to the observer. That is certainly the implication of some of the questions I have been asked about what is really going on with Prosperity Christians, or who is authentically a Christian or a Pentecostal. But consider how many religions teach some variant of a message that the 'world' is merely a temporary veil or vessel for true reality, or that the unseen transcendent trumps the immanent here-and-now. This is not a trivial point. If a person maintains the idea that it is a religious imperative to see everyday reality as deceptive or irrelevant to truth, should we understand any actions prompted by such a view as baldly deceptive of non-believers – or of themselves? Surely, such an attitude would again provide a limited view of how religious practice works.

Let me give a brief example of what I mean. I have spent some of my fieldwork in Sweden listening to Pastor Ulf Ekman, the most famous Prosperity Preacher in the country and one of the most famous in Europe, justifying his actions and convictions to hostile audiences in Uppsala and elsewhere. In another piece (Coleman 2006: 49–50), I have described his linguistic approach as involving a kind of double-talk, by which I mean his tendency on such occasions to use secular, civil idioms of language that are readily comprehended by mixed audiences, even as he later, in front of his congregation, interprets these events as being deeply spiritually loaded under the surface. In using the term 'double-talk' to describe Ekman's public rhetoric am I accusing him of being disingenuous? I think not. Rather, I am attempting to show how preachers and other believers bridge linguistic divides, attempting to speak powerful, performatively charged language *over* audiences even as they appear at a different level to be merely speaking *to* such audiences. The point is that the same phrase can be interpreted to have religious as well as secular significance, and believers sometimes talk of possessing 'spiritual ears and eyes' that help them appreciate the true power behind words uttered by a divinely appointed speaker. It is hardly unusual, after all, for human action to operate in several registers at the same time. Double-meanings or even motivations (or the use of language that teeters ambiguously between the literal and the metaphorical) do not imply deception in any simple sense.

Finally, there is the problem of what is meant by 'minority' in relation to the fraudulent. After all, the beliefs of many religious movements seem especially odd or irrational precisely because they are new or espoused by the few rather than the many. However, from the point of view of a putative visitor from Mars who knows nothing of human history, is it any more plausible that an entity called 'God' created the world in six days (Christianity) than that a life force called 'theta' created matter, energy and time (Scientology)? Furthermore, referring back again to the wider, global Prosperity landscape of movements and congregations, we see how Pentecostalism and neo-Pentecostalism are largely normal and normative in many parts of West Africa, while such is hardly the case in urban Sweden. Broadly, the same belief or action might seem morally upright in one place, but deeply suspect in the other.

Assumptions and Ambiguities

So what should we do with the notion of the fraudulent as an analytical lens? Drawing on arguments made thus far, I consider that its moral charge should be expected but also analysed – not taken for granted. We clearly need to be aware of how accusations of fraud can function as the witchcraft accusations of our time, revealing how moral frameworks are frequently constructed around and in protection of local systems of authority and law, but also how believers and their opponents, 'cults' and 'anti-cults' (Beckford 1985: 7), co-create religious controversy – and themselves – through their interactions. As David Bromley has put it (1998: 4), both established and challenging religious groups contest for control over powerful symbols and individual loyalties. In the process, he notes, they reveal perspectives on 'legitimate' and 'illegitimate' religion, and we might add that they also gain a voice in public realms of social debate, as in the case of Pastor Ekman. Thus, when I wrote my PhD dissertation on Swedish Prosperity Christians (Coleman 1989), I found myself unable to write about one ministry alone, even though much of my focus was on Ekman's 'Word of Life' (*Livets Ord*) congregation and Bible school in Uppsala. It became necessary to see how debates over the group were refracted and constructed in many other conversations and institutions in Sweden, ranging from other churches to media to local inhabitants of the city. In turn, these debates helped to form the future development of the group itself. My approach took accusations of fraud as an example of a moral panic, reflecting particular tensions within Swedish society at the time over Americanization, tolerance, political representation, and so on (1989; see also Coleman 2000).

In this chapter, I retain a concern with examining the implicit assumptions contained in accusations of fraud, but I want to shift my level of analysis to explore the interactions between fraud and prosperity discourses in a slightly different way. What interests me most here is my point about the ambiguities and multivalences of action and motivation, of address and register, that much religious practice expresses. If accusations of fraud, like legal discourse itself, tend to reduce human action to black and white for the purposes of deciding on a course of (redressive) action, what happens when we go in the other analytical direction, to seek what I hesitate nowadays to call 'shades of grey' but think of as the forms of double-voicing and seeming inconsistencies and ambiguities in Prosperity attitudes and actions? From one perspective, these characteristics of religious practice might be seen as inherently deceptive. From another, they could be taken to refer to the 'subjunctive', 'as if' sides of the religious imagination, funnelled into particular forms of ideology and engagement. In making this argument, I do not deny that there have been many occasions when Prosperity preachers or other adherents have actively set out to deceive or defraud others in a 'secular' and/or 'legally defensible' sense; but the point is that this is not the whole story, and certainly not the part of the story that is counter-intuitive, yet vital, to understand. I shall also want to claim that the trajectory of my own argument, in one sense a typical academic and ethnographic seeking for complexity, need not be regarded as a fleeing from the moral responsibilities or consequences of studying a controversial religious movement.

In the following, I shall provide an all too brief summary of what is meant by Prosperity Christianity, before suggesting that a particular way to explore the ambiguities and 'subjunctivities' of its ideologies and actions is to focus on how an examination of notions of 'sincerity' and 'sacrifice' encapsulates why this form of religious practice seems to get under the skin of so many academics, fellow believers and secularists. Briefly put, when filtered through a Prosperity lens, both of these notions pose certain questions about personhood and materiality that are challenging to certain normative models of what 'proper Christianity', especially Protestant Christianity, are in the modern world. We shall see how the Prosperity approach can be understood as about much more than living a luxurious life, or fooling others into funding such a lifestyle: it is also, and more often, about how to construct a certain ideal of the 'authentic' self. My argument is inevitably a general one, but it will focus most specifically on the contexts of

Sweden and the United States – both western democracies, though ones where the public role of religion is very different.

What is Prosperity Christianity?

Recall the variety and ambiguity of the terms I mentioned at the beginning of this chapter: 'Movement', 'Gospel', 'Club'. The point is that, depending on one's point of view, Prosperity Christianity is either a specific movement with a clearly identifiable genealogy in relation to the history of Pentecostalism, or it is a tendency that also spills into (or, in some people's eyes, 'infects') numerous other, already established, congregations and denominations; it is either an unapologetic export of politically loaded, Americanized mission (Brouwer et al. 1996), or a much more multi-centred, complex set of networks and ideologies which have their own histories in the United States, West Africa, Latin America, Europe, and so on. Stephen Hunt's (2000) useful survey of the worldwide spread of Faith or Prosperity Christians describes it as not so much a movement and more an aggregation of roughly similar ministries, with the United States constituting a centre of diffusion through the mobility and wealth of its pastors, the popularity of American ministries' training courses, and other mission and media activity (see also Coleman 2011: 25). Some powerful Prosperity-oriented denominations, such as the Brazilian Universal Church of the Kingdom of God, spread round the world, creating diasporic landscapes of activity that both track and go much further than Portuguese-speaking populations; yet such transnational spread does not necessarily mean that they maintain close relations with other Prosperity denominations. Furthermore, as I discovered in Sweden but is also evident elsewhere, the apparently uncompromising rhetoric of much Prosperity discourse is not accompanied by exclusivity of membership: the Word of Life ministry has some closed meetings, to be sure, but much of the time it is open to people of other theological persuasion, or none. When the ministry was emerging in Uppsala in the 1980s, it was very common for regular visitors to maintain their membership in another congregation (Lutheran, Pentecostal, Methodist, and so on). Similarly, in his analysis of the Southwest Believer's Convention in Fort Worth, Texas, one of many Prosperity-oriented revival rallies organized by Kenneth Copeland Ministries (KCM) in North America and Europe, Jonathan Walton (2012: 109) juxtaposes the theological consistency of the Word of Faith movement with the creative interpretations and appropriations of it by the demographically and denominationally diverse attendees whom he encounters. Of course there is always a mismatch between message and interpretation in any religious context, but as noted below we should still looks for patterns of appropriation and what they might signify.

In any case, what kind of theological message might one encounter at the convention in Fort Worth, or even at the Word of Life in Sweden? Dennis Hollinger's (1991) profile of what he refers to as the Health and Wealth Gospel is now over two decades old but its main points are still valid. He notes that preachers tend to accentuate not only the goodness and bounty of God, but also how such bounty (healing, prosperity, general well-being) is activated and accessed through the believer's faith (ibid.: 53). While ultimate salvation is in the hands of God, divine prosperity is disbursed according to reliable laws of the cosmos, through which success comes 'to those who have the faith to believe it and who are themselves a giving people' (ibid.: 56). Indeed, drawing on Mark 10:29–30, the argument is sometimes made that a hundredfold return is guaranteed by God, though not always immediately, or in ways predicted by the believer. (At other times, the return is 'merely' said to be tenfold, or is not specified in terms of its multiplier.)

Two aspects of such theology need to be stressed. First, the fact that divinely inspired success is often said to be primarily oriented towards helping others, either materially or through mission, rather than providing a luxurious life for the self. Secondly, that much prosperity is accessed and released through what is sometimes termed 'positive confession' – a laying claim to one's own salvation and to divine prosperity that is made 'in faith', in other words by a born-again person who is expressing their conviction in words. Similarly, Walton uses the image of a contract to describe the relationship between believers and God – a relationship through which the person comes to 'know their own higher self in Christ according to the laws of the scriptures' (2012: 111). And while (ibid.: 112) Walton emphasises the importance of 'positive confession' (or 'name it and claim it', based for instance on Proverbs 18:1), he adds the important point that faith is constituted by going beyond verbal action into material, contractual giving, the 'sowing and reaping' that will result in God returning one's gift many times over.

Of course, different preachers have different emphases, and the ones with transnational ministries adapt their message to context. Furthermore, much Prosperity worship looks like standard neo-Pentecostal practice, with short and repetitive songs of praise, speaking in tongues, altar calls, and so on. But I think what tends to be (relatively) distinctive and carried across different Prosperity contexts is the tendency towards externalizing one's faith, by which I mean reaching out with words, gifts, ambitions into a world of resources and mission, and expecting some kind of return on one's investment of language, donations, effort. This is where we see confession, conversion and contractual giving resonating with and reinforcing each other in their outward orientation – or rather orientation that involves constant dialectic between inner and outer, self and other. Moreover, words can go beyond 'confession' into forms of exchange, in the sense that one person may feel no compunction in taking over and quoting (with or without attribution) the words of another, much as they might cite from the Bible. This is not a form of externalization that can ever be seen as stable or completed: the cycles of giving, confession and attempting to convert others are chronic, just as resources that are hoarded are regarded as losing their power through inactivity, and words that remain unspoken have little value as they have no potential for influence over the world.

One of the better known – and more excoriating – critiques of such theology has come from within evangelical circles, represented by D. Hunt and T.A. McMahon's (1985) *The Seduction of Christianity: Spiritual Discernment in the Last Days*, where their notion of seduction refers to what they see as mere technique, close to self-improvement psychology and positive thinking, almost a form of sorcery (ibid.: 12). Along with others, these authors point to the possible roots of Prosperity ideology in nineteenth-century New Thought and Mind Cure Philosophies (see also, for example, Walton 2012: 111). Indeed, Kenneth Hagin Sr., the late father figure of Prosperity Christianity in the US and beyond, is sometimes accused of plagiarizing the works of a previous preacher, E.W. Kenyon, who seems to have been influenced by Mind Cure. Here is not the place to go into these critiques in much detail, other than to point out that they suggest two further metaphors for thinking about why Prosperity Theology may easily be presented as not what it seems. The image of 'seduction' implies a leading astray from a true path of properly ascetic, or at least humble, Christianity, while the pointing to New Thought suggests that Prosperity thinking was never on a conventional holiness path in the first place, so that its genealogy again leads away from an expected trajectory from mainstream Pentecostalism.

If such criticisms provide examples of how the Prosperity Gospel can be presented as *systematically* flawed in relation to an alternative (and purer or more orthodox) model of faith, there have also been plenty of examples of preachers as *individual* bad apples. For instance the co-founder of PTL, Jim Bakker (who has since renounced his connections with Prosperity Theology), faced criminal charges in the late 1980s relating to accounting irregularities, including fundraising strategies promising luxury hotel packages that could not be honoured, and he was eventually jailed for fraud and conspiracy. Even when accusations are less serious, the suspicion that 'there must be something to be uncovered' remains. Walton (2012: 117) mentions the negative media attention a number of Prosperity Preachers have received in the US since the launching in 2007 of Senator Charles Grassley's investigations into patterns of ministry spending and potential abuses of tax-exempt statuses.

In Sweden, over the last quarter of a century, I have certainly witnessed considerable speculation about the financial status and seemingly mysterious sources of revenue of the Word of Life, as it has evolved from being a small prayer group into an international mega-church. In the early years of the group, critiques of the group's alleged brainwashing techniques also reminded me very much of controversies over the New Religious Movements of the 1970s. The group was seen as targeting younger people, vulnerable victims of what was seen as a somehow irresistible – indeed seductive – message for the unwary and the innocent. As an image, brainwashing not only highlights the importance of intellect but also implies that boundaries between self and other are breaking down, even as it removes culpability from the brainwashed person. Again, the distinctions between the irrational and the fraudulent blur in these moral concerns, as gullible people are perceived to be drawn towards a message that is inauthentic and exploitative, yet emotionally and physically engaging.[1]

Parallel concerns have come together most recently and strikingly in a fresh set of worries over this branch of Christianity. Reflecting the latest moral panic (this time articulated at a much larger scale and in more secular terms), some commentators have suggested that Prosperity Thinking lies at the root not merely of foolish actions of individuals or ministries, but of the global credit crisis itself. Thus in December 2009 (see also Coleman 2011), a headline article of the American magazine *The Atlantic Monthly* asked: 'Did Christianity Cause the Crash?' and went on to state:

> America's mainstream religious denominations used to teach the faithful that they would be rewarded in the afterlife. But over the past generation, a different strain of Christian faith has proliferated – one that promises to make believers rich in the here and now. Known as the prosperity gospel, and claiming tens of millions of adherents, it fosters risk-taking and intense material optimism. It pumped air into the housing bubble. And one year into the worst downturn since the Depression, it's still going strong. (Rosin 2009)

Here again, worries over the irrational and the inauthentic come together, in the sense that Prosperity Christianity is presented as a 'new' kind of faith –

---

[1]   I do not address here the Comaroffs' (2000: 315) analysis of what they call 'occult economies' in relation to Prosperity ideologies, but see my analysis in Coleman 2011.

theological matter out of place – that promotes unreasonable optimism. In contrast, the reference to a previous, putative mainstream is akin to what the anthropologist Herzfeld refers to as 'structural nostalgia' (1997; see McIntosh 2009: 35–6), a kind of longing for a return to a past, Edenic order before decay set in.

The *Atlantic* article argues that even given the current economic downturn, millions still find the Prosperity message to be plausible. We might well dispute its assumption that a single religious orientation can have a direct impact on the world economic order, but one aspect of the argument does resonate with Walton's (2012) discussion of how Prosperity Christians may respond to economic crisis. He quotes the well-known preacher, Jerry Savelle, as urging his audience:

> American households have lost 14 trillion dollars in wealth ... But that will not affect me. Dow Jones is not my source. United States government is not my source. Social Security is not my source. God is my source of supply! ... Stop worrying and start sowing ... If you don't have enough money to pay your bills sow a seed. When a worry about money pops into your mind, sow – this is the spiritual law. (Ibid.: 107–8)

There is no sign of holding back here. God is an infinite source and resource, but one that can only be accessed through externalization of resources from the self, even at a time of personal lack.

So is Savelle's message fraudulent, deceptive, or at the very least downright irresponsible? Perhaps. But by now I hope that we can also perceive fraud as a multivalent category, and one that shades sometimes uncomfortably into forms of action whose moral charge is far harder to assess from a single perspective. In the following, then, I want to argue that the frequent unease that Prosperity Christianity prompts, particularly though not exclusively in western academic, religious and media circles, goes deeper than its possible culpability in tax evasion or dubious theology. More interestingly, it points to and complicates some deep-seated assumptions as to the proper place of religion, and especially Christianity, in what is often called 'modernity'. To explain this point, I move briefly to notions of sincerity and sacrifice, especially as they have been discussed in recent debates over the anthropology of Christianity. At this point, my argument becomes necessarily somewhat abstract, but I hope that the main points will none the less emerge.

Sincerity, Sacrifice and Externalization

In her introduction to *The Anthropology of Christianity*, Fenella Cannell (2006: 7–8) refers to some of the ways in which an ascetic stereotype of Christianity remains influential in anthropological circles. She argues that the dominant view of scholars is still that transcendence is somehow at the heart of the religion. This view is derived in part from a Hegelian distinction between Greek traditions where the divine is assumed to be present in the world and Christian ones where it is said to be radically incommensurable with the immanent world of time and space. Particularly significant is the way these perspectives have gone on to reinforce a notion of 'interiority' that has been applied to understandings of Protestant, particularly Calvinist, thought. Such thought, after all, has often been seen as formative in the creation of modern, western personhood and consciousness under capitalism (ibid.: 20).

In making her case, Cannell draws on the work of Webb Keane, who has explored the gradual introduction of Protestant understandings of interiority in the colonial context of the Indonesian island of Sumba. He shows how the encounter between Sumbanese and Protestant missionaries highlighted the latter's efforts to abolish local practices involving fetishism, ritual exchange, and formalised, ceremonial speech precisely because these practices were regarded as confounding distinctions between the believer and external materiality, thus threatening the moral autonomy and putative transcendent aspirations of the believer (see Keane 2007, Wilf 2011).

Keane's arguments also point insightfully to wider notions of both autonomy and sincerity in contemporary western understandings of the self, even as they reveal something of the Protestant genealogy of such understandings. His piece in Cannell's volume is called 'Anxious Transcendence' (2006: 310) and he discusses the ambivalent relationship contemporary westerners have to a particular kind of materiality – language – which acts as both a shared vehicle of expression existing prior and external to the self and a means through which to convey personal meaning and intention. Language in this sense can be seen as acting as a form of self-objectification 'by which human subjects know themselves and make themselves recognizable to others' (ibid.: 310–11). We cannot avoid using language to express ourselves; but whether Protestant believers or not we should try to be as clear – as transparent – as possible in conveying our meanings and motivations to others as well as to ourselves. Or, in Keane's summary (ibid.: 316): 'To be sincere is to utter words that can be taken to be isomorphic with beliefs or intentions.'

As implied in missionary attitudes to Sumbanese religion, a valorization of spontaneous human activity that centres on the cultivation of direct access to interior consciousness is likely in many religious situations to perceive double-meanings, multiple registers of action, the surrendering of agency to external forces and the trappings of materiality as deceptive or even, in some cases, dangerous. What should be evident however is that Prosperity Christianity as I have described it orients believers towards such 'suspicious' actions and orientations. I have talked for instance of the importance of processes of externalization, where exchanging and moving material resources are seen as an important part of the making of the person as an active and entrepreneurial Christian. Materiality and mediation in these terms are explicitly valued as long as they are kept moving, constantly providing an index of the presence of faith.

I am dealing in crude contrasts here, and reality usually involves a mixture of orientations, but my point resonates well with Jon Bialecki's recent analysis of what he sees as the 'unstable subject of Protestant language ideology' (2011: 683). Bialecki posits that 'Christian language use can be understood by delineating two sharply contrasting, but both valued, forms of speech—"centripetal" and "centrifugal"—each of which has different implicit concerns about the importance of self-identity and the sorts of boundaries that comprise the ethical subject' (ibid.: 679). If the centripetal model highlights the *outward* origins of language and 'the exterior cardinal orientations' that help to create subjectivity, the centrifugal model is oriented to 'lock down language's polysemous nature, deny its physical substrate, highlight personal agency' (ibid.: 682). In Bialecki's account, these two models take concrete expression precisely in the two fieldwork contexts I am juxtaposing. Webb Keane's model of the Calvinist Sumbanese generalizes towards a tendency of Christianity in general, and Protestantism in particular, to valorize both sincerity and an ethic of linguistic 'spontaneity', which ideally locate proper agency and meaning as arising from 'the individuated speaker, and not from larger external networks or material items' (ibid.: 682). In contrast, Bialecki uses my analysis of the Swedish Word of Life Prosperity Gospel ministry to illustrate a religious logic 'where the borders of the self are much more porous, and where the concept of speech acts as being rooted in the specificities of the individuated person' is not valued in the same way (ibid.: 683). In the Word of Life context, words have power because of their exterior source, while spiritual agency is carried forth beyond the limits of the person by a further circulation of both words and money.

Perceived thus, the externalization inherent in so much Prosperity practice is not only or fundamentally about indulging in the benefits of capitalism or mere egocentrism, as its critics allege, but rather about a mediation and reconstruction of the spiritually empowered self through interaction with others as well as through certain forms of materiality. And while such action may seem the opposite of an ascetic model of 'self-sacrifice' through abnegation and cultivation of interiority, it presents an alternative model of such action. So what kind of sacrifice might Savelle be implying when suggesting that one should 'sow' even – or especially – at a time of economic crisis? Perhaps a combination, a multivalent mode of submission and a means of externalizing the self as a person who transcends economic rationality, indeed who engages in risk that seems irrational from a secular perspective but gains significance through doing so (see also Harding 2001). Such sacrificial gifts are distinguishable from careful financial management, but help to index the commitment of the believer (see also Coleman 2011). A kind of authenticity emerges precisely through acknowledging the power and the necessity of the material in remaking the self through risks that objectify commitment to the faith.

In juxtaposing these different models of Protestant practice, we might think back to Cannell's (2006) arguments about significant gaps in the anthropology of Christianity. Her position emerges out of the fieldwork experience of working on another hugely popular but controversial religious grouping: Mormonism. For Cannell, we need to allow anthropology (and, one might add, other disciplines) to stop ruling out of court apparently heterodox (Protestant) Christianities when they seemingly fail to offer a radical separation between either body and spirit. Deviation from an ascetic model need not imply mere or simple deception.

Conclusions

Let me finish by reflecting initially on another question that has been posed to me. This one boils down to: 'Stop being so academic; what do you *really* think about the Word of Life?' In a way, this is also an inquiry about sincerity, since it contains the assumption that the supposed neutralities of an academic stance somehow hide what a person truly thinks behind their mask of professional objectivity. Responding properly to such a question would take another chapter but for now I merely note that I would not be working as a social scientist of religion if I did not consider that the academic perspective offered has integrity. The fact that I have no conscious religious axe to grind has perhaps helped me to study the group without attempting to present a critique of its theological credentials. Yet, I think one aspect of the social scientific approach that is both problematic and politically charged does need to be mentioned here. It seems to me that ethnographers and others tend still to adopt generalizing modes of description that run the danger of implying a greater degree of coherence and consistency in people's beliefs than is likely (see also Robbins 2007). For descriptive and analytical purposes one might say, for instance, that 'Word of Life members believe that health and wealth come to those who possess a sufficient amount of faith.'

The point I want to make here is that such descriptive modes, if misinterpreted, lend themselves too easily to the kind of reasoning that condemns a whole movement or ideological orientation as fraudulent or inherently deceptive of the self and/or others. Patterns of religious commitment, engagement and practice are much more complex, contradictory, situationally based and ambiguous than that description implies. This is a point that is raised usefully if briefly by Walton (2012: 127) when he stresses that 'The seeming clarity and coherence of the Word of Faith message provides the authoritative baseline from which persons, like those represented in this chapter, can then appropriate, negotiate, and religiously interpret on their own terms'; in other words, 'these are not closed ethical systems.' He continues (ibid.: 128): 'Rather than a means to deny or obscure harsh material realities such as unemployment, financial strain, or social chaos, the Word of Faith movement offers a theological chord structure from which persons can theologically riff and spiritually improvise.' Well said. But I have implied in this piece that there is still more going on than just reinterpretation of the theology of preachers. Inherent in the very practice of 'externalization' is a kind of risk taking (and riff making), a chronic remaking of the self through material and objectifying acts that make a claim on the world and the self. This is a mode of exploration, a 'subjunctivizing' of one's Christian subjectivity to see how far one can go. Under such circumstances, a rhetoric of certainty and self-assurance acts as a complex means of encouragement as much as a definitive statement about the world.

Pointing to such complexity is not to criticize such faith; nor to condone it. It is to indicate some of the ways in which ideological boundaries that often appear unambiguous and rigid are not quite what they seem. And proposing this message is perhaps the fundamental intellectual and political job of the ethnographer of minority religions.

References

Abbink, J. and T. Salverda (eds) (2013). *The Anthropology of Elites: Power, Culture, and the Complexities of Distinction*. New York: Palgrave Macmillan.

Beckford, J.A. (1985). *Cult Controversies: The Societal Response to the New Religious Movements*. London: Tavistock.

Bialecki, J. (2011). 'No Caller ID for the Soul: Demonization, Charisms, and the Unstable Subject of Protestant Language Ideology', *Anthropological Quarterly*, 84(3): 679–703.

Bromley, D. (ed.) (1998). *The Politics of Religious Apostasy: The Role of Apostates in the Transformation of Religious Movements*. Westport, CT: Praeger.

Brouwer, S., P. Gifford and S. Rose (1996). *Exporting the American Gospel: Global Christian Fundamentalism*. London: Routledge.

Cannell, F. (2006). 'Introduction: The Anthropology of Christianity', in *The Anthropology of Christianity*, ed. F. Cannell. Durham, NC and London: Duke University Press, pp. 1–50.

Coleman, S. (1989). 'Controversy and the Social Order: Responses to a Religious Group in Sweden'. PhD Thesis, University of Cambridge.

— (1991). *Livets Ord och de Svenska Samhället. Tro och Tanke*. Uppsala: Svenska Kyrkans forskningsråd.

— (2000). *The Globalisation of Charismatic Christianity: Spreading the Gospel of Prosperity*. Cambridge: Cambridge University Press.

— (2002). '"But Are They Really Christian?" Contesting Knowledge and Identity in and out of the Field', in *Personal Knowledge and Beyond: Reshaping the Ethnography of Religion*, eds J.V. Spickard, J.S. Landres and M.B. McGuire. New York: New York University Press, pp. 75–87.

— (2006). 'When Silence Isn't Golden: Charismatic Speech and the Limits of Literalism', in *The Limits of Meaning: Case Studies in the Anthropology of Christianity*, eds M. Engelke and M. Tomlinson. Oxford: Berghahn, pp. 39–61.

— (2011). 'Prosperity Unbound? Debating the "Sacrificial Economy"', in *The Economics of Religion: Anthropological Approaches: Research in Economic Anthropology*, eds L. Obadia and D.C. Wood, (31): 23–45.

Comaroff, J. and J. Comaroff (2000). 'Millennial Capitalism: First Thoughts on a Second Coming', *Public Culture*, 12(2): 291–343.

Garriott, W. and O'Neill, K.L. (2008). 'Who is a Christian? Toward a Dialogic Approach in the Anthropology of Christianity', *Anthropological Theory*, 8(4): 381–98.

Harding, S. (1991). 'Representing Fundamentalism: The Problem of the Repugnant Cultural Other', *Social Research*, 58(2): 373–93.

— (2001). *The Book of Jerry Falwell: Fundamentalist Language and Politics*. Princeton, NJ: Princeton University Press.

Herzfeld, M. (1997). *Cultural Intimacy: Social Poetics in the Nation-state*. New York: Routledge.

Hollinger, D. (1991). 'Enjoying God Forever: An Historical/Sociological Profile of the Health and Wealth Gospel in the USA', in *Religion and Power Decline and Growth: Sociological Analyses of Religion in Britain, Poland and the Americas*, eds P. Gee and J. Fulton. London: British Sociological Association Sociology of Religions Study Group, pp. 53–66.

Hunt, D. and T.A. McMahon (1985). *The Seduction of Christianity: Spiritual Discernment in the Last Days*. Eugene, OR: Harvest House Publishers.

Hunt, S. (2000). '"Winning Ways": Globalisation and the Impact of the Health and Wealth Gospel', *Journal of Contemporary Religion*, 15(3): 331–47.

Keane, W. (2007). *Christian Moderns: Freedom and Fetish in the Mission Encounter*. Berkeley: University of California Press.

McIntosh, J. (2009). 'Elders and "Frauds": Commodified Expertise and Politicized Authenticity among Mijikenda', *Africa (Journal of the International African Institute)*, 79(1): 35–52.

Robbins, J. (2007). 'Continuity Thinking and the Problem of Christian Culture: Belief, Time and the Anthropology of Christianity', *Current Anthropology*, 48(1): 5–38.

Rosin, H. (2009). 'Did Christianity Cause the Crash?', *The Atlantic*, December http://www.theatlantic.com/magazine/archive/2009/12/did-christianity-cause-the-crash/307764/.

Walton, J. (2012). 'Stop Worrying and Start Sowing! A Phenomenological Account of the Ethics of "Divine Investment"', in *Pentecostalism and Prosperity: The Socio-Economics of the Global Charismatic Movement*, eds K. Attanasi and A. Yong. New York: Palgrave Macmillan, pp. 107–29.

Wilf, E. (2011). 'Sincerity Versus Self-expression: Modern Creative Agency and the Materiality of Semiotic Forms', *Cultural Anthropology*, 26(3): 462–84.

Chapter 5

Folk Healing, Authenticity and Fraud

Stuart McClean and Ronnie Moore

Introduction

In this chapter, the authors focus on critically examining and analysing contemporary healing beliefs and practices in relation to prevailing debates and discourses about fraudulent and/or 'quack' healers. We examine folk-healing practices in the UK, exploring in particular the example of crystal and spiritual healing, and we offer ethnographic data to help ground some of the discussion. Folk healers typically have no formal training, or at least minimal quasi-formal training, but claim some ability to heal, and most will not charge a standardized rate for the services they provide. Less professionalized than other complementary and alternative health practices, they frequently exhibit a 'folk' understanding of, and approach to, health and illness. More often than not they are seen as part of a community resource (Moore and McClean 2010).

Practices like crystal and spiritual healing – part alternative health practice, part 'New Age' belief system – are located in a broad field that can be defined here in an anthropological sense as minority religion. These have sometimes been constructed as 'marginal' and esoteric healing practices concerned with spirituality and self-actualization (personal growth and improvement), analysed in the broader context of what is termed the 'New Age' (especially in the sociology of religion). In the US, McGuire's *Ritual Healing in Suburban America* (1988) for example, was a classic study that explored healing groups in suburban New Jersey, and is a good illustration of the 'exotic' in middle-class America. Other texts such as English-Lueck's *Health in the New Age* (1990), Hess's *Science in the New Age* (1993), and Brown's *The Channeling Zone* (1997) made important inroads into understanding the nature of 'New Age' healing practices in American society. The 'New Age' can be defined as a social movement incorporating 'diverse goals', but which may be likely to promote a variety of personal and interpersonal values such as self-responsibility, psychological growth and creativity (English-Lueck 1990: 1). This complex and diverse movement also attracted the attention of the social sciences in the UK (Heelas 1996, Prince and Riches 2000, Heelas et al. 2005), with the focus on 'soft' capitalism, and its growth clearly reflected in the magazines and books now dedicated to the esoteric, healing and self-help literature. The use of crystals and stones to heal the body is typical of such New Age marginal religious and healing activity.

As well as being defined as broadly New Age, such practices can just as usefully be described as 'folk' healing, as the following should illustrate. In the broadest sense, folk healing refers to what we would call informal (that is, lay) health practices that are rarely advertised and for which formalized payments are not always pursued. They are different from other more complementary health practices in the UK, or what has increasingly been called CAM (complementary and alternative medicine), in that complementary practices have mimicked other specialized biomedicine as a fee-paying model. Lay people practice folk healing, but they are not legally recognized as professionals (Stone 2010). Given that they are stigmatized as a 'primitive and backward remnant of magico-religious thinking of the past' (Lazar 2006: 36), questions about fraud are never very far away.

Crystal healing, for example, as it is understood and practised today, has its origins in New Age western healing practices of the 1980s and 1990s, but we note that the use of crystals for healing purposes has a longer history (see McClean 2013). Since the 1990s, a steady stream of crystal-healing texts have been published that aim at providing an 'expert' view on crystals; small centres in the UK (and further afield) have been established in order to provide tuition and guidance in crystal healing (though there are some significant differences between crystal-healing centres about how to do this and what would be included in the curriculum), but mostly the training offered is minimal and does not compare with the more professionalized approach of many complementary health practices.

We begin by defining fraud and deception and considering the social construction of fraud, against the backdrop of changing views about 'quackery' in health-care contexts. We go on to highlight anthropological perspectives on health and healing, which are inevitably linked with discussions about cosmology, spirituality and magic, and we offer some relevant discussion about the ways in which authenticity has been constructed in the pre-modern and modern era. We then offer some key ethnographic illustrations from one of the authors' research (McClean), in relation to constructions of 'bone fide' crystal and spiritual healing, authenticity, and the problems of financial gain, all of which are introduced to help ground the theoretical and conceptual issues.

Defining Fraud and Deception in Folk Healing

One popular (media) discourse surrounding crystal healers suggests they are perceived as 'crackpots' espousing 'mumbo jumbo' and 'silly nonsense' for astronomical fees (Moir 1993), a view also noted in the academic literature (Hornborg 2012). Yet, it is fair to say that there has always been a difference between the healers that are considered to be deserving of some credit (regardless of the evidence-base) such as to be found in more commonplace complementary health practices, and those who are beyond credulity; that is to say, individuals who are seen as 'charlatans' and 'quacks' – a throwback to the times past when people were perceived as peddling mostly harmless but expensive cures, potions and tricks for a diverse demographic in British society (Porter 1989, 1993, 1994).

There have been repeated and concerted campaigns against the quacks and the charlatans and hucksters of healing medicine. In Britain, these campaigns are well established and documented: campaigns against the quacks, charlatans, mountebanks, cranks and hucksters of medicine in Britain go back at least as far as the sixteenth century, when the kingdom's first Parliament Act regulating the practice of medicine was passed in 1512 (Wahlberg 2007: 2307).

Early sellers of patent medicines were accused of 'quacking', which meant exaggerating the curative properties of these medicines. A 'quacksalver' (an Old Dutch word) meant boasting about the virtues of their salves (or remedies). Quackery has been applied to a wide range of healing systems and forms of alternative medical practice and knowledge. Others have referred to them as hucksters and snake oil peddlers (Diamond 2001, Morrall 2008). Wahlberg (2007) states that the reason these healers were referred to as quacks in the past was not just because the nature of the therapies that they provided or the products they offered (though this was relevant), but more commonly it was because of their unorthodox beliefs: ones that provided a counter to scientific biomedicine during the period of biomedicine's emerging dominance.

So there is nothing new in this rooting-out of fraudulent healing activities, and more recent campaigns, such as that from the House of Lords (2000) to rid the UK of incompetent, dangerous and distrustful practitioners of complementary health is but one manifestation of this. Science and evidence-based medicine is the creed and ideology under which it is believed it can be achieved. However, rather than seeking outright ban of some practices, the strategy has, according to Wahlberg (2007), been about the 'normalization' of its practice and use – that healers must be regulated and seen to be fit to practise through the use of certification, healer competency, use of qualifications, and so on – modes of professionalization from which folk healers by definition become excluded. In our ethnographic example below, we highlight some of the ways in which folk healers have engaged with this agenda in order to appear authentic.

Indeed, under the House of Lords Select Committee report on complementary medicine (2000) a classification of CAM was produced, which resulted in three distinct groups: those that demonstrated some scientific efficacy for a limited number of ailments (for example, acupuncture); those that may lack scientific evidence-base but provide comfort as support to patients; and the last group of 'alternative disciplines' that were described as indifferent to the science of conventional medicine and lack any credible evidence base (for example, crystal healing and other folk-inspired healing practices). This report was published at a time when other public watch forums in the US like Quackwatch (www.quackwatch.com) started to emerge, and the US National Council against Health Fraud (www.ncahf.org), as well as medical practitioners and writers in the UK such as Ben Goldacre who have had a role in overseeing health activity and identifying what they see as health fraud or what has been termed 'pseudoscientific' therapies. Almost by definition this has become anything non-biomedical. As such, scientific (and biomedical) knowledge is more valued (see Lee-Treweek 2005), which reflects a battle between medical systems for authenticity, legitimacy and acceptability.

As a theme, quackery is quite strongly reinforced in writing about CAM, and we can see how issues connected to fraudulent activity are tied up with the debate on quackery. A firm critic of complementary health and certainly esoteric healing practices – Edzard Ernst (2006) – talks about complementary health moving from quackery to science in the surge for legitimacy, public acceptance and the need for regulation and to ensure public safety. In the new era of some acceptance of non-orthodox health practices, the issue is about the internal split of the CAM field, using practitioners to help the public distinguish between the competent, incompetent and/or dangerous (Wahlberg 2007). The issue of quackery is focused on practitioner competence and accreditation and not necessarily the efficacy of the treatment (mirroring in some ways the debates and controversies in the US over the distinction between drugs and supplements, the latter not being based on clinical efficacy).

So, how should we define fraud? With difficulty, seems to be the answer. There are those who have acted with active and conscious deception to commit fraud (sometimes financial or status-related), such as the work of Daniel P. Wirth and the now-discredited fraudulent study on IVF and prayer (Ernst 2006). And yet, one of the key problems of much healing activity and research is that there is little formal evidence in peer-reviewed publications, so any claims may be perceived as fraudulent (Lee-Treweek 2005). Fraud usually involves some level of deception (to oneself, but primarily to others who will be unwitting players in this deception). This is central to the issue: in the modern era, healers play a role in society (as do orthodox doctors) and even those who feel what they do works do not do it without some doubts as to its efficacy, and so some level of deception is involved. However, the issue is not just focused on whether something does or doesn't work. If a placebo is offered or if a GP recommends a homeopathic remedy for a strain, when they know it doesn't work, is this fraud? CAM practitioners themselves are interested in and concerned with perceived fraud amongst their community, partly in their self-interest to defend what they do and see their own activities as honest and trustworthy, to avoid litigation, but also to protect their clients.

Bolton (2011) discusses the self-belief required to carry out healing acts, and the notion of belief in the performance of medical practice. For Bolton, the crucial definition and criterion of quackery/fraud is one's self-belief in the practice, regardless of effectiveness. The GP that prescribes the drug that proves to be ineffective is not a quack if they believed it had a chance of working. The GP that tells a patient to take homeopathic remedies believing it not to work, but thinking that this may help the patient through placebo is not a quack. Equally, the healer with genuine self-belief in what they are doing, irrespective of actual effectiveness and objective benefit is not a quack. Few healers must be interested in deception for the sake of it (or through monetary gain, which is unlikely to be significant). And yet, few healers could be described as fanatical (having absolute confidence in their effectiveness). And so, there are a large number of healers between those statuses: they have a degree of self-belief that what they are doing is helpful, but there is also self-doubt, and uncertainty is the normal state. This issue is raised by Taussig in an essay about faith and scepticism, where he argues that sceptical attitudes towards the practice may even be normal as an approach to learning amongst the practising healers (in this case, Shamans): ' … it would surely not be unfair to venture the hypothesis that learning Shamanism means doubting it at the same time and that the development of such a split consciousness involving belief and non-belief is what this learning process is all about' (Taussig 2003: 284–5).

In this case, are they quacks, and are they committing fraud, or does this distinction raise problems with this definition? The view that I would add here, is due to the conditions of modernity that we consider here, there should be few fanatics in modern society who have no level of self-doubt over their practice. The debate over the Shamanic healers is equally interesting as writers have referred to some poor healers who cannot believe either in themselves or what they are practising (Schieffelin 1996), or they fail to learn the skills of innovation (see Kendall 1993) and equally make poor healers.

In Langford's (1999) study of the modernization of Ayurveda doctors' practices in India, and the notion of mimetic action, she was led to question whether the Ayurveda doctor was authentic or a quack. She explains that medical anthropology leads one to be discomforted by notions of quackery, explaining:

> ... quackery is a concept used by medical practitioners and others to discredit medical practices other than biomedicine (which is sometimes also termed modern medicine, cosmopolitan medicine, or allopathy). Some biomedical doctors consider all Ayurveda to be a kind of quackery, based on a bogus view of the body and dispensing treatment the biological effects of which are scientifically unproven. As a medical anthropologist, however, I was prepared to put biological efficacy aside in favor of symbolic efficacy. (Langford 1999: 25–6).

She also explains how such discussions and debates about efficacy and quackery are debated at the local level, where there are as much contested views as there would be between orthodox and non-orthodox medicine.

Quackery could hardly mean simply a mimicry of medicines or methods or qualifications, since such mimesis is essential to the training and identification of any medical practitioner. Quackery could also hardly mean a mimicry with intent to deceive, since deception may be used beneficially to inspire the trust of the patient (ibid.: 41).

It should be remembered that healers in history (Jesus and Rasputin provide but two notable examples) have also been regarded as fraudulent and not to be trusted. But such concerns with the fraudulent raise issues about not just the efficacy of the act (whether it works and whether the healer knows or doesn't know that it works), but the idea about what is authentic and sincere in modern societies. What does it mean to anthropologically examine healing practice, and say something is fraudulent? On what basis is it fraudulent? Who has the power to define what is or isn't fraudulent or trustworthy? How does one position of authority come to define these things for others?

Magic, History and Authenticity

Anthropological perspectives on health and healing are inevitably linked with discussions about cosmology, spirituality, other-worldliness, ritual and magic. Evans-Pritchard's (1937) classic work is an important illustration of this, but examples are likely to be found in virtually all human societies. There is also a temporal as well as spatial imperative here, which helps highlight the ways in which healing and fraud is constructed. Historically, we also see the connection between health, healing and magic. The pre-Enlightenment way of thinking was very much bound up in these central ideas and, as Kassell (2005a, 2005b) illustrates, beliefs are evident in the early modern period and have coexisted (and continue to coexist) with biomedical scientific systems in what sociologists term late/post modernity (Moore and McClean 2010). Taussig (2003) has discussed the ways in which Shamanic healing in societies has drawn attention to the exposure of the trick of healing (as well as concealment), and by doing does not lessen the magic of healing. For Taussig, one may substitute the word 'fraud' with the word 'simulation' or 'mimesis', as the relationship between belief and non-belief is not straightforward.

As discussed above, 'fraudulent' is taken to mean, by deception, inappropriate action for personal gain. We suggest that localized beliefs about health and illness (whether they affect a cure or alleviate suffering or do not) are deemed to be held as authentic since (as with religion) communities believe in the power of the cure rather than rely on biochemical/medical models of proof. In other words, the notions of fraudulent and authentic healing are not unrelated to the belief system in which a person or community is immersed, that is, health systems. The cure is held to be the manifest function while social solidarity of communities may be held to be the latent function of folk healing and other marginal religious beliefs and healing systems.

If we hold this to be true, we should turn our attention away from quackery in informal healing systems and look at quackery within the biomedical system. Experienced physicians, particularly general practitioners, know full well the importance of the lay perspective in terms of efficacy and successful practice. The patient-centred approach is deemed important in modern biomedical practice. Some have even resorted to what might be considered as magical practice in the medical encounter:

> Mexican miners liked and respected Dr Wilson, the company Doctor and came to him with a great variety of complaints ... 'Well', he said, Nine tenths of the [Mexican] people who came to see me for treatment are really not in need of medicine at all, but if I don't prescribe something, they feel I have no interest in them, or do not understand their case, and consequently will lose confidence in me. So I give them some non medicated tablets with directions to take one after each meal, one at bedtime, and I tell them if they don't get to feeling better in a

few days to come back. If they return, I change the colour of them and in a few
days they will get well and I get the credit. (Cited in Graham 1985: 175–6)

One might argue that this represents pragmatic medicine. Helman (2006)
presents a similar case for the importance of the power of placebo or suggestion
in medicine. However, the ethics and authenticity of this may be legitimately
questioned and it might be argued that this is the thin edge of a dangerous
wedge. The boundaries of biomedicine then appear to be problematic,
sometimes resulting in harm or fatality (see, for example, the extreme cases of
Dr Neary in Ireland in 2006, who performed an inordinate number of Caesarean
hysterectomies without good reason, and Dr Shipman in England who murdered
many of his patients). Such behaviour may be held to be fraudulent and, in these
cases, criminal.

The *raison d'être* for biomedicine and its general principles (first do no
harm) have been questioned by scholars, even within the profession itself. The
sociologist and social critic Ivan Illich (1976), for example, classically detailed
medical iatrogenesis as a consequence of modern medicine, while Szasz (1961)
and others denounced the prescriptive, inhuman and forceful medicalization
of people deemed to be mentally ill. More recent medical practice also raises
the issue of authentic medicine further with the rise and popularity of body
enhancement procedures. Yet the authority of this medical system is not
seriously challenged, even if the ethics are.

Discussions and analysis of what is fraudulent also relates to the broader issue
of what we find authentic and how this authenticity is established. The discussion
of authenticity is a familiar one in the social sciences where the dominant model
has been to utilize social constructionist conceptual frameworks to question the
nature of authenticity in culture and society. In the description of 'culture' many
social practices can come under scrutiny as to their authenticity, such as foods,
music, styles of dress, music artefacts, and so on. What counts as authentic
in many of those cases, where it involves some level of syncretism, is fraught
with difficulty.

The anthropologist Richard Handler, in his analysis of authenticity, argues
that authenticity is a 'cultural construct of the modern Western world' (1986: 2).
He explains that in the West we seek out authentic cultural experience, but that
this desire for authenticity is our modern western problem and is tied up with
other notions of the individual in western society. Utilizing the theory of Lionel
Trilling's *Sincerity and Authenticity* (1972), and the concept of sincerity (the
absence of feigning or pretence), Handler argues that such modern notions arise
in conjunction with our modernity and the rise of social mobility (and thus,

the possibility of changing social status). Prior to the modern era, in medieval society, nature and the cosmic order was God-ordained and individuals were assigned a social status that was granted by God and was therefore not in question (in other words, it did not become a social status); nor did it alter: That a king can be imagined as playing the social role of king suggests how greatly the modern outlook differs from the medieval, in which, presumably, the king simply was king, by virtue of the essential being God had granted him (Handler 1986: 3).

In earlier times, pre-modernity, gods and kings could heal with their touch. In the modern era, with the rise of individualism and the absence of ordained social status, it emerges that individuals (including kings) 'play' social roles – they 'act' and 'take a position'. The present concern for authenticity comes from the very modern problem of perceiving status (that is, healer) and role playing (playing the healer) as one and the same thing. The authentic role of the healer in the modern era is, by default, always in question and their sincerity always in question as there is no 'naturalized' healer status. Not just critics, but those who heal are aware of this and the tensions surrounding healing practice draw attention to this problem of authenticity and legitimacy, as we shall see with the ethnographic example below. The healer's desire for authenticity arises mostly from needing to not draw attention to the role playing, although there are exceptions.

In pre-modern society in Europe, if one could heal they were considered a healer (as 'naturalized status') and one ordained by God to carry out that work; they did not play the role of healer. Today, despite the legitimacy claims of those who heal, the essential problem is that the figure of healer has become a social role that one adopts and adapts according to the 'management of the self' strategy (see Goffman 1959). All forms of action are therefore under scrutiny and questioned for their authenticity and sincerity, even amongst healers themselves, as we shall see. All medical practitioners then are not healers as a natural state – they are performers and they must be convincing in their acting-out of this role (see Bolton 2011, McClean 2013). Healers, as well as doctors, and those who practice religious beliefs, must try and convince with their performance – self-belief in the performance is not a prerequisite for its effectiveness (Lévi-Strauss 1963).

Crystal and Spiritual Healers in Northern England

In the remainder of this chapter, we refer to ethnographic research to illustrate and deepen understanding of some of the issues raised so far, but also to ground these conceptual issues. The ethnography referred to here was based on research into the lives and practices of crystal and spiritual healers in the North of England. The healers made use of a Centre (a Victorian terraced house located in the centre of a provincial town) to provide their healing activities, to learn, to socialize, and to seek out and offer information about a whole range of healing and non-healing related issues. The researcher (McClean) conducted participant observation over a two-year period and as part of this also learnt to become a healer – this was, in fact, essential to becoming accepted as part of the healing community at the Centre.

'Bone Fide' Crystal Healing

In the literature on complementary health, the issue of the trustworthiness of practitioners often focuses on professional status, licensure and accreditation to a professional body, to protect the public from unscrupulous practitioners. In the field of crystal healing and other less professionalized, certainly less organized, healing practices, the issue surrounding the scrutiny of healers is less clear-cut. On one level, all the healers who took part in the research knew how they might be perceived by others, and so questions about their activities and the training that was provided were raised frequently. Much of this issue focused on their concern about being seen as fraudulent, and the practitioner issue of being competent and proving that competency. How to be 'bone fide' crystal healers, as opposed to ones that were illegitimate, was something they were concerned with.

The head of the Centre, and the individual who led the healing courses – Teresa (pseudonym, as are names of all participants) – maintained the view that the organization of healers in the UK was authentic. This was formed in 1988 by a group of crystal healers to promote training in crystal healing and to ensure that their courses 'adhere to the minimum training standards set by the organisation', and that regulatory standards are met by the affiliated schools (that is, the healing Centres distributed across the UK). Its existence suggests that even esoteric healing activities such as crystal healing are closely regulated and standardized by a national body. More importantly, Teresa was keen to point out that these are 'bona fide' organizations, unlike the other 'quango' groups that she argued could be set up at any time. Teresa explained what happened to healers whom she taught. They were given certificates and told they could officially practice. For Teresa, this meant that the individual is insured and their details are placed on a national register organized by the main body of healing organizations. Teresa's responsibility was to oversee the courses and to ensure that training standards were being set. In many ways, the business model here was very similar to a pyramid scheme, in that trainee healers that Teresa taught could themselves go on to set up a healing course that Teresa would oversee and vouch for. The offshoot courses, for example, had to be based on Teresa's model, and she explained how she would check up on their trainees' practice and assignments. As Teresa explains, this involved a lot of work:

> It just gets busier. I don't know how I'm going to cope with all the work. I've got tutors working for me now, one in Newcastle, one in Sedgefield, Beth in Northamptonshire, and Jane in Malvern. They're all over-subscribed on their courses. I have a little arrangement with all of my tutors. I give them a syllabus – the tutors are part of my group by appointment only, they have to be just right – I tell them how to structure the course and once they start I visit them once in the two years and assess how the course has gone. If it's all okay I'll give them a lovely little certificate. In return I ask for 5 per cent of the course fees that they receive. I like them to teach a course that is similar to the one I designed, but obviously they make it theirs, otherwise it would lose its spontaneity.

In many ways, this also tells us something about the economic incentivization of the pyramid scheme in healing. It may appear to be one of the hallmarks of problematic or fraudulent activity, but also represents some mimicry of other more professionalized health sciences. Also, Teresa clearly had an input on other courses around the UK, of which she was patron. She emphasized that linked healing centres did toe the line when it comes to the message they communicate publicly. For example, on one occasion I asked Teresa, 'Do you have any conflict with any of the healers, over difference of opinion or anything like that?' She replied, 'Well, we have a tutor who I've got to go and talk to Jane about, as she recommended her ... she is cutting corners with the course. I don't think she is doing it right, she won't do the work for the course so we are going to have to talk to her to sort it out.'

Teresa stressed the level of organization that her diploma demanded. This issue and what it signifies in terms of 'professionalism' is an important part of the Centre's legitimacy – that is, the way 'significant others' (patients, regulators, CAM therapists) perceive and comment on these regulatory activities. A good example of this foregrounding of professionalism is the way Teresa distributed certificates to newly qualified crystal healers. These were awarded on completion of the first and second year of training, and another was given once the tutor was capable of conducting their own courses. Although healing trainees said they didn't care much for the certificate, they admitted that its presence would help legitimate (and authenticate) their practice to prospective patients. Healing practitioners, then, in order to head off accusations of fraud and to distinguish themselves from other healing organizations such as faith healing, may use training, education and accreditation to show how they have embarked on professionalizing strategies, as they seek to build upon their standing and legitimacy (legally and otherwise). We could argue that these moves show a certain convergence in the ways in which all healing and complementary health organizations have presented themselves, similar to the biomedical profession.

More crucially, in order to raise the legitimacy of their practice and to separate themselves off from other 'problematic' healing practices, the healers spoke frequently about their dislike and distrust for Reiki healing. They frequently compared themselves to other healers from different traditions, but there was particular suspicion for Reiki healers in the UK, whom they felt did not receive the necessary training – the unscrupulous and ill-trained was reserved for others and not themselves. For example, one of the younger male healers – Charlie – had laughed at the suggestion that Reiki healing was in the same league as hands-on spiritual healing:

> Reiki though, that wasn't learnt through twenty years of understanding the symbols and the methods of healing. It was taught from the masters to the students, now though, you just do three days a year for a while and they give you a certificate and you're a Reiki healer. It's ridiculous, and who knows what they are doing, they don't understand the symbols they are using in the healing, and in the initiation they are put things in their aura that are ways of controlling them [the clients] and they don't know what kinds of things they're carrying around with them.

Adele, another trainee healer at the Centre, had said that Teresa had taught them not to trust modern Reiki healing and that something fraudulent (and dangerous) was at the heart of what they did:

> You wouldn't really think it seeing the people that go along to the Reiki meetings, middle-aged women, very nice people and everything. You see, it works by them visualising symbols being thrown into your chakra points. They usually ask you to close your eyes and then they do their symbol and put it in your energy field, but what people don't realise is that it is wrong and it is actually stunting their development. It's like the Moonies, from the outside we all might think they're a

bunch of nutters, but when you're in it you feel differently, but they all use a form of control over the people.

For Charlie, and others at the Centre, their feelings of uncertainty at the authenticity of healing practice are displaced on to 'other' less credited healing beliefs – in this case, Reiki. The healers at the Centre were aware of the discrediting of healing practices, and the ranking of CAM practices, and so were keen to further discredit practices perceived as more charlatan-like. Suspicions are aimed at the accreditation and standards of the healing, as well as what Charlie and Adele hint are the intentions of the healers to control their clients. Professionalizing strategies like the ones listed above were also there to mark themselves as different than Reiki and more in line with other more credible healing traditions.

The Problem of Financial Gain

Healers maintained an ambivalent relationship to money and payment, which is common with many folk healers who are not committed to a fee for service model present in other private CAM services (McClean and Moore 2013). Such ambivalence is also present amongst New Age healers, who know that any financial benefit from their activities leaves them open to accusations about their motives (Brown 1997). Teresa saw herself as a businesswoman and a healer, and did not see these identities as necessarily incompatible (given her interest in charging others to use her course), but there was a tension about this.

For example, Teresa suggested that the healer's role was incompatible with any desire to possess status or money. Teresa stated that healers are not highly remunerated, as the higher spiritual authorities or 'upstairs', as she referred to them, ensured that healers had just enough money to work. For Teresa and others at the Centre, healers who seek purely financial gain could be perceived as fraudulent. Adopting this rationale, to practise something that may or may not work matters less than the motivation for doing it. There is a problem here, as the desire to serve and be spiritual raises other concerns: spiritualism confers the promise of high ritual status when it is carried out satisfactorily, and such promise increases the competition for status amongst healing groups. In this respect, the issue of status amongst healers (or healer reputation) was more important than the ability to command a high fee (although some healers also sought this).

Like Charlie, Teresa had criticized other healing practices such as Reiki that she felt were being used in a potentially fraudulent way, and that much of the criticism was directed as a perception that money and financial gain was the primary motivation for the healers:

> You see you can become a Reiki master after just three weeks, where normally it would have taken someone a lifetime to develop like that. You see, over time the symbols [used in the healing] have been bastardised and so the kind of Reiki they are doing is different from that in the past, it's like a game of Chinese whispers. There are an awful lot of corporations involved in making this so, by changing little things in the healing so it is slightly different and you pay to access the other symbols, so for them it brings in an awful lot of money. They are 'raking' it in, if you like!

Healers, in their desire to personalize the healing practice (to make it more individual), may do something risky and/or fraudulent (deliberately deceptive) in order to make themselves more important, though not necessarily any more remunerated. Charlie in particular, as we shall see below, was a young healer who had a desire to do well in the healing world, but Teresa had voiced her concern openly about getting caught up with the obsession with money and status.

But there is some ambiguity over this as well. Given that most of the healers are more accurately classed as folk healers than CAM practitioners, then the issue of charging for their healing becomes fraught with difficulty and can be seen as a signifier of potentially fraudulent activity. At the Centre run by Teresa, healers were able to give free healings on a Wednesday evening, but at other times they were expected to charge a fee, and 20 per cent of this went to Teresa. She realizes this is a problem with the way healers perceive their own skills and it is a tension, as Teresa explains:

> There's the problem of fees. Some people [healers] make an awful fuss of charging for healing, but I think you have to charge a fair fee. Charlie today gave a lady a healing for which he used the 'Doctor' [Charlie's spirit doctor approach] and he charged £10 for it, but I think he is going to have to ask for more than that really. My prices are suited to the local area really; nobody has any money here. A healer in the US who advertised through the television was asking for $1000 for a psychic reading – I think he should be strung up! I'm not sure about the American healers, though.

Authentic vs Fraudulent Healing Practice

The issue of who is allowed to be seen as 'real' healer and who is not is a central issue for many healers themselves, and it is clear that this issue vexes many of them. Healers are acutely aware of charlatans and would regularly refer to 'well-known' or infamous healers who they perhaps had met before, seen demonstrations from, and they made evaluations and judgements about who and who not to trust. When healers at the Centre recalled seeing other people heal, they would be careful to refer to the character of the individual healer – whether they were trustworthy, kind, or gentle, as increased validation for their healing intentions, whether they made much money out of the 'act', and whether they thought there could be any 'tricks' going on – like the magic conjurers with which the term is attached.

Healers are also fully aware of the situation of being called frauds, and this was something that came up in conversation naturally. One evening at the healing Centre, Teresa had explained how her husband – a local farmer – had long been critical of her activities: 'Derek doesn't really believe in what he calls all this rubbish. He's a businessman ... He still calls me a charlatan and that we are robbing people, and that hurts a little bit.'

The nature of his work led to some tension with Teresa, particularly as it impacted upon their lifestyles, and on numerous occasions Ruth – her daughter – who also worked at the Centre, would mention examples of their general hostility. She explained how when they met people on holiday that her husband would insist she didn't say what she did for a living. Teresa managed to get her own back by saying that she beat him up in a past life (in their past lives, her husband was a Druid priestess and Teresa was a Viking), and this helped to explain his current hostility.

Nevertheless, an awareness of what might be considered to be fraudulent or acceptable practice had let into critiques of healers they knew. For instance, one day Teresa was discussing the work of a healer she knew who developed a crystal healing therapy called 'electro-crystal therapy', but Teresa was ambivalent about its efficacy as well as the motivations behind it. Teresa had been talking to me about the fact that computers, radios, watches and other forms of sophisticated technology utilize the quartz components, but says that although quartz had clearly been crucial to modern life, the selective combination of crystal and technology cannot be a good thing. Inserting a manufactured electric current through crystal to increase its energies did not seem right to her and this led her to question his motives and the reasoning behind it – the idea of it becoming a discredited practice amongst healers was on her agenda.

As such, healers establish some boundaries over acceptable and therefore fraudulent and authentic practice. One way authenticity can be established is through the performance of healing, and this is crucial to the credibility and authenticity of the act, as well as aiding its effectiveness (McClean 2013). Performing healing is scrutinized carefully at the Centre. For example, during the healer training sessions, Teresa had been clear about the fact she closely observed trainee healers to see that they were doing it right. She had said how many people think that when they wave a crystal about that they are doing a healing, when in fact they are doing nothing. When one of the trainee healers seemed nervous and joked about whether Teresa thought any of us were doing that, she said she would if she thought that was the case.

Charlie's healings were a case in point. Charlie started off practising fairly conventional hands-on spiritual healing at the Centre, but over time developed this into a 'spiritual surgery' approach, with the use of trance-channelling spirit doctors into his healing repertoire. In other words, using spirit doctors made Charlie's healing more performance-like and gave a sense that what he was doing was different to the others, but the issue of actually playing a role of the healer playing at channelling spirits through him, was never far from the conversation. Charlie explained how he developed the skills after visiting a trance healer in Germany and he would often compare his healing style and performance to his, knowing that credibility and authenticity of the act has much to do with the style and panache of the performance. However, Charlie had explained how when the other trance healer did the healings it seemed to look good, but when he conducts them himself it never feels as convincing. Other healers present at the time had said that being convincing (that is, putting on a good show) would grow with confidence.

Another time Charlie had given one of his spirit doctor healings that I was able to witness as a trainee healer, and while Charlie was in his trance and playing the part of the spirit doctor he had nodded to different areas of the room while saying it was busy in the room. Ruth giggled slightly at the comment and looked over at me; noticing this, Charlie qualified the statement, by saying it was 'busy in the spirit world'. Though Ruth giggled at Charlie's verbal 'slip', she does not later question Charlie on the authenticity (or lack of) in his actions. Why is this? I argue that Ruth keeps quiet as it would not be a good idea to question another healer's innovatory practice. To do so would perhaps threaten the legitimacy and cohesion of the group, and it would threaten the ideology upon which healer membership is based. This reluctance to question practice (but holding an awareness that some healers are fraudulent) is problematic, but is based on trusting the healer's motivations, and not questioning the credibility of the acts. Charlie knows that he relies on the other healers for their approval, but is able to stretch the boundaries of acceptability.

One day I was discussing Charlie's progress with Teresa, and finding it difficult to reconcile some of these tensions in my own mind, I asked her, 'What Charlie does, I suppose that's shamanism in a way?' Teresa looked at me intently and shook her head slowly:

> No, Charlie is trying, well, what he's aiming to do is to be a spiritual surgeon. It's like the Filipino psychic surgeons, except without the physical tools and so on. With the Filipinos, they actually do the healing with all the scalpels and there's blood and something comes out of the body and it goes into a bucket, and when you look into the bucket, there's nothing there. You have to be careful though, there's a certain amount of charlatanism out there, but a lot of it is genuine.

Filipino psychic surgeons and spirit surgeons from other parts of the world are documented elsewhere (Easthope 1986, Graham 1990, Lazar 2006), and the similarities with what Charlie is trying to achieve are evident. On one level, Charlie's interest in psychic surgery brings to light some credibility issues, in that the conventional-sounding 'surgeon' appeals more than the exotic nature of shamanism. But, what is authenticity in this context? What is fraudulent? Handler's (1986) analysis of authenticity, as discussed above, is useful here, because the concern for authenticity comes from the very modern problem of perceiving status (that is, healer) and role-playing (playing the healer) as one and the same thing. Charlie is in the position of having to play the role and know that others watching know that he is playing the role of the spirit doctors, but if the intentions are good (to try to effect healing or some level of comfort for the client) then the other healers do not question it; fraudulent healers are perceived as ones with the wrong intentions.

Conclusions

As discussed above, 'fraudulent' is taken to mean, by deception, inappropriate action for personal gain. But what is fraud and or fraudulent action in folk healing is not unrelated from the local and particular context as well as the localized belief systems that support the healing system. The healers mostly demonstrated strong self-belief about the usefulness and genuineness of their healing practice (and healing more generally). This genuine self-belief, combined with some doubts about practice, such as its effectiveness, led one to believe that they are not quacks and they are not acting fraudulently, but there is a thin line between authentic and inauthentic healing in this context.

We have showed how authentic action and healing in pre-modern times was relatively unproblematic as healer was a 'naturalized' status; the absence of social roles (that one 'played' and 'performed') enhanced the power and legitimacy of the healer in society. In our modern or what we may now call late-modern era, authenticity is always in question and healers must establish their own norms about this and how one can tell authentic from inauthentic healing practice and belief.

As an example of a minority religion and a folk-healing practice, crystal and spiritual healing has taken a marginal role as a complementary health practice and practitioners have been perceived (even amongst other complementary health practitioners) as quacks and charlatans, almost by definition. Against the backdrop of this, crystal healers are aware of the perception and their response to it has been outlined above. Healers have sought to manage this by engaging in healing practice that questions its own authenticity (such as Charlie's spirit doctor' approach), to innovate healing practice and to relate authenticity to the performance of healing, given that it is a social role that healers play (and are not 'born' into). Healers critique other healing practices (and healers) by questioning the authenticity of their claim and they pursue professionalizing agendas, in order to establish its credibility. An ambivalence to money and formalized payment (as well as to unwarranted success and status) contribute to this view that crystal healers are aware of the public perception and seek to engage in healing that may be of benefit to the whole local community, regardless of ability to pay. And so, even if the actual specific health benefits (the manifest function) are illusory, the secondary (latent) aspects of such a belief system may provide a greater benefit for the wider community and this may be impossible to measure.

References

Bolton, J. (2011). 'Between the Quack and the Fanatic: Movements in our Self Belief', *Medicine, Healthcare and Philosophy*, 14(3): 281–5.

Brown, M.F. (1997). *The Channeling Zone: American Spirituality in an Anxious Age*. London: Harvard University Press.

Bynum, W.F. and R. Porter (eds) (1987). *Medical Fringe and Medical Orthodoxy 1750–1850*. London: Croom Helm.

Csordas, T.J. (1997). *Language, Charisma, and Creativity: Ritual Life in the Catholic Renewal*. Berkeley: University of California Press.

Diamond, J. (2001). *Snake Oil and Other Preoccupations*, forward by Richard Dawkins. London: Vintage.

Easthope, G. (1986). *Healers and Alternative Medicine: A Sociological Examination*. Aldershot: Gower Publishing Company Ltd.

English-Lueck, J.A. (1990). *Health in the New Age: A Study in Californian Holistic Practices*. Albuquerque: University of New Mexico Press.

Ernst, E. (2006). 'Spiritual Healing: More Than Meets the Eye', letter. *Journal of Pain and Symptom Management*, 32(5): 393–5.

Evans-Pritchard, E.E. (1937). *Witchcraft, Oracles, and Magic among the Azande*. London: Oxford University Press.

Goffman, E. (1959). *The Presentation of Self in Everyday Life*. Garden City, NJ: Doubleday and Co.

Graham, H. (1990). *Time, Energy, and the Psychology of Healing*. London: Jessica Kingsley Publishers.

Graham, J.S. (1985). 'Folk Medicine and Intercultural Diversity Amongst West Texas Mexican Americans', *Western Folklore*, 44(3): 168–93.

Handler, R. (1986). 'Authenticity', *Anthropology Today*, 2(1): 2–4.

Heelas, P. (1996). *The New Age Movement: Religion, Culture and Society in the Age of Postmodernity*. Oxford: Blackwell.

—, L. Woodhead, B. Seel, K. Tusting and B. Szersynnski (2005). *The Spiritual Revolution: Why Religion is Giving Way to Spirituality*. Oxford: Blackwell.

Helman, C. (2006). *Suburban Shaman: Tales From Medicine's Frontline*. London: Hammersmith Press.

Hess, D.J. (1993). *Science in the New Age: The Paranormal, its Defenders and Bunkers, aAnd American Culture*. London: University of Wisconsin Press.

Hornborg, A. (2012). 'Designing Rites to Re-enchant Secularised Society: New Varieties of Spiritualized Therapy in Contemporary Sweden', *Journal of Religion and Health*, 51(2): 402–18.

House of Lords Select Committee on Science and Technology (2000). *Complementary and Alternative Medicine, 6th Report*, 28 November http://webarchive.nationalarchives.gov.uk/+/www.dh.gov.uk/en/Publicationsandstatistics/Publications/PublicationsPolicyAndGuidance/DH_4009086 (accessed 4 March 2014).

Illich, I. (1976). *Limits to Medicine. Medical Nemesis: The Expropriation of Health*. Harmondsworth: Penguin.

Kassell, L. (2005a). 'The Economy of Magic in Early Modern England', in *The Practice of Reform in Health, Medicine and Science, 1500–2000: Essays for*

Charles Webster, eds M. Pelling and S. Mandelbrot. Aldershot: Ashgate, pp. 43–57.

— (2005b). *Medicine and Magic in Elizabethan London*. Oxford: Clarendon Press.

Kendall, L. (1993). 'Chini's Ambiguous Initiation', in *Shamans and Cultures*, eds M. Hoppal and K. Howard. Budapest: Akademiai Kiado, pp. 15–26.

Langford, J.M. (1999). 'Medical Mimesis: Healing Signs of a Cosmopolitan "Quack"', *American Ethnologist*, 26(1): 24–46.

Lazar, I. (2006). 'Taltos Healers, Neoshamans and Multiple Medical Realities in Postsocialist Hungary', in *Multiple Medical Realities*, eds H. Johannessen and I. Lazar. Oxford: Berghahn, pp. 35–53.

Lee-Treweek, G. (2005). 'Knowledge, Names, Fraud and Trust in Complementary Therapy', in *Complementary and Alternative Medicine: Structures and Safeguards*, eds G. Lee-Treweek et al. London: Routledge, pp. 3–26.

Lévi-Strauss, C. (1963). 'The Sorcerer and his Magic', in *Structural Anthropology*, ed. C. Levi-Strauss. New York: Basic Books, pp. 167–85.

McClean, S. (2013). 'The Role of Performance in Enhancing the Effectiveness of Crystal and Spiritual Healing'. *Medical Anthropology*, 32(1): 61–74.

— and R. Moore (2013). 'Money, Commodification and Complementary Health Care: Theorising the Role of Personalised Medicine Within De-personalised Systems of Exchange', *Social Theory and Health*, 11.

McGuire, M.B. (1988). *Ritual Healing in Suburban America*. New Brunswick, NJ: Rutgers University Press.

Moir, J. (1993). 'Summer Lives: The Heal Thing', *Guardian*, 4 August.

Moore, R. and S. McClean (eds) (2010). *Folk Healing and Health Care Practices in Britain and Ireland: Stethoscopes, Wands and Crystals*. Oxford: Berghahn.

Morrall, P. (2008). '"Snake Oil Peddling": CAM and the Occupational Status of Doctors and Nurses', in *Complementary and Alternative Medicine in Nursing and Midwifery*, eds J. Adams and P. Tovey. London: Routledge, pp. 52–69.

Porter, R. (1989). *Health For Sale: Quackery in England 1660–1850*. Manchester: Manchester University Press.

— (1993). *Disease, Medicine and Society in England 1550–1860*. London: Macmillan.

— (1994). 'Quacks: An Unconscionable Time Dying', in *The Healing Bond*, eds S. Budd and U. Sharma. London: Routledge, pp. 63–81.

Prince, R. and D. Riches (2000). *The New Age in Glastonbury: The Construction of Religious Movements*. Oxford: Berghahn.

Schieffelin, E. (1996). 'On Failure and Performance: Throwing the Medium out of the Séance', in *The Performance of Healing*, eds C. Laderman and M. Roseman. London: Routledge, pp. 59–89.

Stone, J. (2010). 'Beyond Legislation: Why Chicken Soup and Regulation Don't Mix', in *Folk Healing and Health Care Practices in Britain and Ireland: Stethoscopes, Wands and Crystals*, eds R. Moore and S. McClean. Oxford: Berghahn, pp. 226–53.

Szasz, T. (1961). *The Myth of Mental Illness: Foundations of a Theory of Personal Conduct*. London: Secker.

Taussig, M. (2003). 'Viscerality, Faith and Skepticism: Another Theory of Magic', in *Magic and Modernity: Interfaces of Revelation and Concealment*, eds B. Meyer and P. Pels. Stanford, CA: Stanford University Press, pp. 272–306.

Trilling, L. (1972). *Sincerity and Authenticity*. Cambridge, MA: Harvard University Press.

Wahlberg, A. (2007). 'A Quackery with a Difference – New Medical Pluralism and the Problem of "Dangerous Practitioners" in the United Kingdom', *Social Science & Medicine*, 65(11): 2307–16.

Chapter 6

Sex-Work and Ceremonies: The Trafficking of Young Nigerian Women into Britain

Hermione Harris

The internationally recognized definition of trafficking comes from the UN document commonly referred to as the Palermo Convention:[1]

> 'Trafficking in persons' shall mean the recruitment, transportation, transfer, harbouring or receipt of persons by means of threat or use of force or other forms of coercion, of abduction, of fraud, of deception, of the abuse of power, or of a position of vulnerability or of the giving or receiving of payments or benefits to achieve the consent of a person having control over another person, for the purposes of exploitation. Exploitation shall include, at a minimum, the exploitation of prostitution of others or other forms of sexual exploitation, forced labour services, slavery or practices similar to slavery, (or) servitude ... .

The question of fraud is therefore intrinsic to the official description of trafficking. Fraud is a multi-layered concept; I include its first cousins of deceit, lying, duplicity, trickery, falsehood, manipulation and the whole gamut of deception. The Palermo statement also refers to the essential precursors to the exercise of fraud by the perpetrator: the abuse of power and the victim's situation of vulnerability.

Many of these aspects of fraud underlie the rapidly growing trade in the trafficking of human beings. Trafficking comes in a variety of guises: it covers domestic servitude, the use of children for begging and benefit fraud, labour in agricultural, manufacturing and service sectors, and the harvesting of organs.

---

[1] The UN Convention against Transnational Organized Crime was ratified by the General Assembly in 2000. The supplementary protocol on the trafficking of persons, especially women and children, came into force in 2003.

However, a major aspect of the trade is in trafficking for sexual exploitation. Although boys and men may also be recruited, the majority of the victims are young women and girls.

Trafficking into sex-work is big business. By its very nature, much of which will be clandestine, estimates of the profits to be made from trafficking for prostitution can only be speculative, but are on a par with the trade in drugs and weaponry. Kara (2009: 19) calculates that in 2007 the sale of what he refers to as 'sex slaves' generated US$600 million in profits, while their exploitation rendered US$35.7 billion. He speculates that there will be 1.48 million trafficked sex-workers by the end of 2012, with Europe as the leading destination (ibid.: 17). As to their origin, Nigeria is a main source of supply: it has been estimated that some 40,000–50,000 women were trafficked from Nigeria between 1990 and 2005. There is not even a rough estimate for how many of these passed through, or remained, in the UK, but we know that the majority of referrals to an organization supporting rescued victims concerned Nigerians (Cherti et al. 2013: 28).

Conditions in Nigeria provide fertile ground for trafficking. Those at the bottom of the heap, as the victims, long to escape; those on the way up, like their traffickers, see a chance to make easy money from their desperation. Despite its recent economic growth, and its great resources of oil and agricultural products, Nigeria is beset with economic mismanagement, corruption and political instability. Disparities of wealth leave a majority of the 150 million population in poverty: some 80 per cent of the oil wealth goes to the richest 1 per cent (UKBA 2012: 15). The lack of infrastructure and unreliable water and power supplies stand in the way of national economic development; opportunities for education and employment are low. The effect of globalization on the movement of peoples and resources, plus the revolution in technology and the means of communication, have encouraged the growth of a Nigerian diaspora which now spreads across the world. Travel overseas is a common part of contemporary Nigerian culture, either in aspiration or reality.

Nigerian traffickers find markets worldwide. But the main destination for their human merchandise is Europe. There are various conduits into Europe from Nigeria. Journeys across North Africa and the Mediterranean may be lengthy and arduous, but travel to London tends to be by aeroplane. The UK may be the final stop, but is often used as a staging post before the young women are sold on to Italy (the main destination for Nigerians), Spain, Greece, Holland, the Czech Republic, or other European countries. Although there are female traffickers, the majority are men, based either in Nigeria or Europe. Women tend to dominate in the next stage, once the girls have been trafficked. The contact in

Italy and elsewhere in Europe is usually a 'Madam' who will house and control the girl and take a substantial part of her earnings (Okojie 2009: 156).

Several people may be involved in the initial procurement of potential sex-workers. The trafficker may already know the family, or make contact directly with the parents or spouse, who will benefit financially from cooperation. If the girl is adrift, the trafficker may approach her himself. Whether he is working on his own account, or as part of an organized ring, he will have a network of contacts to facilitate travel. He may hand the victim over to another in the UK, or house her himself.

The Victims of Trafficking for Sex-Work

In Britain, an attempt to track down and prosecute these traffickers is under way. Since 2011, several young Nigerian girls have appeared in court to testify against their captors. What follows here is taken from the testimonies of six such victims, contained in extensive interviews conducted by the police, social services and other concerned bodies.[2] They were originally detained by authorities at British or European border controls for being in possession of false documentation, and subsequently identified as victims of trafficking. Although their papers stated that they were over 20 years of age, all except one were minors at the time of entry to the UK. One young woman whom we will call Ruth was 14 when picked up for being in possession of forged papers at the Spanish border; Precious only got as far as Stansted Airport before being detained. Hannah, supposedly 29 but actually 16, handed herself over to airport officials on arrival in Italy. Esther, then 15, was bound for Athens when her documents were found to be forged; Sarah's trafficker was trying to get her into France when she was arrested; Grace was on her way to Italy.

Despite individual details, the experience of these young women is remarkably similar, containing substantial elements in common.[3] Such a small number of stories in no way constitutes a sample of women trafficked from Nigeria, nor do these cases aim to represent the experience of migrant sex-workers in general. But the accounts illustrate particular aspects of trafficking which appear in the

---

[2]　Access to the transcripts and DVDs of police interviews, additional documentation and reports, together with attendance at court hearings, were gained through acting as an expert witness providing cultural background to cases of trafficking.

[3]　This information is now in the public domain, but cases have been anonymized by changing names and some personal details.

burgeoning literature on the Nigerian trade.[4] These testimonies also challenge the imagination of judge and jury when the traffickers come to court. The duplicity of traffickers, and the potential web of deceit in which young women can be ensnared are, if proven, straightforward examples of fraud that fall within the scope of the Palermo Convention. But these accounts also stray into less familiar territory of religion, of ceremonies, curses and the occult. They offer an insight into the particular role played by religion in some instances of trafficking. In practical terms, this has bearing on the credibility of the victims' testimonies in their reluctance to give evidence. But it also raises the question on the status of belief in the assessment of fraud.

The Experience of Grace O

All facets of fraud appear in the case of Grace O. Arriving in the UK early in 2011, her documentation stated that she was 29; in fact, she was only 15. She landed full of hope that she was at last escaping her miserable existence in Nigeria through this 'holiday' she had been promised.

Grace was born in a small isolated village in Edo State, Central Southern Nigeria. She was an only child; her mother died in childbirth and her father followed a year later. She then went to live with an older woman, 'Auntie' Joy. As elsewhere in Nigeria, the terms 'Auntie' and 'Uncle' do not imply an affectionate caring relationship; they are rather ubiquitous terms of respect to a senior, as personal names cannot be used when addressing an elder. Certainly there was little positive for Grace in this arrangement; she lived a wretched life of domestic drudgery with physical and psychological abuse; she was both beaten and starved. She was also told that she was responsible for the death of her parents, an accusation which implied that she was a witch (La Fontaine 2009).

When she was 12, she was packed off to a neighbouring village to live with an older man as his wife, in exchange for a plot of land. She was constantly raped and assaulted by her drunken 'husband', and consequently miscarried when she became pregnant.

She was still only 13 when a man arrived to talk to her husband, asking him to 'find him a girl from the village'. This 'Uncle' was kind to Grace, and bought her presents, which she had never had before. So when later he offered to take her to England for a week's holiday, she was thrilled. Her husband travelled with

---

[4]   There is little research specifically on the UK with the exception of the comprehensive recent report by Cherti et al. (2013).

her to Abuja, the Nigerian capital, where he bought her clothes and make-up and had her photo taken – 'to hang in the house', he said. He also secured her documentation, and before seeing her off on the plane, drilled her in the details of a new identity.

These she successfully repeated to the Heathrow immigration officers in London, and was met again by Uncle who took her to the house where she was to stay. The reality of her situation began to sink in. She found herself locked alone in a curtained bedroom, while Uncle went to work in his British public-sector job. She was then subject to his sexual assaults. No longer the caring friend, he told her that she was to be sent to Italy as a prostitute in order to repay her husband, and cover all the expenses he himself had incurred in bringing her to Europe. Then began the process of recasting her identity once again. She was slapped and threatened with gang rape if she could not remember details of the elaborate alias, supported by a plethora of documents and photos.

Grace was also subject to other procedures. Uncle pinned her on the bed, and cut her on the chest with a razor. He then rubbed black powder into the cuts, and smeared her bra and knickers with her blood. These, together with pieces of head and pubic hair, he wrapped in a white cloth. Later, Uncle administered an oath. Knocking on the table with a small piece of metal, he made her swear that she would never betray him. If she ever revealed the truth, she would face madness and a lingering death.

However, when the day came for her to be trafficked on to Italy, they were intercepted at the airport. Grace was brought to a place of safety and Uncle was detained.

Deception, Abuse and Vulnerability

One significant factor in the stories of Grace and the other young women is their common ethnic origin. All their traffickers and five of their victims come from Edo State, which suffers markedly from national socio-economic problems (Okojie 2009). Edo State lies at the heart of Nigerian trafficking; nearly every family in the capital, Benin City, has a member involved in the trade, either as a victim or a perpetrator. Okojie and colleagues (2003) found that the 'overwhelming majority' of Nigerian sex-workers repatriated home came from Edo; 90 per cent of the Nigerian sex-workers in Italy come from the region (Onyeonoru 2004: 17). There was once a flourishing legitimate trade between Edo and Italy, Nigerians purchasing gold and clothing, and supplying migrant workers to service Italy's informal sector. But as the Nigerian economy worsened during the 1980s and unemployment rose, Italian employment and commercial opportunities also declined. Female migrants then moved into prostitution, and, using long-established networks, women gradually became the commodities to be traded (UNESCO 2006: 16).

Although Benin City is the epicentre of the trafficking trade, Edo State itself is largely rural, composed of isolated hamlets (Bradbury 1970). The victims describe the poverty-stricken conditions of their childhood in their small villages, or as in the case of Precious, another of the six, the 'ghetto' housing (her word) in the chaotic back-streets of Lagos. The families with whom they lived were themselves mired in poverty, scraping a living from farming or petty trading. These were not their own parents; it is common practice for Nigerian children to be reared in households other than those of their biological mother and father, often with relatives. This may be a satisfactory arrangement for both parties, the child providing domestic service in exchange for education. But in the cases here, as with Grace, the experience was one of physical and psychological abuse. Ruth was orphaned as a baby, and brought up in the household of an uncle. Here she was treated as a household drudge, quite differently from the children of the family. Hannah had been living with Mary, a relative of her dead father. At the age of 12, she was sent to work for a Lagos family 'as a slave', as she now says. Here she was beaten, stabbed and starved. She worked from 4 in the morning until late at night, but her wages were sent back to Mary. Esther and Sarah suffered similar exploitation in foster homes in their villages; Sarah was so hungry that she would sneak out to scrounge food whenever she could. Precious had a less abusive foster situation in Lagos, but had to abandon her plans for her future and engage in petty trading to make ends meet.

These foster children had no value beyond their labour. So when a chance came to make some money out of them, they were treated as expendable commodities. Grace, Ruth and Esther were sold directly to traffickers by those in authority over them. The others were approached personally by a trafficker with an eye for a vulnerable and unprotected target. Hannah had been thrown out of her Lagos household when she was made pregnant by the father of the family. She was living on the streets until approached by 'John'. Sarah's trafficker befriended her in her village; Precious was selling vegetables in the market when she met 'Joseph'.

Naïve young women, living in miserable circumstances and unaccustomed to kindness, were easily seduced by offers of help, by promises of employment or education abroad. They trusted their new friend, and the exciting picture he painted of their future. The victims describe how nice the men were when they first met, their own pleasure at the new clothes, make-up and jewellery, the attention they had never had before. Coming mainly from remote areas with no knowledge of the outside world, these young women were prime targets for traffickers' deceptions: Esther had never heard of Europe and had no idea where 'abroad' might be; Ruth had never encountered a European, and thought they would go to 'Canada' by car.

This vulnerability was compounded by a lack of education. Although theoretically the 2003 Universal Basic Education Policy stipulates universal free education, this is not reflected in practice. Of the 30 young sex-workers deported back to Nigeria interviewed by Attoh (2009: 168), 27 had dropped out in primary or junior secondary. In the case of these six young women, three could neither read nor write; Uncle would mock Grace as a 'village girl', and her illiteracy meant that she could have no purchase on travel documents forged in her name. The promise of education abroad is a powerful one; all the victims here record the hopes raised by their traffickers. Precious had reached secondary level, but had to leave school at 15 as she could no longer afford the fees. She was therefore delighted when she encountered Joseph who assured her of schooling plus 'super-stardom' as a singer in Britain.

Nigeria is a hierarchical society, and two further relevant factors in the victims' circumstance are their gender and their age. The structure of gender relations is more complex than simple female subordination; Nigerian women have long had significant economic roles in agriculture and trading, and now in the professions. They are in charge of domestic affairs within a marriage, for which they demand respect. Nevertheless, the majority of both men and women accept that the man is the head of the household, who will expect compliance. Respect and obedience is also required by seniors from juniors. The majority of women trafficked from Nigeria are young, between the ages of 14 and 22 (Buker 2007). Of the 40 victims interviewed in Cherti's recent research, half were under the age of 18 when trafficked, as were five of the six young women discussed here. These girl-children, both through cultural expectations and their own life experience, would be conditioned to obey anyone set in authority over them.

In normal circumstances, the primary authority figures would be the family, but the particular victims considered here had no parents. Of the 39 female and one male interviewees in Cherti's study, well over a third were orphans. This is a critical factor both in their own feelings of vulnerability, and in having no one to protect them. When Grace pleaded not to be raped again, Uncle taunted her that her mother should come from the grave to help her; that her dead father should take her to school. He told her that he always looked for people with no parents, 'because they have no one to fight for them'.

Lack of immediate family also deprived the victims of access to wider webs of support. Personhood in Nigerian society depends very much on the membership of a group; whether it be an extended family or social, geographical, economic, ethnic, or religious affiliation. It is these networks which will provide essential contacts for assistance and exert influence on a member's 'patron', a person with power, whose status is evident by the number of 'clients' they support. None of the six young women had any such advantage. Precious commented on her failure to get work beyond the market, 'I had nobody to help, nobody to assist.'

Offers of help from a friendly older man therefore seemed not only to be the way into a wider world, but also the way out of a wretched situation. This was despite their previous experience of men which had been largely abusive. In five of the six cases here, this included sexual exploitation. Grace was constantly raped by her 'husband'; Hannah was living off sex-work when she was put out of the house after rape and pregnancy by the man of the family. Ruth was sexually assaulted by her uncle; Sarah was living hand to mouth by exchanging sex for food. Esther had already been sold to a Lagos 'madam' before being trafficked on for sex-work in Europe.

Precious had reached London before she was accosted by her trafficker and the 'friend' turned into a rapist. It was only when the young women arrived in London that they realized how they had been duped, and experienced the changed behaviour of their captors. Like Grace, they were kept incarcerated in one room, subject to mockery, violence, forced alcohol and sex. As Ruth said, 'he treated me like an animal', while she was being prepared for further trafficking to Europe. The girls had been in no position to have a perspective on the future they were being offered, or effectively to resist when the reality of their predicament became apparent.

The Operation of Fraud

In theory, Nigerian agencies and legislation have existed for some time to combat trafficking fraud and to offer protection to victims. In 2003, the Trafficking in Persons (Prohibition) Law and Enforcement Prohibition Act came into force, restating earlier legislation, followed by the establishment of the National Agency for Prohibition of Traffic in Persons (NAPTIP) (Okojie 2003: 3.3). But, despite the Palermo Convention, as of 2004 there was no evidence of a subsequent reduction in the procurement of girls from Edo State, and no convictions (UNESCO 2006: 3.A.4). It appears that 'The agencies charged with investigating and prosecuting crimes do not quite appreciate the seriousness of the phenomenon of human trafficking' (Okojie 2003: 3.3).

Since that time the government has developed a National Plan of Action (2008) and a number of Nigerian NGOs have taken up the issue, but the official protection for trafficked victims is not yet well developed. Successful prosecutions have been few (UKBA 2012: 25.36), and often result in fines rather than imprisonment. NAPTIP has come in for criticism for maladministration and misdirection of funds. Overall, in 2011, 'the Government of Nigeria did not demonstrate progress in its anti-trafficking law enforcements efforts to combat trafficking' (USSD 2011: 3d).

Part of the problem is the collusion of Nigerian authorities with traffickers. Apart from the fact that certain members of the Nigerian police are themselves involved in prostitution and trafficking, corruption is widespread throughout the force (Smith 2007; UKBA 2012: 33–43). The question of corruption is complex. Given the significance of social and kinship ties, the duty to assist members of the extended family or other dependents is paramount, and meagre salaries do not stretch to meet obligations. While this may account for low-level bribery, fraud at senior levels can involve substantial sums for self-enrichment; both are backed by intimidation and the threat of violence. Either way, traffickers can buy their way through the system at the expense of the victim. As Esther said of traffickers: 'In my country, if the boy have money then he would give the police money and they will let him go.'

The reputation of the Nigerian police spills over into assumptions the victims make about British authorities, and make trust difficult to establish. Hannah was afraid if she talked to the police, her captor would pay them off, and she would be detained in his place. These fears were constantly reinforced by traffickers, who use these negative stereotypes to their advantage. Ruth was placed in a children's home when she was picked up at Heathrow, but, as instructed by 'David', absconded to meet her trafficker. He told her that if she returned to the institution, the police would find her, would disbelieve the story of a young girl, and would either deport her to Nigeria or kill her. When later she refused to have sex with him in the locked room where she was held captive, he threatened to give her up to the police himself. As they are 'wicked', he said, they would beat her up and throw her in jail. They would also discover that her 'papers' were false.

The collusion of members of the migration authorities in Nigeria also undermines attempts to stem the brisk trade in false documentation, particularly the supply and doctoring of passports both for traffickers and their victims (Carling 2006: 23–4). When the young women witnessed money changing hands, they saw that their traffickers had 'friends' in visa offices and at the Lagos

Murtala Muhammed Airport. Once inside Britain, the traffickers have complex ways of covering their tracks. Their fraud can only be uncovered by painstaking forensic investigation by the police: interviews, examination of mobile phones, computers, credit cards, bank accounts, CCTV footage, shop records – piecing together enough evidence to mount a case. A trafficker convicted in 2011 used seven different identities and eight addresses. Through his web of contacts, both in Nigeria and Europe, he could easily obtain false identity cards and passports.

Then there is the victims' drilling in the false information to be given at Britain's borders: their change of name, age, marital status, ethnic origin, and the purpose and length of their visit. One young woman was told to say that she was a lesbian, seeking refuge in Britain. They may go through this charade more than once, with different details, first when leaving Nigeria for the UK, and again when being trafficked on to Spain, Italy, the Netherlands, or Greece. Through their assumed names and the imposed narratives of their lives, the victims were therefore stripped of their own identities; physical and verbal abuse further wears down their sense of self. Living a lie, they thus become embodiments of fraud.

There are therefore two areas of fraud involved in Nigerian trafficking into prostitution which fall under Palermo's criteria of abusing both vulnerability and power. The first is the fanciful promises made to young women, the imaginary vision of their future presented to them by their trafficker. Secondly, the forged documentation and invented identities with which the victims operate constitute the means whereby the traffickers' deception can be realized.

But there is yet another attack on victims' personhood, which in the spirit of the Palermo Convention could be classified as a further aspect of fraud: a form of deception 'to achieve the consent of a person having control over another person, for the purposes of exploitation'. This is the handing over of the girls' autonomy to their controllers by means of the occult. Through rituals known by the indigenous term 'juju', the victims are sworn to secrecy. In the context of disturbing ceremonies, such as that experienced by Grace at the hands of Uncle, they take an oath that they will never disclose their experiences, that they will obey whomsoever is put in authority over them, and that they will repay any 'debt' owed to those involved in their migration. Breaking of the promise will activate the effects of the curse, resulting in misfortune, illness and death. This oath of obedience constrains their resistance through fear of supernatural reprisals, resulting in effective self-censorship and enforced collusion in the deprivation of their own liberty.

Oaths and Rituals

In expressing their fear of the oath, the young women often make little distinction between physical and supernatural sanctions. Hannah's trafficker finally told her that she was to be sent to Italy for sex-work rather than schooling: 'That night I told him that I would not go he said that the oath I took would kill me – or he would kill me himself.' When she was taken into protective police custody; she was terrified that her traffickers would say that she had absconded. They would kill her. She was not sure how, perhaps by 'gun' or 'machete' or 'by the juju they use'.

This interpenetration of the material and occult illustrates implicit West African belief in the reality of both visible and invisible worlds (Ellis and ter Haar 2004). This is not a smattering of superstitions, but a way of seeing the world that permeates Nigerian culture. The universe of gods and spirits is the ultimate source of the unseen power that binds the two realms together and bears upon mundane existence. This spiritual power in itself is neither good nor evil, but may be used for either. Misfortune and sickness are often thought to be inflicted by others' spiritual malignity; individuals must therefore equip themselves with superior force with the assistance of priests and ritual practitioners. Juju, the manipulation of objects and gestures which have been empowered through incantation to bring about a desired result, is a ubiquitous practice. In oath taking, and the imposition of a curse, it is the words themselves which are imbued with performative power. Strictly speaking, witchcraft is the exercise of an individual's innate power to affect others, but is often used interchangeably with juju – and both stand in to refer to indigenous religion.

Of all the 36 Nigerian states, Edo State is commonly said to have the most pervasive adherence to an enchanted world-view, and has a widespread reputation for the occult. It is only in this region that pre-trafficking rituals are common currency. Precious, who was brought up in Lagos, was the only one of the six who did not undergo a ceremony, although she was told that a curse had been put upon her to ensure her obedience.

While Grace's ritual took place in London, the others were subject to their ceremony before they travelled. Esther was taken to a river near her village by the father of her surrogate family. He was, as she put it, a 'native doctor'. Smeared with white clay, he placed 'something' into his mouth and chanted incantations. He then gave her instructions never to reveal anything of her experience, on pain of death. When delivered into prostitution in Lagos, her 'madam' made her eat a raw egg and wash with black soap. She was not sure about the meaning of this, except that it was a form of juju that was being used against her.

Hannah was taken from Lagos to a house 'in the bush' where she encountered a group of men with red clothes tied around their chests. Their leader wore feathers in his hair and was smeared with chalk. The room smelled foul, she says, and she could see knives, various pots and other objects together with blood on an altar. She immediately felt afraid 'because the place was like a place of witchcraft'. One of the pots contained a snake; another held a stinking liquid that looked like blood with white worms floating on the surface. She was told to wash in this concoction, and to wrap herself in a red cloth. This done, one of the men cut off some pubic hair and took hair from her head and armpits with a razor. This he put in a smaller pot, together with toe and finger-nail clippings, and her underpants and bra, and placed the container on the altar. He then took a syringe-full of blood from her arm, which also went on the altar. One of the most frightening parts of the ritual was seeing her face appear in a mirror when her name was recited before it, even though she felt she was nowhere near. As part of the ritual, Hannah was told to take an oath not to run away, to repay the money that she would owe for her journey, and to remain silent about her experience. If she rejected her false identity and her instructions, or tried to escape without meeting her debts, the oath would kill her: 'He said that if I ran I would die. Tell anybody, I would die. Or argue anything, I would die. Wherever I was their charm would find me'.

It took Ruth nearly two years to give the story of how 'black magic has been put on me'. She was shut in a room by her uncle, the man of the Edo household where she had been living and who had sold her to John. Two men then carried in a brown coffin, containing a mask and a wig. Cutting her with a razor, her blood was also placed inside the coffin together with her underwear. As she refused to get into the box, she was left to sleep on the floor. But the next day, they forced her into a white coffin where she stayed until the following day. She then was stripped naked, with her hands tied behind her back while they shaved her underarm and pubic hair which was put into a pot. She was then taken to another location where she was made to eat a raw chicken's heart, and drink a concoction.

Indigenous ritual practitioners are entrepreneurs: they will have their own specialities and incorporate additional elements in their ceremonies – snakes, worms, mirrors, coffins – but the basic elements accord with accounts by Kara (2009: 90, 91) and others. Fundamental to the rituals is the belief that personal items and bodily substances are imbued with the spiritual essence of their owners, and so act as a conduit of control. Hence the significance of blood. As containing the owner's life-force, their spiritual power, blood is an extremely potent substance. The blood of animals (and humans) is often a required ingredient in sacrifices to gods and spirits; in the Christian tradition, the blood of Christ is a central element, whether in the Mass, or in the Pentecostal insistence on the blood of Jesus to empower. Grace was clear as to its cultural significance: 'I was so scared because in Nigeria ... if somebody collected your blood or your hair, it's like he wants to go and use it for something that may kill that person.'

Nail-clippings are a common ingredient in Nigerian juju spells; in many traditions, hair is another repository of an individual's vital force – hence Samson of the Old Testament (Judges 13:16–30), Rasta dreadlocks and the reluctance of male members of certain religious groups to cut their hair. The collection of hair from particular places in the body has additional significance. Pubic and armpit hair represents dominance over the woman's sexuality. Hair from the head indicates control over thought and reason, as well as over the person as a whole: the head has particular meaning in Nigerian epistemology as the centre of God-given destiny. Ruth's mask and wig are clear symbols of her identity, to be replaced by an assumed persona; the mirror captures Hannah's image for others to control.

Spiritual power knows no geographical boundaries. When the victims are cut with razors, this is not only to collect their blood, but to rub a powerful substance into the wounds. The victim's body is therefore permanently invaded by the power of the juju – a form of remote control. When Sarah was asked how she might be killed, she replied that she didn't know, but it would happen because of the black substance in the cuts. Her scars also serve as a reminder of the curse: 'Every time I look at my body ... I remember what was done to me. I don't know if I'll be able to forget in my life.' She also remembers the fear she felt at the appearance of the practitioner at her ceremony. His white face masked his earthly identity, with his red and black clothing symbolizing danger and death. Now, Sarah says, 'whenever I think of him, my heart jumps because I think that I will die.' The trauma that the victims have suffered haunts their dreams, which are thought to provide an insight into invisible powers. Dreams of being pushed and hit, of being attacked by dogs reveal the activity of witches, while nightmares of medicine men and traffickers indicate their continued influence. The young women constantly mention their fear of the oath. A cold, a headache, signals the beginning of the end.

Juju: Fraud or Conviction?

Those now involved in the care of these young victims often express puzzlement over the apparent co-existence of their fear and their Christianity. Surely their faith would convince them that occult threats are part of the traffickers' deceit? Grace is a firm believer in God, and ardent member of her Pentecostal church, yet explains: 'I'm so scared of those things, worshipping idols, juju and the native doctors – it's horrible – there's nothing they can't do.' 'With juju they can call a person's name – and they will die in their sleep.' But in the Nigerian scheme of things, there is no contradiction here. 'Religion' can usefully be defined as 'a body of beliefs and practices arising from the supposed operation of spiritual forces in the universe, whether invested in objects, words or gestures, or embodied in spirits or gods' (Harris 2006: 12). This encompasses all invisible powers. For Christians, the ultimate source of life force is the Holy Spirit. The efficacy of juju, witchcraft and indigenous deities and spirits are not denied, but are categorized as agents of the Devil deploying satanic power. The drama of the pre-trafficking ritual impresses the force of this power on the victim. Hannah's ritual terrified her – as was intended. The priest told her that 'he did it so I'll believe everything that was happening, so I would realize this was not a fake ... Before that I had not believed these things, but after that I started to have fear about these things and believe ... .'

For the victim, then, the rituals, the juju and the curses are not fraudulent – they are real. But what do they represent for their well-travelled and worldly captors? To the largely secular authorities involved in the prosecution of traffickers – police, social workers, judge and juries – these rituals seem to be the epitome of fraud: the invention of elaborate performances to frighten the victims, play on diffuse ideas about the occult, and lock them into perpetual silence. Coercion it may be, but is it fraud? Does the definition of fraudulent activity depend on conscious deception? As yet, there is no ethnographic research on those conducting pre-trafficking juju ceremonies, or of those who commission them; the focus is on victims, not their abusers. Juju certainly adds a dramatic dimension to the trafficker's deceit, but whether the ceremonies themselves can be classed as trickery depends on the perspective from which they are analysed – by those involved in the drama, or by sceptical commentators with a different cultural orientation. Various indigenous medicine men may add on their ritual specialties, but there is no evidence to suggest that they, or the traffickers who commission their services, do not believe in what they are doing. Carling (2006: 29) argues that 'It is conspicuous that the traffickers themselves often have the same faith in the magical powers as the victim' – perhaps he should omit the word 'often'. Madams in Italy and Nigeria consult each other about 'magical rituals' to keep the police at bay, and siblings at home in Benin City use juju to attract well-heeled clients for their sisters abroad.[5]

This is not to say that ritual experts claiming supernatural powers always believe in what they are doing. Leaving aside obvious quacks and charlatans, practitioners' relationship to their occult craft varies. Take, for example, the question of divination and fortune-telling. Judith Okely (1996: 100) found that gypsy fortune-tellers never consulted one another; they knew the chicanery of their own practice – a clear-cut case of deception. But other situations are more ambiguous. In his classic study of Zande oracles, Evans Pritchard found indigenous sceptics: some witch-doctors as well as clients derided the authenticity of certain other diviners, whose miracles, they said, were fraudulently produced. Witch-doctors also combined fakery with what they believed to be genuine dealings with invisible powers (1937: 183–201). Similarly, in prophecy through possession by the Holy Spirit in Nigerian Aladura churches, visioners are warned against offering 'false visions', concocted by themselves, or introducing earthly embellishments into otherwise God-given revelation (Harris 2006: 201–2).

But in both these latter cases, it is the cheating operator, or rogue element, not the whole underlying system of belief which is in question. Although it may be acknowledged that there are impostors within a particular ritual practice, this does not, for practitioners as well as clients, necessarily invalidate belief in the occult powers involved. Indeed, as errors and misjudgements can be explained by human dishonesty, rather than as proof of the system's futility, the rituals themselves are protected from scepticism and doubt.

There also will be a difference between the victim's and the practitioner's reading of the juju; the girls often say that they do not understand the meaning of individual items in the ceremony – for example, the piece of metal in Hannah's bedroom ritual. Hannah herself could offer no explanation for what she described as the knocking of the table with a pen-like stick of iron. 'John' could have been adding this feature merely for theatrical effect. But he also could be making a genuine attempt to reinforce the power of the promise with that of a relevant deity, in this case Ogun, the god of iron, believed to underwrite oaths including those in trafficking (Carling 2006: 28). If John was not communicating this specific symbolic message to Hannah which she would understand, then he was speaking to the spirits.

---

[5] Nelson Edewor, personal communication, 29 November 2012.

Fear of Disclosure

Whether we take the insider's or the outsider's view of the rituals, and see them as 'genuine' or not, the traffickers' use of juju is central to their main tactics of force, fear and fraud. By instilling fear of death, the oaths impose self-censorship on the victims, drawing them into the cycle of deceit, and silencing their protest. This can also destroy the girls' credibility as witnesses when traffickers come to court.

Hannah tried to challenge John, baulking at telling UK immigration authorities that she is married:

> I said to him, 'I have never been married so why would you do a marriage visa for me?' He said the name on the passport ... had been changed. He said he had added more years to my age. I asked him why. He said that without that I would not be allowed [into the country]. I didn't like what he was doing ... because all these things to me was like it was all fake. I became discouraged. He told me that whatever he told me I should take it or else the oath would kill me. So I didn't speak any more.

Even when picked up by immigration officials at British or European borders, when their trafficker had already disappeared, two of the young women still adhered to their false identities. Because of this, Sarah, then aged 14, was held for several months in a British adult jail for being in possession of forged documents, until a social worker realized that she was a trafficked minor. She still found it hard to talk. At the time of their interviews by the police, all six young women were in a place of safety, being granted leave to remain in the UK or claiming asylum with the help of lawyers, social workers and psychiatrists. But their fear keeps seeping back. Their testimonies are at times confused, contradictory and evasive: 'I don't know', 'I can't remember'. Their body language speaks of apprehension and fright. Ruth was shown an identity video of potential traffickers, but she felt their eyes following her from the screen, threatening to come and take her away if she dared to speak. It was some months before she asked for the test to be repeated – and picked out her abuser. Esther exhibited the same fear when the police showed her photos recovered from her trafficker's computer. She clearly featured in the pictures, taken when she was held captive in Lagos and in London, but denied any recognition of the place, people, or events. It took her several months for her to 'remember' the location and the identity of the others present, including that of her captor.

The reason for this silence is now being understood. The recent Home Office *Plan to Tackle Child Abuse Linked to Faith or Belief* mentions 'use of the fear of the supernatural to make children comply with being trafficked for domestic slavery or sexual exploitation' (2012). The Crown Prosecution Service recognizes the effects of 'witchcraft and juju rituals inherent in their culture' (CPS 2011: 15). Trafficked children, the CPS explains, 'may be reluctant to disclose the circumstances of their exploitation ... Experience has shown that inconsistencies in accounts given are often a feature of victims of trafficking and should not necessarily be regarded as diminishing the credibility of their claim to be a victim of trafficking' (ibid.: 16). In practice, gradual disclosure of information depends on a dawning conviction of the oath's impotence, and a sense of personal security. For young people who have suffered so much deception in their lives, this is a lengthy process, and will depend very much on the sensitivity and support offered by carers and questioners. 'I'm so free', said Sarah, after a lengthy period of rehabilitation. 'That is why I cannot hide anything ... that is why I'm saying it now.'

Victimhood and Agency

The concept of fraud implies two agents: the fraudster and the defrauded – in this case, the deceiving trafficker, and the victim, tricked into servitude. But despite the universal label of 'victim', young women trafficked into sex-work are not inevitably passive objects, devoid of agency. Rutvica Andrijasevic (2007), in the context of Eastern Europe, contests the dichotomy of malevolent criminal and innocent victim, and challenges the representation of trafficked women as violated prisoners. She argues that women often make an informed choice to travel, to escape domestic poverty and earn a living unavailable at home. The trafficker, then, would be more an enabler than an exploiter.

Although not applicable to the six cases detailed here, this scenario is more apposite to the situation of many Edo women migrating to Italy.[6] They also may undergo juju rituals, but in the full knowledge that their future lies in prostitution, with their oath enlisting invisible powers to protect them (Okojie 2004. Carling 2006, Kleeman and Jones 2011, von Einsiedel and Ruhfus 2011). Deception still plays a part. The trafficker provides their false documentation, and may offer a vision of life in Italy which does not include standing half-naked in cold streets

---

[6]   It is estimated that over 80 per cent of African sex-workers in Italy come from Nigeria (Okojie 2009: 151, UKBA 2012: 147).

serving up to 20 men a night. But this is not a hidden industry; in Benin City, the capital of Edo State, it is common knowledge that a family's relative prosperity will be derived from a daughter's earnings. The stigma of prostitution is waning; it is often relatives and 'boyfriends' who arrange the travel. In the absence of other sources of income, the migrant sees no alternative future beyond poverty, and feels responsible for her family's welfare (Onyeonoru 2004).

These variations in trafficking underline the danger of generalizations, whether between different countries of origin, or within Nigeria itself. But even the young women pictured here do not fit a stereotype of pure passivity in the face of fraud. Given the apparent psychological stranglehold of the curse, their final decision to tell the truth and to identify their trafficker constitutes an act of significant bravery. Such was Hannah's defiance over her re-trafficking to Italy. When John had selected a passport from his collection with a photo that bore some resemblance to her, he arranged her clothing, make-up and hair style to match. However, when the time came for travel, in spite of her fear and John's constant reminder of her oath, she sabotaged his plans. On the plane, she scrubbed her face clean of cosmetics, and redid her hair. On reaching Italy, she was waved through immigration, but she refused to move. She signalled that she needed help, and was returned to a place of safety in England.

The stories of the other women also reveal resourcefulness in small acts of resistance, and determination to survive within the limitations of their situation. But at the same time, their own eagerness to make something of their lives in spite of their circumstances in Nigeria rendered them all the more susceptible to fraudulent promises of a better life.

Conclusions

The topic of juju is a tricky one. It provides a sensationalist dimension to afro-pessimism, the notion that little good will arise from a continent riddled with corruption and disarray. Or at least, dwelling on details of the occult fosters what we might call afro-negativity: Africa as a land of cruelty, superstition and abuse of power. Publicity around child witchcraft and the case of a young boy's torso found floating in the Thames (Hoskins 2012) provide grist to the media's mill. Headlines on trafficking cases follow suit: 'Blood rituals forced on sex slave orphans'; 'Trafficked girls controlled by juju magic rituals'; 'The slave trader in

Britain who sold women around Europe for sex under the spell of his "juju" witchcraft'; 'Juju traps terrified girls into sex slavery.' When taken out of context, the details of pre-trafficking rituals provide a titillating mix of sex and magic, obscuring other aspects of the case.

Van Dijk (2001), from his research on Nigerian women trafficked into the Dutch sex trade, argues that sensationalized accounts of 'voodoo' rituals being inflicted upon the girls created a 'moral panic'; these sinister African practices were believed to threaten the very fabric of civil society. In Britain, despite the occasional headline and the best efforts of NGOs[7] to disseminate information, there is not yet enough publicity surrounding trafficking to engender such a crisis. But what van Dijk also found was a deep concern on the part of the police for these young women, a personal bond not typical of relationships between officials and illegal migrant labour. This does have resonance with the British experience, whereby certain officers in the Metropolitan and other police forces go to great lengths not only to uncover fraud and prosecute traffickers, but to ensure the well-being of victims. It is from their detailed research that the stories retold here emerge. Part of their endeavours is the attempt to gauge the significance of juju. This is not to exoticize their investigations, but rather to convey the ordinariness of demonic powers in West African life-worlds. They, and other concerned parties, are anxious to account for the young women's reluctance to give evidence, and to make sure that these understandings are communicated to judge and jury. They know that it is vitally important to identify both the exercise of unequivocal fraud, and of the manipulation of belief, in order to bring the women to safety and put their traffickers behind bars.

References

Andrijasevic, R. (2007). 'Beautiful Dead Bodies: Gender, Migration and Representation in Anti-trafficking Campaigns', *Feminist Review*, 86: 24–44.
Attoh, F. (2009). 'Trafficking in Women in Nigeria: Poverty of Values or Inequality?', *Journal of Social Science*, 19(3): 167–71.
Bradbury, R.E. (1970). *The Benin Kingdom and the Edo-speaking Peoples of South-Western Nigeria*. London: International African Institute, pp. 46–7.

---

[7]   Such as: End Child Prostitution, Pornography and the Trafficking of Children (ECPAT) and Africans Unite Against Child Abuse (AFRUCA). See also the policy recommendations in IPPR's report (Cherti et al. 2013).

Buker, H. (2007). 'Transporting Women Sex Workers from Nigeria to Europe', *Crime and Justice International Magazine* www.ncjrs.gov/App/publications/Abstract.aspx?id=242693 (accessed 10 April 2012).

Carling, J. (2006). *Migration, Human Smuggling and Trafficking from Nigeria to Europe.* Geneva: International Organization for Migration (IOM).

Cherti, M. et al. (2013). *Beyond Borders: Human Trafficking from Nigeria to the UK.* London: Institute of Public Policy Research (IPPR).

CPS (Crown Prosecution Service) (2011). *Human Trafficking and Smuggling; Legal Guidance.* London: CPS, p. 15.

ECPAT (End Child Prostitution, Pornography and the Trafficking of Children) (2008). *Vulnerablity and Control of African Child Victims of Trafficking; UK Experience.* London: ECPAT

Ellis, S. and G. ter Harr (2004). *Worlds of Power: Religious Thought and Political Practice in Africa.* London: Hurst.

Evans-Pritchard, E.E. (1936). *Witchcraft and Oracles among the Azande.* Oxford: Clarendon Press.

Harris, H. (2006) *Yoruba in Diaspora: an African Church in London.* New York: Palgrave Macmillan, p. 12.

Home Office, Department of Education (2012). *National Action Plan to Tackle Child Abuse Linked to Faith or Belief* https://www.education.gov.uk/publications/standard/publicationDetail/Page1/DFE-00094-2012 (accessed 25 February 2014).

Hoskins, R. (2012). *The Boy in the River: A Shocking True Story of Murder and Sacrifice in the Heart of London.* London: Pan Books.

Kara, S. (2009). *Sex Trafficking: Inside the Business of Modern Slavery.* New York: Columbia University Press, p. 90.

Kleeman, J. and J. Jones (2011). 'Sex, Lies and Black Magic', *Unreported World* series, Channel 4, 8 April.

La Fontaine. J. (2009). *The Devil's Children. From Spirit Possession to Witchcraft: New Allegations that Affect Children.* Farnham: Ashgate.

Okely, J. (1996). 'Fortune-tellers: Fakes or Therapists?', in *Own or Other Culture*, ed. J. Okely. London: Routledge, pp. 94–114.

Okojie, C.E.E. (2009). 'International Trafficking of Women for the Purpose of Sexual Exploitation and Prostitution the Nigerian case', *Pakistan Journal of Women's Studies*, 16(1 and 2): 147–78.

— et al. (2003). *Report of Field Survey in Edo State, Nigeria.* Turin: United Nations Interregional Crime and Justice Research Institute (UNICRI).

Onyeonuru, I.P. (2004). 'Pull Factors in the Political Economy of International Commercial Sex Work in Nigeria', *African Sociological Review*, 8(4): 115–35.

Smith, D.J. (2007). *A Culture of Corruption: Everyday Deception and Popular Discontent in Nigeria.* Princeton, NJ: Princeton University Press.

UKBA (Home Office, UK Border Agency) (2012). *Nigeria: Country of Origin Information Report.* London: UKBA.

UNESCO (2006). *Human Trafficking in Nigeria: Root Causes and Recommendations,* Policy Paper 14.2 (E). Paris: United Nations Educational, Scientific and Cultural Organization (UNESCO).

USSD (US State Department) (2011). *Trafficking in Persons Report.* Washington, DC: US State Department.

van Dijk, R. (2001). '"Voodoo" on the Doorstep: Young Nigerian Prostitutes and Magic Policing in the Netherlands', *Africa,* 71(4).

von Einsiedel, O. and J. Ruhfus (2011). *People and Power; the Nigerian Connection.* Al Jazeera English http://www.julianaruhfus.com/the-nigerian-connection/ (accessed 22 November 2012).

Chapter 7

Food, Faith and Fraud in Two New Religious Movements

Marion S. Goldman

Introduction

Throughout history, prohibitions, rituals and celebrations involving food have been associated with faiths in all parts of the world (McGuire 2008). In nineteenth-century America, new religious movements exalted some foods' life-giving properties while they banned others. For example, the Transcendentalist commune, Fruitlands, promoted strict vegan diets, but outlawed some vegetables, like carrots, because they grew down into the earth and symbolized man's base nature (Hankins 2004: 36). The Mormon Church still forbids all alcoholic beverages, coffee, and tea, while caffeinated soft drinks remain debatable. However, despite the strict dietary rules, the Church of the Latter Day Saints (LDS) made food an effective and profitable part of its outreach and recruitment in the nineteenth century.

Mormons established trading posts along the emigrant trails between Utah and California in the 1850s, selling supplies to church members and other travellers as well. These trading posts generated revenue and also goodwill, because helpful LDS members obviously belied the widespread demonization of their faith and they openly explained their religious commitments to outsiders who stopped for provisions (Howard 2000: 48). Contemporary new religious movements own and manage a number of restaurant and food businesses that serve the same purposes as the old Mormon trading posts: bringing in money, spreading their group's beliefs about food, and demonstrating their members' likeable personal qualities.

Both the food wholesale businesses and restaurants run by new religions, however, may be troubled by tensions that reveal some of the contradictions that develop when alternative faiths enter the retail marketplace for goods and services. This chapter explores controversies within two contemporary new religions where allegations of fraud and abuse of power emerged in their high-profile restaurants. The demands of restaurant work tested devotees' stamina and loyalty, hired outsiders' tolerance, and also their leaders' honesty.

Greens and the small Café Gratitude chain were founded on the Pacific Coast, where there is a concentration of new religious movements (NRMs) in the United States (Bader and the BSIR Study Group 2006: 45–8). Their customers tend to be middle-class 'foodies', interested in exploring personal growth and having enough disposable income to pay at least $35.00 for a dinner with a glass of wine or beer (Goldman 2012). Serving this clientele, both Greens and the small Café Gratitude chain became profitable within two years of their founding. The restaurants initially attracted positive media attention, while their later problems generated a number of articles, posts and other non-fiction publications that served as documentary sources for this chapter. The first dispute unfolded during the 1980s, when San Francisco Zen Center members ousted their charismatic leader, who had benefited from devotees' long hours of labour at the Center's bakery, organic farm and renowned vegetarian restaurant. Questions about leadership and exploitation also surfaced in 2011 in the Café Gratitude restaurants, where hired hands disputed labour practices that Landmark Forum believers took for granted.

Social Contexts

Despite Mormon outreach and an occasional health food restaurant founded by devotees of minority religions, the restaurants operated by alternative faiths were barely visible until the 1960s, when affluent seekers sought out eating experiences that appeared to both sustain their bodies and expand their spiritual capacities. Although most of these establishments were founded after 1965, the first of the wave of NRM restaurants that attracted affluent mainstream customers started in 1957 with the Aware Inn on Hollywood's Sunset Strip. Its charismatic co-owner, Father Yod, later founded the Source, a vegetarian restaurant that was staffed by very attractive young women who made up a large proportion of his 200-member group, the Source Family (Harvey 2007). A number of other small spiritually oriented restaurants emerged in other California communities during the early 1960s, but the connections between new religions and food and restaurant businesses became more visible in the late 1960s, after the Immigration and Nationality Act of 1965 made it easier for Asian teachers and their devotees to settle in the United States (Melton 1993). Many of these groups incorporated vegetarian diets into their doctrines and practices, sometimes using free food as outreach and offering recipes to interested outsiders (Rochford 1985). In the early 1970s, the International Society for Krishna Consciousness's Govinda's Buffets and the network of small cafes owned by devotees of Sri Chinmoy helped make Americans aware of new religious movements (Goldman 2012: 10–12).

Other groups contributed innovations to popular cuisine by introducing Americans to new kinds of food. For example, the San Francisco Zen Center's Tassajara Bakery brought specialty breads like ricotta olive bolso or lemon challah to the West Coast (Brown 1970) and Stephen Gaskin's Tennessee spiritual community, the Farm, marketed the first commercial tempeh in the US in the mid-1970s (Shurtleff and Aoagi 2001: 10).

While the culinary innovations that NRMs introduce may endure and become part of mainstream diets, most of their restaurants, like the Source, survive for less than a decade. Resembling the alternative faiths that create them, these ventures flourish briefly and then fade away as new enterprises rise up to replace them. Public controversies about exploitation are rare, because the restaurants usually close quickly in the face of financial losses or leaders' shifting priorities. A memorable case of mismanagement in the early 1970s involved a small intentional community of devotees of an obscure Indian guru who briefly ran the Diamond Sutra Café in San Francisco's Haight-Ashbury district. Despite the establishment's very reasonable prices, few diners ever returned. When I visited in 1972, our table of four waited at least an hour for our curries, while the lone chef slowly prepared each entrée individually in order to honour every customer's inner divinity. In another case of unrealistic organization at Bhagwan Shree Rajneesh's airy Zorba the Buddha Bakery and Café in Portland, Oregon, customers rarely had to wait long for delicious sandwiches and pastries. However, the popular restaurant regularly lost money, because its managers had not calculated the cost of transporting their luscious baked goods from communal kitchens located 200 miles away (Beckman 1985). Both of these short-lived restaurants illustrate some of the difficulties of bringing spirituality into the marketplace, where it may collide with the rules for successful commerce. Nevertheless, some enterprises associated with alternative religions thrive when they focus on making profits and fully utilizing their employees' commitments to their group.

One recent success is Supreme Master Ching Hai's worldwide chain of more than 120 Loving Hut Cafes that sell well-priced vegan dishes to enjoy on site or take home. Supreme Master, a sixty-something Vietnamese woman, tells the world to eat vegan, honour the natural environment, and seek serenity through her Quan Yin meditations on inner light and sound. Each restaurant is a franchise that devotees manage and most workers belong to Supreme Master's burgeoning movement. They are efficient, courteous and eager to answer questions about their spiritual commitments. Like the earlier Mormon trading posts, Loving Huts represent both outreach and revenue. The employees are happy to labour for love of their leader, their friends and the entire planet; so they often see their work as a kind of worship. Until a devotee's commitment begins to fray, even boring tasks like wiping down tables or emptying garbage can take on spiritual significance. The Loving Hut chain's success rests on each owner's financial and managerial skills, on the direction of the movement,and on the faith that Ching Hai's devotees place in her and in one another.

If workers' faith is shaken by external events or internal dissent, however, it is probable that there will be accusations of fraud, as there were in the two restaurants that are the subject of this chapter. The cases of Greens and the Café Gratitude chain illustrate some of the complicated dynamics that can unfold when spirituality mixes with commerce.

To make their businesses successful, religiously committed workers often suspend judgement about what might be considered manipulative and exploitative employment practices that increase their group's profits. They are labouring for a higher cause and they rarely pause to consider the many statutes that protect workers from exploitation. Judgements, however, surface when devotees or outside employees no longer trust the leaders and join together to critique the business models that they once supported. As Jacobs (1989) notes, devotees are committed to their charismatic leader and also to one another. Mutual support is vital to the development of negative definitions of the leader and the workplace. The two cases under consideration illuminate the ways that members of new religious movements come to define deception and fraud. In each restaurant, some workers asserted that they had been exploited and their leaders had defrauded them of both wages and also human dignity. Others believed that they were neither victimized nor misled, although their working conditions were problematic because food services demand high commitment and selfless labour. The decision to define a situation as fraud or not rests on three interdependent relationships: loyalty to the group's leader, connections to other dissidents, and the interdependence of perceived spiritual growth and restaurant work. Each case illuminates how individuals chose to frame their experience either as intentional exploitation or view it as part of the price for spiritual fulfilment. Both cases illustrate the complicated dynamics that can unfold when spirituality and commerce. mix together.

Troubles at Greens

In the early 1980s, Greens Restaurant was the flagship of the group of high-profile commercial enterprises developed by Richard Baker Roshi, an imposing, intensely charismatic figure. He was the designated successor to Shunryu Suzuki Roshi, the first West Coast Buddhist priest to invite ordinary Americans to sit zazen, a lengthy sitting meditation to suspend judgement and focus on the moment (Chadwick 2000). Suzuki envisioned a vital group of Zen temples that were connected to the first American Soto Zen monastery, which he established in Tassajara, a remote hotsprings that is located inland from the central California coast.

Richard Baker studied Zen and sat zazen with Suzuki, while he also worked tirelessly to increase the visibility and impact of the Zen Center, cultivating donors and starting new projects. As his teacher grew increasingly frail in the late 1960s, Baker's passionate commitment and closeness to Suzuki created a sense of inevitability around the dharma transmission that made him the next Chief Priest. One devotee described Richard's charisma: 'He was a human vortex, drawing everyone in toward the Zen Center' (Downing 2001: 85). Another asserted, 'Richard had the capacity to make us feel we could see way up the road into the future' (Downing 2001: 106).

While Suzuki was still alive, Zen Center students cleared land and built the monastery at Tassajara, while Baker raised money from elites like the founder of Xerox and the chairman of Fidelity Mutual (Downing 2001: 106). In addition, Baker organized a huge San Francisco benefit concert for Tassajara, a 'Zenifit' (Zen benefit) that featured the Grateful Dead and Janis Joplin (ibid.: 107). These projects set a precedent for a lasting division of labour: Baker was the leader and the spokesman for the Center, while Zen students worked at varied Center ventures with little or no financial compensation.

When Suzuki Roshi died in 1971, Baker was at the helm of an expanding organization with a budget that had reached $4 million by 1980. Only 350 students lived at Zen Center properties, but thousands of Americans had ties to the Center through visits to Tassajara, their own Zen practice, or just reading. An edited compilation of Suzuki Roshi's lectures, *Zen Mind, Beginner's Mind* (Suzuki 1970) was its publisher's biggest success ever (ibid.: 177) and *The Tassajara Bread Book* (Brown 1970) sold 150,000 copies in two years after it was first published (ibid.: 177). The Zen Center owned and operated a number of San Francisco businesses: a neighbourhood market, a bakery, a small bookstore, and Greens, its celebrated restaurant. The main temple and living quarters, the Tassajara Zen Monastery, and Green Gulch organic farm were other major assets that Baker had developed. However, in 1984, Richard Baker left San Francisco in disgrace and all of the businesses except Greens collapsed soon after his departure. The Board rebuked him for betraying their trust through sexual relationships with several women who depended on his guidance and forcing devotees to live at the edge of poverty while he enjoyed a lavish lifestyle that was built on ordinary members' hard work. Baker, however, believed that his three well-staffed households, his new BMW, his priceless Japanese antiques, and his celebrity friends reflected well on his students and were a means of heightening the Zen Center's visibility and influence on American culture (ibid.: 30, 282, 296–7).

A later Zen Center Abbot asserted, 'Dick would say things like, "'I'm only hanging around with all these glorious people [celebrities] so that Zen will penetrate the world.'" (ibid.: 320). It seemed as if Baker genuinely believed that a network of unique small businesses could be the impetus for a self-sustaining Zen community (ibid.: 282). Moreover, according to Baker, gruelling work assignments represented personalized spaces where Zen students could grow emotionally and learn to practice compassion and mindfulness in secular contexts.

Greens has been the jewel in the Zen Center's crown since it opened in 1979 and it is still flourishing, although an outside non-profit corporation responsible to the Zen Center now manages it. The best tables at Greens overlook the Golden Gate Bridge from an inspiring room that was once a huge deserted warehouse at Fort Mason. Skilled Zen Center artisans raised the floor, carefully carved seating areas out of burl wood, and added immense windows to frame the spectacular views. For more than three decades, Greens has been celebrated for haute vegetarian cuisine like Bengali potato croquettes with coconut, chillies, and coriander.

For a time, the workers who built and staffed Greens took their leader's explanations on faith, despite their growing doubts about his expensive lifestyle. However, as Baker's affairs with his students became common knowledge at the Zen Center, some of the restaurant workers began to question every aspect of his leadership. Many resented the ways that they were pressured to give up their personal meditation and study time in order to labour for 12–16 hours a day, with no personal spiritual or material benefit. Some sought public assistance because, in 1979, the year that Greens opened, senior students received room and board and an average monthly stipend of only $115 to cover their health insurance and other necessities.

Despite low wages and long hours, however, others gave Baker the benefit of the doubt, because they believed that their restaurant work had led them to a personal calling or a deeper understanding of service. Two of Greens' leading chefs acknowledged gruelling working conditions and little appreciation of any kind. In the same context, however, one accused Baker of exploitation and the other remained loyal despite her misgivings (2002 interviews, for Goldman 2012).

Edward Espe Brown, the author of the best-selling *Tassajara Bread Book* (1970), became increasingly bitter about his marginal lifestyle, when he compared it with Baker's houses, luxury car and personal staff. His book had earned hundreds of thousands of dollars of royalties that he had unthinkingly signed over to 'Chief Priest, Zen Center, San Francisco', when Suzuki Roshi was still alive. Brown never received any money for the book until it went to new editions beginning in 1986, after Baker's departure. As Brown started to voice his complaints and talk with other dissidents, Baker ordered Brown to move around in different jobs from manager to busboy at Greens, with the rationalization that each job would contribute to his spiritual growth (Downing 2001: 280). And while he had been the head chef at Tassajara and a well-known cookbook writer, Brown never had the opportunity to cook at the restaurant.

When the Zen Center's Board came together to discuss their Abbot's misdeeds, Brown realized that he had given his life to Richard Baker and the Zen Center, but suddenly he wanted it back for himself (ibid.: 40–42). At that point, he redefined Baker's activities as exploitation and fraud. He suddenly saw his teacher's rationalizations and justifications as masks for a desire for limitless personal power.

One 1983 Board meeting focused on Baker's inappropriate sexual liaisons with an emotionally fragile Center member and with the wife of a major donor who was studying Zen with him. When Baker tried to deflect the discussion and blame the Board for a witch hunt, Brown finally rejected the leader: 'Here's the person who has been taking responsibility publicly for building *all* of Zen Center, and the problems are our fault? ... No, no, no, it's an old trick of spiritual teachers' (ibid.: 41).

After Baker's departure, Brown briefly became head of the Zen Center's Board, but he left the Center to teach meditation and cooking, and write new books about Zen and the art of food preparation. A decade later, Brown collaborated on the *Greens Cookbook* (Madison 1996) with chef Deborah Madison. While he still offers various classes at the Zen Center, Green Gulch Farm and Tassajara, Brown continues to view Richard Baker as deceitful and resolutely avoids any contact with him. He blamed Baker for exploiting him and others, but Brown sustained his connection to Zen, the San Francisco Center, and his fellow devotees after Baker was ousted.

In contrast, Deborah Madison, the woman who first developed Green's unique approach to vegetarian cuisine, still regularly meditates in zazen alongside her disgraced teacher, who now heads the isolated Crestone Mountain Center high in Colorado's Sangre de Christo Mountains. She left the Zen Center and the US with her ex-husband soon after Baker was expelled, she studied cuisine in Rome, and then returned to Santa Fe, New Mexico, where she teaches cooking and writes articles and highly praised cookbooks (Madison 2002). Madison was the chef in Baker's household before Greens started and she never became part of the Center's dissident faction. She was lastingly grateful to her teacher for directing her toward a lifelong spiritual path of cooking and writing, so she viewed his actions as misguided, but neither fraudulent nor deceitful. Her experience resembled Edward Espe Brown's but she defined Baker as a flawed soul rather than a deliberate perpetrator of fraud (ibid.: 198–9). She even rationalized Baker's lavish lifestyle: 'This is how many people live, to be fair. Right? If you were to think of Zen Center as a corporation, and Richard as CEO, all of this would make perfect sense' (ibid.: 199).

When she prepared elaborate dinners for Baker's distinguished guests like the governor of California or celebrities like Rolling Stone Mick Jagger, Madison and other household staff members were instructed to remain in the background. She described her frustration: 'But in Richard's house, I was not supposed to open my mouth or enter into an event. You were a little wooden thing that displayed perfect behavior. You were not an equal. The student should be seen and not heard. It was a bit like a prolonged childhood (ibid.: 224).

She also resented the fact that Baker peppered his dharma talks to Zen Center students with vivid descriptions of his travels and fascinating adventures. Then, within a minute, she rethought her criticism and stated that he may have described his experiences in order to benefit Zen Center students by expanding their horizons: 'Richard was living a life on the outside for the rest of us' (ibid.: 222). He had always encouraged her to acknowledge and expand her gift for cooking and he tapped Madison to invent an extraordinary vegetarian menu long before Greens opened.

Although her extraordinary culinary innovations were widely recognized outside the Zen Center, Madison, like other Greens staff, was not allowed to step into the spotlight or accept public praise in person. In fact, Baker appeared to be ambivalent about Madison's success. She described a triumph that Baker diminished after she had planned and prepared a dinner for 150 in honour of the Dalai Lama:

So, we planned and planned and put together an amazing meal ... and the next morning I was called in for dokusan [private instruction], and Richard told me very strictly that people did not like working with me. I was too demanding. And when people got interested in Greens, and wanted to interview me, I was told not to care about that stuff, to be a modest Zen student. So I did no interviews. (Ibid.: 292).

Madison's first husband, Dan Welch, was on the Zen Center's Board, and he was one of only two members who voted not to accept the Chief Priest's resignation in 1983. Soon after Baker's forced exit, the couple went to Rome and worked together in the kitchen of a wealthy family while they studied cooking. They divorced, but remained close friends when they returned to the US, and each of them separately moved to Santa Fe. After maintaining his distance for four years, Welch reconnected with Baker. He now resides at the Crestone Mountain Zen Center, where he has become Baker's dharma heir. For both Madison and Welch, the exhausting work at Greens never signalled fraud or deception, but instead represented a version of the rocky path that every seeker must travel. Said Welch about the trouble at Greens, 'Everyone who feels hurt has work to do' (ibid.: 380).

Where Edward Espe Brown saw malice, Madison and Welch saw inevitable human frailty. Their circumstances were much the same as Brown's, but their personal relationships to Baker, their weak ties to dissident factions, and the rewards that they gained from discovering a fulfilling vocation through Baker's guidance led them to very different interpretations of their work lives.

Baker envisioned Greens as another means to bring Zen into the world and demonstrating the spiritual possibilities in everyday life, but there was never any concerted plan to bring outsiders into the Zen Center through the restaurant (ibid.: 272–4). In contrast, customers and staff at Café Gratitude are asked to participate in spiritual affirmations and consider exploring the Landmark Forum's approach to personal actualization and the cultivation of lives filled with spiritual and material abundance.

Ingrates at Café Gratitude

Late in 2011, several employees filed complaints alleging that Terces and Matthew Engelhart violated California labour laws at their San Francisco Café Gratitude, part of the small chain of vegan organic restaurants that are connected to Landmark Forum. Landmark is a personal and spiritual development group that is related to the controversial *est* movement that began in the Bay Area in the 1970s. The Engelharts currently own five restaurants in California, but they have owned as many as seven. Another Landmark devotee recently opened a franchised Café Gratitude in Kansas City, Missouri.

Terces and Mathew Engelhart have been involved with Landmark for at least two decades, but they have no formal positions with the group. Landmark-friendly employees always refer to the owners of Café Gratitude as Matthew and Terces, never by their last name, and each devotee has a real and/or imagined relationship with them. The Engelharts started their first restaurant in 2004 with some of the profits from the multi-million dollar sale of the successful clothing chain, Flax, that Matthew had founded with his first wife, Jane.

The cafes grew out of Matthew's and Terces's determination to promote sacred commerce, where the marketplace can become a path to self-realization. In rustic cafes filled with greenery, customers and employees are asked to consider Landmark's philosophies of abundant possibilities and personal accountability. The Engelharts want to turn every Café Gratitude into a workplace community of like-minded staff who are committed to changing the world one person at a time, beginning with themselves (Engelhart, Engelhart and Brown 2008). Each cafe becomes a sacred space where the movement's ideals are enacted and there is no separation of work for the benefit of the business and work as a personal spiritual practice.

Landmark characterizes its approach as spiritual, not religious, but it is grounded in the religious belief that everyone has a core spark of divinity within them that can be connected to some amorphous cosmic force (Goldman 2012). The Engelharts view Landmark as a way of connecting everyone with the divine spark that lies within them and they see Café Gratitude as a means of facilitating customers' awareness of Landmark's services (Engelhart and Brown 2008). Their restaurants' early successes, however, made it necessary for them to employ a mixture of Landmark devotees, seekers interested in its approaches, and experienced workers whose only quests involved earning a living. That mix led to lawsuits.

Seasoned chefs and servers were recruited for busy restaurants, because some devotees were not efficient workers. Moreover, the Engelharts opened several new restaurants in the wake of their early success and the start-ups required skilled staff rather than eager Landmark graduates. By hiring outsiders, the Engelharts created a context where practices that had been taken on faith, like affirmations, were likely to be challenged as exploitation and other routine procedures involving compensation and taxes could even be classified as criminal.

At every Café Gratitude, customers and employees alike are asked to participate in affirmations of an abundant world where everyone can reach their full human potential. There is a whiteboard at each cafe's entrance with a question of the day such as, 'What makes you happy?' A server may also ask, 'What are you thankful for?' A sarcastic answer: 'I am thankful to be able to afford this place', would not please a Landmark devotee. While a reply such as 'I am grateful for the rain that draws us together in community', would be greeted with a supportive grin and possibly a hug.

Each dish on the menu has a designated affirmation, such as: 'I am Dazzling', 'I am Fulfilled', or 'I am Strong'. To order, customers are supposed to state the affirmation and when a dish is served they are asked to restate it. These rituals represent a context where the believers and the sceptical personnel often part ways. If a server brings an order to a table and looks around and asks who *is* the 'I am Dazzling Caesar Salad', the appropriate response is a joyful: 'I AM DAZZLING!' However, on a bad day, it's easy to say something like 'I ordered the damned salad and I Am Wiped Out.' Even in the face of this sort of resolute disconfirmation, a devotee may congratulate a customer on an inner dazzle that is only hidden by his or her exhaustion, while a sceptical hired hand is likely to laugh out loud at a smart rejection of the culture of affirmations.

Although its rituals sometimes provoke laughter, Café Gratitude's vegan organic menus attract many diners who are willing to pay fairly high prices and go along with the programme, with no intention of exploring Landmark Forum's approaches to personal and spiritual growth. The cafes are known for tasty dishes such as plump enchiladas topped with mushrooms and cashew cheese or grilled summer squash filled with sweet corn from the Engelharts' Be Love Farm in Vacaville. While doing research for this chapter, I ordered the 'I am Adoring Tiramisu', a cake soaked in espresso with vegan whipped cream and chocolate frosting, and it looked and ultimately tasted so delicious that I gladly explained 'I am Adoring' because I loved my cats, Bruzzer and Simon, so much.

None of the employees who filed lawsuits had been involved in Landmark Forum before they were hired. They alleged that if they did not pay a high fee to participate in an introductory Landmark Seminar weekend, it was impossible for them to be promoted to managerial status. Despite their resistance, however, sceptical employees still had to practise some of Landmark's approaches to personal and spiritual growth, because Café Gratitude requires every worker and manager to participate in daily 'clearing' programmes. These are group sessions where workers examine their personal lives to clear out the causes of their bad attitudes and learn to express gratitude for life's abundant blessings (Engelhart, Engelhart and Brown 2008: 25–32). The plaintiffs questioned this requirement, but they did not file any complaints, because the sessions are not explicitly illegal and they can be framed as organizational 'team-building'. However, their other charges had legal merit.

Several workers filed complaints about demands to put in extra hours without overtime pay and also pool their tips with managers and workers at an off-site kitchen (Grub Street 2011). A bookkeeper alleged that he had been illegally classified as a full-time employee so that he would not receive higher hourly wages. He also complained that the Engelharts denied him adequate caregiver's leave when his wife had cancer. The lawsuits were settled within four months, with the stipulation that no one on either side could publicly discuss the resolution.

While their attorneys negotiated, the Engelharts encouraged their supporters to write to newspapers and post on media websites. This employee's post uses the language of Landmark Forum and repeats themes found in dozens of other posts:

> As an actual employee of Café Gratitude, having worked for this company for five years, and having experienced the practices and mission of Café Gratitude in its actuality I would love to be heard. Negativity breed's [*sic*] negativity and everyone is looking for something to be a victim of, or someone/something to blame. Let me assure all readers that Café Gratitude is of the highest integrity and has the highest generosity of any employer I have ever worked for and is the most compassionate and truly wonderful company that I have ever come across. (Primm 2011)

Another devotee asserted that troubles began when Café Gratitude started to hire staff on the basis of their restaurant experience rather than their commitment to Landmark (Grub Street 2011). Old and new employees who had passed through Landmark saw their work as an avenue for spiritual expansion and membership in a community of like-minded believers, while those who maintained a distance from the Engelharts and their spiritual organization viewed it as paid labour and nothing more. Like the individuals at Greens who remained loyal to Richard Baker, Café Gratitude workers who discovered a sense of community and personal meaning through their jobs saw their extra hours without overtime, pooled tips and Landmark participation as meaningful and intrinsically rewarding. According to Matthew Engelhart, the co-owner, 'We promise our employees a life breakthrough.' The dissidents desired only overtime pay and appropriate salaries. Soon after the legal settlement, the Engelharts closed the two restaurants where the plaintiffs had worked and two other unprofitable establishments. But two others have taken their places. However, so long as most or all of their employees have high levels of commitment and minimal scepticism, it is unlikely that more internal conflict will develop and some of the Café Gratitudes will become enduring enterprises.

The new Kansas City and Los Angeles area restaurants try to hire individuals who are involved with Landmark Forum and/or the Engelharts' related seminars on sacred commerce and building workplace communities. Every job applicant must complete a statement of interest that asks questions such as: 'What inspires you about the possibility of Sacred Commerce?' or 'What are your thoughts about service and spirit?' These open-ended questions are designed to select for individuals who will be cognizant of Landmark or at least open to the Engelharts' demands for high commitment and workplace community.

When Business as Usual is Not Exactly Business

Outreach and revenue are explicit common functions of restaurants that mix food and faith, while personal spiritual practice may be more variable. It is central in some places like Govinda's Buffets or the reorganized Café Gratitude chain, but of minor import at Greens in the twenty-first century. Even when they are told that their restaurant work is a spiritual practice, devotees, like those at the Zen Center's Greens, often try to sustain a separation between work and worship. Because of the presence of outsiders, workplaces are not sacred space and members usually separate their primary spiritual practice from their workplace activities. Their food service businesses operate as 'audience cults' (Stark and Bainbridge 1985: 27) that attract diverse customers, who learn something about a group's message and might want to find out more over time.

When the high demands of the restaurant industry take time away from devotees' practice and distract them from their spiritual priorities, they may resent their work and come to define those obligations as products of deception and exploitation. At Greens in the 1980s, devotees bowed to the divinity in all things when they began their shifts, but had no other spiritual obligations. Dissidents at the Zen Center began to discuss their misgivings about Richard Baker with one another when they no longer had enough time to study or engage in the seated meditation zazen practice that was foundational to the Zen Center's spirituality. However, no public disputes surfaced until the Head Priest's financial excesses and sexual misdeeds became widely known.

In contrast to the Zen Center, Landmark Forum maintains no unique sacred space where devotees live or enact their spiritual priorities. Novices and seasoned members alike practise the movement's approaches to personal and spiritual growth at work, in their intimate relationships, and in seminars that are designed to cement their bonds to the group and implement its doctrines. Landmark is primarily a 'client cult' (ibid.: 28–9) that is focused on helping individuals make emotional breakthroughs that facilitate their leading happier, more meaningful lives. Every server and cook is supposed to exemplify the benefits of the Café Gratitude philosophy and supportive community and attempt to recruit outsiders. Personal authenticity and commitment within Café Gratitude are affirmed by the recruitment of family members, friends and acquaintances to the Engelharts' and Landmark's other workshops.

Unlike the early Zen Center and other movements in their first generation, including its own predecessor *est*, Landmark Forum has no single charismatic leader. Instead, workshop leaders or Landmark-associated business owners such as the Engelharts come to embody the group's doctrines and practices for other members.

There were public allegations of deception and fraud at both Café Gratitude and Greens. However, under similar circumstances in both venues, some workers believed that the leaders had exploited and deceived while others did not. Dissidents at Greens restructured the Zen Center by forcing Baker out and they changed working conditions at the restaurant by implementing state and federal regulations for all employees. They clearly indicated that work at Greens was not a primary spiritual practice, although employees cultivate attitudes of attentiveness and service. In contrast, the plaintiffs at Café Gratitude never changed the organization and they had already departed when they filed suit in order to receive just compensation for their past work.

In both cases, there was little dispute about conditions that were problematic and often illegal: low pay, minimal benefits, no overtime compensation. The different responses within each group indicate that the workers' standpoints were crucial in determining whether or not they had been deliberately deceived and exploited (Neitz 2004). If they were fully committed to the movement and its leaders and believed that their work offered them spiritual rewards, they were unlikely to voice serious allegations of deception and fraud; although they might complain about some conditions, as Deborah Madison did at Greens.

Whether they supported Richard Baker or not, Zen Center devotees at Greens uniformly believed that their restaurant work failed to provide them with space for spiritual practice or enough time to commit themselves to the regular rituals at the San Francisco Zen Center. In contrast, dissidents at Café Gratitude rejected all of Landmark Forum's spiritual priorities. They viewed the Engelharts' commitment to sacred commerce as rationalizations for exploitive and fraudulent labour. Landmark graduates and those open to Landmark, however, welcomed opportunities to build spiritually oriented workplace communities and did not object to their compromised pay or working conditions.

Because leaders could justify questionable activities in both contexts and no allegations noted physical violence or other extreme abuse, there was room for competing definitions of deception and fraud. Fraud was not obvious in the workplace situations at Greens or Café Gratitude, but was instead a socially conferred label (Erikson 1966). These cases demonstrate the ways that faith may negate dissent and initial scepticism may encourage it.

Three sets of relationships shaped responses to questionable activities at Greens and Café Gratitude: relationships to the leader, ties with other members, and the intrinsic rewards that work provided. If someone were close to the leader, they were likely to dismiss questionable activities as either simple missteps or an intentional challenge that would allow them to grow spiritually and emotionally. However, if someone never bonded at all with the leader or if they no longer did, they were more likely to protest against deception and fraud in their workplaces.

Dissidents at Café Gratitude took their jobs for money rather than love of their leaders or affinities with other members. Their key personal relationships were outside the group and they did not bond with one another until after they contemplated legal action. They judged their workplace by standards external to Landmark Forum. At Greens, dissidents who had serious questions about their leader's intentions and actions were still committed to the Zen Center and its spiritual goals. They began to talk with one another in order to return to lives shaped by Zen practice and they judged Baker by Zen standards of righteous conduct. The rumblings began between couples or small groups of close friends who gradually coalesced into a group of dissidents within the movement.

The third and least easily observed element that led individuals to define their work as fulfilling or exploitative involved the intrinsic rewards that they experienced. Workers who found community at Café Gratitude and felt that workplace spirituality and Landmark seminars benefited them, accepted working conditions that dissidents found intolerable. Similarly, at Greens, some Zen Center devotees accepted the gruelling work schedules and lack of recognition because they discovered that cooking or serving was a path to personal enlightenment.

Faith, food and fraud are a volatile mixture. If bonds to the leader, relationships to other devotees, and the work/worship connections never existed or shift, restaurant workers may come to view elements of their work as the product of deception and fraud. These cases illustrate how definitions of fraud in minority religions change and how changing definitions can close down restaurants or even threaten the foundations of new religious movements.

References

Bader, C. and the BISR Study Group (2006). *Selected Findings from the Baylor Religion Survey*. Waco, TX: Baylor Institute for Studies of Religion.

Beckman, A.C. (1985). 'Zorba the Baker', in *The Rajneesh Papers*, ed. W. McCormack. Portland, OR: New Oregon Publishers, Inc., pp. 93–4

Brown, E.E. (1970). *The Tassajara Bread Book*. Boston, MA: Shambala Publications.

Chadwick, D. (2000). *Crooked Cucumber: The Life and Teachings of Shunryu Suzuki*. New York: Broadway Books.

Downing, M. (2001). *Shoes Outside the Door: Desire, Devotion, and Excess at the San Francisco Zen Center*. Washington, DC: Counterpoint Press.

Engelhart, M., T. Engelhart and M.M. Brown (2008). *Sacred Commerce: Business as a Path of Awakening*. Berkeley, CA: North Atlantic Books.

Erikson, K.T. (1966). *Wayward Puritans: A Study in the Sociology of Deviance*. New York: John Wiley and Sons.

Gaskin, S. (2005). *Monday Night Class*. Summertown, TN: United States Book Publishing Company.

Goldman, M. (2012). *The American Soul Rush: Esalen and the Rise of Spiritual Privilege*. New York: New York University Press.

Grub Street (2011), November 29. 'A New Side of the Café Gratitude story, and Their Potentially Shady Commerce' http://sanfrancisco. grubstreet.com/2011/11/a_new_side_of_the_caf_gratitud.html accessed 1 February 2012.

Hankins, B. (2004). *The Second Great Awakening and the Transcendentalists*. Westport CT: Greenwood Press.

Harvey, D. (2007). 'Father Yod Knew Best', *LA Weekly*, 30 August http:// www.laweekly.com/2007-08-30/news/father-yod-knew-best/ (accessed 6 June 2013).

Howard, T.F. (2000). *Sierra Crossing: First Roads to California*. Berkeley, CA: University of California Press.

Jacobs, J.L. (1989). *Divine Disenchantment: Deconversion from New Religions*. Bloomington: Indiana University Press.

Kaiser, D. (2011). *How the Hippies Saved Physics: Science, Counterculture, and the Quantum Revival*. New York: W.W. Norton and Company.

McGuire, M. (2008). *Lived Religion: Faith and Practice in Everyday Life*. New York: Oxford University Press.

Madison, D., with E.E. Brown (1987). *The Greens Cookbook: Extraordinary Cuisine from the Celebrated Restaurant*. New York: Bantam.

— (2002). *Local Flavors: Cooking and Eating from America's Farmers Markets*. New York: Broadway Books.

Melton, J.G. (1993). 'Another Look at New Religions', *Annals of the American Academy of Political and Social Science*, 527(1): 97–112.

Neitz, M.J. (2004). 'Gender and Culture: Challenges to the Sociology of Religion', *Sociology of Religion*, 65(4) (Winter): 391–402.

Primm, A.L. (2011). November 30. Post Comment on 'Cafe Gratitude to Close All NorCal Locations' East Bay Express, 30 November http://www.eastbayexpress. com/WhatTheFork/archives/2011/11/29 (accessed 4 January 2012).

Rochford, E.B. (1985). *Hare Krishna in America*. New Brunswick, NJ: Rutgers University Press.

Shurtleff, M. and A. Aoagi (2001). *The Book of Tofu and Miso*. Berkeley, CA: Ten Speed Press.

Stark, R. and W.S. Bainbridge (1985). *The Future of Religion*. Berkeley: University of California Press.

Suzuki, S. (1970). *Zen Mind, Beginner's Mind*. Boston, MA: Weatherhill.

Chapter 8

Miracle Makers and Money Takers: Healers, Prosperity Preachers and Fraud in Contemporary Tanzania

Martin Lindhardt

A central insight of sociological theories of religious markets or religious economies is that competition in unregulated markets tends to produce the kind of religious products that consumers prefer and demand. It follows that religious consumption is higher in a market situation where plurality and freedom of choice prevail. Research, informed by religious markets theories, not only focuses attention on religious consumers but also considers the creative advertising of religious institutions and individual entrepreneurs who aspire to generate visibility for themselves and their products (see Finke and Stark 1988, Iannaccone 1992).

Religious market models provide a fruitful perspective in the study of religious pluralism in contemporary post-liberalization African countries like Tanzania, where new Islamic groups and new Pentecostal/Charismatic ministries regularly pop up and battle to outdo each other in the provision of religious products and services. When it comes to some of the most sought-after spiritual services, such as healing, protection against witchcraft, expulsion of spirits, and not least, the assistance of invisible forces in economic and work-related affairs, world religious institutions and entrepreneurs find themselves in harsh and direct competition with another powerful group of providers, the traditional healers. In this market situation, where the provision of spiritual services is in obvious ways becoming a potentially profitable endeavour, more and more suspicions of fraud are emerging. Making money by providing spiritual services to others is not in itself as morally suspicious as it is in other places and contexts. Historical research on church membership in the United States in the early twentieth century has shown that the clergy were more persuasive when they did not benefit materially from their followers' faith and that people were outraged when they heard of religious leaders amassing large personal fortunes (Finke and Stark 1988). In the case of contemporary Tanzania, such a clear pattern cannot be found. As in other African countries, many people see both wealth and political power as possible indications of a person's potent alliances with the spiritual world. And in so far as consumers seek spiritual assistance in economic affairs, it seems both logical and reassuring that providers appear to be living proofs of the efficiency of their services. But when traditional healing or the running of a Pentecostal/ Charismatic ministry in too obvious ways becomes a business venture and when adherents or consumers fail to see the material fruits of spiritual assistance, doubt can easily be shed on the honesty of providers.

Based on long-term research in Iringa, a regional sub-capital of south-central Tanzania, this chapter sheds light on popular scepticism towards both traditional healers and Pentecostal/Charismatic preachers. I shall refrain from passing judgements as to whether some healers and preachers *are* frauds who deliberately and consciously lie about their skills and spiritual powers in order to make money. The issue to be explored here is how complex circumstances and developments within Tanzania's traditional medical and religious fields have contributed to the emergence of a culture of distrust towards providers of spiritual services and products. This distrust does not discourage people from seeking spiritual assistance in everyday affairs, but it does inspire critical reflection and an increased awareness of the necessity of being able to distinguish between genuine healers or preachers and frauds. In what follows I relate suspicions of fraud being committed by healers and preachers to processes of commercialization of the occult and of Christianity in neo-liberal Tanzania. But I also argue that the scepticism many people feel towards providers of spiritual services stems from deeper epistemological insecurities in relation to invisible forces and not least from the inherent difficulty of gaining certain knowledge about the nature of unseen spiritual powers that produce material effects in the visible world (see Lindhardt 2012).

Background

Iringa is a pluralist city in terms of religion and ethnicity. Although locally rooted beliefs and practices are still common, most people, including all 'traditional healers' (*waganga wa kienjeje*) I have spoken to, have some institutional affiliation with one of the world religions. Islam has a strong presence, but as in most Tanzanian inland cities, Christians are the majority in Iringa. While the Roman Catholic Church counts the most members, the city also has one of the highest concentrations of Lutherans in the county (unfortunately reliable statistic material on religious adherence is hard to find). In addition to the historical mainline mission churches, a number of Pentecostal/Charismatic ministries have been founded in and around Iringa. In response to the Pentecostal competition, Pentecostal-inspired charismatic revival movements have grown within mainline Protestant churches and the Catholic Church.

The main ethnic groups are the Wahehe, the Wabena and the Wakinga, but several people from other parts of the country such as the Wachagga from northern Tanzania and the Wanyakusa from southern Tanzania have also settled in the city. The Wahehe, the Wabena and the Wakinga all have patrilineal descent systems and share many beliefs, religious practices and linguistic features. The main language in Iringa is Kiswahili. Inter-ethnic marriages are common, all the Christian churches I have visited are multi-ethnic and traditional healers treat all patients regardless of ethnicity.

Modern Traditional Healers

The study of traditional healing in Africa has provided a solid empirical foundation for challenging views of tradition as static and bounded. A significant body of literature portrays African healers as creative cultural innovators whose (strategic) claims to tradition do not prevent them from adapting to modern frameworks, exploring new, external (for instance Christian and Islamic) sources of spiritual powers and addressing contemporary concerns and life problems of urban Africans such as AIDS, unstable marriages, legal troubles or success and failure in business, politics and soccer (Geschiere 1997, West and Luedke 2006). An overwhelming majority of Tanzanian healers I have met refer to themselves, and are referred to by others, as 'traditional healers' (*waganga wa kienyeji* or *waganga wa asili*). But many also add English words such as 'professor' or 'doctor' to their titles (for instance 'Doctor Mduba. Mganga wa asili') to stress that they both keep up with modern medical standards and possess the wisdom and power needed to deal with problems that biomedicine cannot solve. In addition many, especially Muslim but also some Christian, healers claim to be assisted by *majini*, non-ancestral spirits, commonly associated with Islamic coastal culture.[1] *Majini* have different ethnic and national characteristics, which are reflected in

---

[1] The existence of *majini* (*jinn* in Arabic) is substantiated in several verses of the Qu'ran. As a general rule, Tanzanian Sufi Muslims see such spirits as the creatures of God, though they also distinguish between good, protective and harmful *majini*. Many, especially Pentecostal-Charismatic Christians, insist that *majini* are really satanic spirits.

their stereotypical division of labour. Some healers told me that their Chinese, Indian and Arabic *majini* can assist people trying to succeed in business, whereas British *majini* can help persons who have to present themselves in court.[2] When interviewed about their knowledge and powers, many healers both pointed to their spiritual assistance from deceased ancestors and/or *majini* and stressed that they had done a good deal of *utafiti* in order to learn about healing herbs. *Utafiti* can be translated as 'research' and the same word is commonly used to refer to scientific investigations. By making simultaneous claims to tradition and modernity and to ancestral and global spiritual forces healers situate themselves as transgressors of boundaries and as powerful mediators of different systems of knowledge and practice (see also West and Luedke 2006).

Within recent decades, the practice of traditional healing (*uganga*) in Tanzania has undergone processes of commercialization, professionalization and bureaucratization. Many of Tanzania's traditional healers are now members of a national association of traditional healers and are becoming more integrated into the formal medical system. These healers have government-issued documents for clients and anthropologists to see, and in order to obtain such documents they must pass an examination. One of the most famous traditional healers in the country, Anthony Mwandulami, runs a hospital of traditional herbal medicines, strategically located along a highway between the south-central cities of Makambako and Njombe and easy to reach via public transportation, where patients can stay in dormitories for several days. Another nationally famous traditional healer, Shaibu Magungu (the grandson of the legendary late healer Bibi Kalembwana) presents his witchcraft cleansing rituals as a public service (though one for which people must pay) and has written proposals for external financing in the same format as that used by developmental agencies applying for funds (Green and Mesaki 2005).

Though personal networks, local reputation and recommendations of satisfied clients are still the most important way of letting new potential clients find healers, the latter have also adopted modern marketing strategies. Some have stalls with big posters and different kinds of medicines on display in city markets, and many who operate from their homes put up sign boards, never neglecting to display their mobile phone number, along main roads, or they have small identity cards which they pass out. The liberalization of the mass media in Tanzania in the 1990s also provided traditional healers with new channels for

---

[2]   Tanzania is a former British colony and the country's present judiciary combines jurisdictions of Islamic, tribal and common British law.

asserting a public presence, and nowadays many use the radio and newspapers to advertise their services.

Healers have also successfully adapted to the needs and demands of both large- and small-scale entrepreneurs in Tanzania's neoliberal economy. In the 1980s, the International Monetary Fund and World Bank dictated implementation of structural adjustment programmes, which resulted in a significant expansion of the informal economic sector, as it became increasingly difficult for ordinary citizens to make a decent living through formal employment (see Tripp 1997). For a majority of urban Tanzanians, including many who have formal employment, the *mradi* (project) has become the most important means of survival. *Mradi* may refer to a wide range of income-generating activities, such as selling onions from a stall, making doughnuts to sell at a local market, small- or large-scale commercial farming, keeping chickens and selling their eggs, buying a sewing machine and making clothes, selling second-hand clothing, buying a car that can be used as a taxi, or opening a small shop, restaurant, or hotel. Harsh competition, low purchasing power of potential clients, and the difficulty of raising enough capital to invest and expand are only some of the conditions that people with a *mradi*, or the ambition of starting one, must face. In this context, it is hardly surprising that some kind of extraordinary support is considered necessary by many. Nowadays, a majority of healers (including each and every one of the thirty I have interviewed) provide their clients with *dawa za biashara* (business medicines), usually in the form of a powder that must be spread out in shops or market stalls, or sometimes rubbed on the body of the owner, in order to attract clients, and to neutralize the powers of witchcraft that may prevent a business from prospering.

Though the services of healers are in high demand, many people also look upon the healers with deep ambivalence. The commercialization of traditional healing and the, sometimes unashamed, concerns of healers with making money make others question their integrity. I will return to this point shortly, but here another reason for the popular and widespread scepticism towards healers deserves a few comments. In the view of many Tanzanians, the link between traditional healing and the world of witchcraft is an intimate and complex one. According to popular belief, witches are persons with inherited and/or acquired spiritual powers that are mainly used to disturb others and obstruct their prosperity, though such powers can also be used to secure the enrichment of witches themselves. The power of witchcraft enables a person to leave his or her body at night and fly around invisible. Though the power of witchcraft is somehow intrinsic to certain persons, witches are also known to be allied with both ancestral spirits and *majini* that assist them in all kinds of matters. Healing, in whatever form, involves power and the possession and employment of specialized knowledge. It is widely believed that healers can only provide protection against witches because they themselves possess powers and knowledge of witchcraft. Deep knowledge about witchcraft cannot be acquired through detached observation, but requires some kind of engagement with the world of witches (see Lindhardt 2012). Healers take pains to distinguish themselves from witches, but to many others, the difference between the two is unclear, and even healers themselves are bound to acknowledge some affinity with the world of witchcraft if they want to appear spiritually powerful. Though most healers will deny that they can leave their bodies and fly around naked, they readily admit that they are assisted by ancestral spirits and *majini*. They distinguish between their own benevolent *majini* (who only require a little incense from time to time) and the evil *majini* of witches (who need human blood), but this clear-cut distinction between different kinds of *majini* is not always convincing to other people.

In significant ways, people's understandings of the developments of witchcraft parallel some of the innovations of traditional healing described above. I was often told that contemporary witches are members of national and pan-African witchcraft associations and hold annual meetings; that witches are constantly studying in order to improve their methods and enhance their powers and; that an increasing number of witches, including rural pagan witches, now ally themselves with *majini*. In addition, within the last couple of decades, the use of business medicines and the marketing and advertising of the occult have been paralleled by an increase in Tanzania and several other African countries of rumours and concerns about rapid accumulation of wealth through witchcraft (Geschiere 1997, Sanders 1999, Lindhardt 2009, forthcoming). According to popular belief, fast or sudden wealth acquired through witchcraft comes with problematic conditions, such as restrictions on the use of money or the sacrifice of a close relative. Though the use of business medicines and the witchcraft of wealth are not the same thing, many people find the exact borderline between the two to be a difficult one to draw. For the same reason, very few people openly admit using business medicines, though everyone suspects others of doing so and healers insist they sell a lot of it. Writing on the Inhagzu of Western Tanzania, Todd Sanders notes that medicines are best used secretly as one person's medicine may always be another person's witchcraft (1999: 126).

The ambiguous and unclear relationship between the powers of traditional healing and the powers of witchcraft inspires certain scepticism and anxiety in relation to healers. This anxiety is reinforced by the growth and proliferation of Pentecostal ministries and charismatic revival groups within mainline churches in recent decades. Unlike traditional Catholicism, which is to some extent characterized by a condescending toleration of popular practices, Pentecostals/ Charismatics (including Catholic Charismatics) are uncompromising in their insistence that all healers must be witches and hence servants of the devil, and they are not shy in expressing this view publicly during open-air revival meetings. For many others who do consult healers, doing so implies trusting that the latter chooses to use their spiritual powers in benevolent ways.

According to one popular theory, healers in search of paying customers cooperate with other witches, asking the latter to make people sick. Or healers may themselves pass on a *jini* (singular of *majini*) to patients after curing them so that they will fall ill again at a later point. I also heard several stories about unfortunate side effects of traditional medicines. Women can use medicines from healers in order to control unfaithful and violent husbands. Such medicines are usually placed into the food a woman cooks for her husband, or discretely placed on his genitals during intercourse, the kitchen and the bedroom being the domains in which a woman can negotiate domestic power relationships. The medicine will reduce a man's interest in other women and make him miss his wife whenever he is away from home. Or it will make him impotent when he is with other women. However, the medicine can have the side effect of making a man lazy, apathetic and impotent at home. Many people also believe that wealth acquired through the use of business medicines is only temporary and that economic ruin and other personal disasters or premature death will eventually follow after a few prosperous years.

The ambiguity with which many people look upon healers has by no means been reduced by the commercialization and increased marketing of traditional medicines and services. As argued by Maia Green and Simeon Mesaki, in Tanzania's post-liberalization free market of traditional healing, the client has become 'reconstituted as a consuming agent who selects from among services on offer' (2005: 382). The availability of a great variety of products with mysterious powers is accompanied by a certain scepticism and critical awareness among consumers who must be careful when choosing. In an ideal neoliberal capitalist world, the dissolution of monopolies and the free market competition will benefit consumers, as providers are bound to enhance their competitiveness by improving their products and services and by keeping prices low. While Tanzanians understand this logic well, many have real-life experiences that contradict it. In the views of many, the free market of traditional healing has also provided new opportunities for unscrupulous charlatans and frauds in search of fast and easy money. Even Pentecostals/Charismatics who insist that all traditional healing is the work of the Devil sometimes add nuances to the picture by distinguishing between different categories of healers.[3]

I was frequently told that most genuine healers are found in the rural areas and that many people in the city prefer to travel to their home villages when they need to consult a healer, though this preference was also in part ascribed to a wish to keep the consultation a secret from urban neighbours and business rivals. Genuine healers possess the power and knowledge, for instance, of healing herbs, to cure people and protect them against witchcraft (even if Pentecostals/Charismatics insist that any involvement with traditional healing will, in the long run, trap a client in a harmful relationship with the Devil). In the city, so several informants explained to me, one is more likely to encounter commercial charlatans and frauds who present themselves as healers and make claims to both medical knowledge and spiritual powers in order to be able to charge high fees, but who are in reality unable to provide their clients with any real assistance.

Though people acknowledge that healers need to develop and keep up with modernity and admire their abilities to do so, the modernization of traditional healing is also associated with some of modernity's morally questionable by-products such as individualism, lack of communal values, excessive, uncontrolled greed and an obsession with money. Traditional healing is a way of making a living and people agree that healers are entitled to expect payment for their services. But when healing becomes too much of a business, the integrity and honesty of healers can easily be called into question. Having the power and knowledge to heal others cannot be easily separated from a certain moral duty to actually do so, and an unashamed concern with making money from healing can be subject to moral condemnation. Several informants explained to me that 'genuine healers' charge small fees, and only ask for payment after a patient has been cured. If patients have no cash, they may even be treated for free, and then maybe pay at a later point if money comes their way. By contrast, many of the urban charlatans who present themselves as healers tend to charge outrageous fees and are hesitant to give credit.

Paradoxically, the fact that many healers who claim to possess great powers and boast of their achievements are not particularly wealthy also sheds doubt on their abilities and honesty. Nationally famous healers like Anthony Mwandulami and Shaibu Magungu are living proof that someone who has the ability to heal and help others and who wishes to use his or her powers and knowledge to become rich can indeed do so. During my latest field trip to Iringa in January

---

[3]   Most Pentecostals/Charismatics I have met had visited healers before they were 'saved' and joined a church or revival group, and can therefore speak from experience.

2012, I did a bit of hanging out with a couple of healers (two brothers) who have a stall on the central city market. They both claimed to be assisted by a considerable but varying amount of *majini* (at one point more than a hundred) that they bought during trips to the coastal cities of Dar es Salaam, Tanga, or the Island of Zanzibar, and sometimes sold on to others.[4] They were nevertheless always short of money and asked me for quite small amounts, for instance, for bus fare or lunch. When I recounted this paradox to other informants, they found it highly unlikely that someone with such powerful spiritual alliances and with an obvious interest in making money would not be wealthy.

It is common knowledge that politicians seek the assistance of healers during election campaigns and that soccer teams rely on healers to win matches. Most people, including a couple of former professional soccer players I interviewed, reckon that healers *can* make a difference in elections and soccer; for instance, by giving political candidates medicines that will enhance their charisma and persuasiveness; by controlling the wind during soccer matches; by making goal keepers see double so that they become unsure about which of the two balls they see they should try to save, or by making forwards see monsters every time they approach the goal of the opposite team. But my Tanzanian friends and acquaintances were unconvinced, though quite amused, when I told them I had interviewed three different healers, none of whom was wealthy, who all wished to take credit for the victory of the same local candidate in the last elections. When a local healer returned to Iringa after a couple of months of absence and claimed that he had been in Dar es Salaam helping the soccer team Yanga win the Tanzanian Premiere League, others found his story ridiculously improbable. First of all, he was not known to be a particular powerful healer, so it was unlikely that he could have landed such an important assignment. Secondly, helping Yanga, one of the biggest clubs in the country, would most certainly be a well-paid job, and he appeared to be no better off financially than before he left.

I was often told that healers try to gain reputation by lying about their origin. People in Iringa consider the coastal city of Tanga and the western city of Sumbawanga to be national witchcraft centres. Tanga, where the majority of the population is Muslim, is associated with Islamic or modern, *majini*-related witchcraft, whereas Sumbawanga is mostly associated with 'traditional' witches

---

[4]   *Majini* are invisible and immaterial, but they can be attached to objects which can be passed on from seller to buyer. Sometimes *majini* come in small bottles. They may also be attached to eggs, which must be kept carefully as it is believed that the *majini* will somehow be hatched from them. Finally, a *jini* may be passed on through a mere handshake, and the original host must then inform the *jini* that it is now attached to a new host.

who mainly rely on ancestral spirits.[5] Considering the popular and widespread belief that witches and traditional healers dig into the same funds of occult power and knowledge, it is hardly surprising that Sumbawanga and Tanga are also seen as national centres of traditional healing. In Iringa, there are many non-local healers who are travelling through and stay for a while before moving on. As they cannot rely on personal networks and contacts to the same extent as local healers, the visiting healers often advertise their services through the radio or by hanging posters in crowded places. With very few exceptions, all visiting healers I met or heard of claimed to be from either Sumbawanga or Tanga, and they never neglected to mention their origin on posters and sign boards, or on the radio. But many people I spoke to suspected that some of these healers came from other places and lied about it because they wished to be connected with the expertise and spiritual powers of Sumbawanga or Tanga.

People agree that many healers tell such white lies in order to convince others that they are more powerful and knowledgeable than they are in reality. A person who consults a dishonest healer in good faith risks losing a significant amount of money. Besides, the chance of getting the proper help or treatment for a condition is much smaller than it would be if a 'genuine healer' were consulted (though even in this case, there are no absolute guarantees). My informants also commented that many healers, and especially the dishonest and incompetent ones, sometimes cause unnecessary conflicts and hostilities between relatives or neighbours when they falsely identify particular individuals as witches and as the source of a patient's problem.

Probably the most overused words in the anthropological literature on traditional healers in Africa are 'ambivalence' or 'ambiguity'. I doubt if there is any society in the world in which the ability to cure people from illness is not a source of prestige. And in societies where most people share a strong conviction that this worldly success and prosperity are partly dependent upon successful management of spiritual forces, persons who claim access to such forces are likely to enjoy a certain amount of respect or awe. But as described, the ambiguous and unclear relationship between the powers of traditional healing and the powers of witchcraft fosters a widespread scepticism towards healers. In addition to being associated with witchcraft, healers can also be suspected of being common liars, cheaters and greedy charlatans who make false claims to power and knowledge in order to make money. These conflicting views on healers are held by the same people. It was quite common for informants to tell

---

[5]   Iringa is located in South-central Tanzania and was often described to me as a city of *mchanganyiko* (mixture).

me that all healers are liars who are unable to help others and then, in the very same breath, go on to warn me against getting too closely involved with healers I was studying as I might expose myself to some spiritual danger. Pentecostals/ Charismatics insist that healers are witches whose powers should be feared and actively combated through prayer. But Pentecostals/Charismatics also point out that healers are lying about their abilities to cure the sick and that only Jesus possesses true powers of healing. Testimonies of salvation typically include an account of illness that inspired a search for healing and spiritual protection. In most cases, the eventual convert first consulted one or several healers, but to no avail, and finally ended up in a Pentecostal/Charismatic ministry where healing and spiritual power were found. However, most Pentecostals/Charismatics do recognize the ability of healers to help people succeed in economic affairs, and they understand that advising people against using business medicines, or any medicine provided by healers, is most effective if an alternative is offered.

The Faith Gospel

The burgeoning market of traditional healing and not least of medicines used to acquire material wealth is paralleled by the increasing impact of the Faith Gospel, also known as the Gospel of Prosperity within Tanzania's ever-proliferating Pentecostal/Charismatic ministries and revival groups. Central to this gospel is an outspoken conviction that every saved Christian has the right to receive divine blessings of health and wealth, as well as the duty to pay tithes and make donations of money to God through a ministry. The Faith Gospel has North American origins (see Lindhardt 2009), but its spread in Tanzania and many other sub-Saharan African countries within recent decades has less to do with processes of Americanization and cultural imperialism than with its resonance with existing ontologies and with the creative processes of appropriation through which it is rendered meaningful and relevant to Africans.

Most prosperity ministries preserve a classical Pentecostal emphasis on personal salvation, a sanctified lifestyle, and the continuous manifestations of the Holy Spirit in ritual life. But in many ways, Faith Gospel preachers also present their 'product' as yet another market option for consumers shopping around for spiritual assistance in economic affairs. During open-air revival meetings where they address potential converts, preachers present the power (*nguvu*) of Jesus as an explicit alternative to medicines provided by healers, whether in terms of success in business or protection against witchcraft and other spiritual dangers. And the parallels do not stop there. Similar to ways in which business and anti-witchcraft medicines must be placed physically or poured out in a shop, stall and home, several Pentecostals/Charismatics explained to me how they walk around in those same places, 'placing prayers' or 'placing the blood of Jesus' (*kuweka maombi* or *kuweka damuya Yesu*) with the imposition of hands, in order to be protected against evil forces and make their businesses prosper. Pentecostals/Charismatics are amused when sharing stories about how they themselves are sometimes suspected by neighbours or business rivals as being particularly powerful witches, because the divine power of Jesus makes their businesses flourish and grants them immunity against attacks from minor witches.

However, more than just providing consumers with another magical or miraculous means for attaining material ends, prosperity ministries also offer ways of dealing with the perceived ambivalence of wealth. In fact, many Pentecostals/Charismatics, and especially those who have not become rich after years of faithful tithing, readily recognize that business medicines/witchcraft are far more efficient than divine power in terms of generating fast wealth. But they insist that money given by God is legitimate and free of the dangers and immoral aspects that haunt wealth generated through occult alliances.

As argued by Simon Coleman in his contribution to this volume (see Chapter 4), Charismatic Christians often conceive of their exchange relationship with God as a sacrificial economy (see also Lindhardt 2009, forthcoming). Pentecostals/Charismatics in Iringa have different cultural strategies, both for addressing sensitive issues concerning the moral legitimacy of wealth and for preventing their relationship with God from turning into an impersonal market exchange in which money, acquired by whatever means, could be used to buy blessings as if they were goods on a supermarket shelf. One strategy is praying intensely over coins and bills before donating them in church and explaining to God what kind of counter-gift one desires. Some informants described such praying as an act of placing (*kuweka*) their request in the money. Praying transforms coins and bills from impersonal mediums of exchange to inalienable gifts, invested with a part of the donor's spiritual essence (Mauss 1954: 12). If this essence is impure, born-again Christians insist that the gift will produce no counter-gift. Money acquired through some sinful activity (theft, corruption, prostitution, the use of witchcraft) may be donated to a church and cleansed through praying, but the donor will receive no divine blessings.

The concern with the legitimacy of wealth acquired through some alliance with spiritual powers is further addressed through practices that emphasize transparency. Public testimonies of Pentecostals/Charismatics who have become wealthy and ascribe their wealth to divine blessings stand in a clear and demonstrative opposition to the secrecy and opacity that surround the use of business medicines and the witchcraft of wealth. And the ritualized offerings during church meetings, where congregants openly pay their tithes (of which churches keep registers) and make donations that will supposedly result in divine blessings, provide a powerful contrast to the secret and immoral sacrifices, for instance, of a relative, that, according to popular belief, are required in order to prosper through the use of witchcraft.

Though Pentecostals/Charismatics take considerable pains to demonstrate the moral legitimacy of wealth and exchange, the fact that running a prosperity ministry can be a lucrative business for some individuals is not lost on people. There is a certain tension here. On the one hand, preachers who deliver the message of prosperity are more persuasive if their personal testimonies serve as examples that God blesses his children materially. An impoverished, humble prosperity preacher with worn-out clothing would be about as convincing as a badly overweight dietician or a toothless dentist. But, as noted by several scholars (Meyer 2007, Gifford 2011), finding ways of coping with the failure to fulfil the promise, made to lay Pentecostals/Charismatics, of prosperity in the here-and-now is probably the greatest challenge of current Pentecostalism in Africa. A preacher who becomes prosperous while many of his faithfully tithing congregants remain less fortunate is likely to inspire certain scepticism, moral condemnation, negative media coverage, and even suspicions that spiritual powers, other than those of God, may be involved in the running of a ministry (Meyer 2007, Smith 2001). A frequently voiced critique of the Faith Gospel, in Tanzania and elsewhere in the world, is that its preachers abuse the faith of their parishioners by enriching themselves through large donations. In Tanzania, such criticisms are articulated by Muslim and mainline-Christian observers, but they also come from within the Pentecostal/Charismatic spectrum as many adherents feel that their doctrines and teachings have become subject to vulgarization and decay. They relate this development to the increased competition in Tanzania's religious market.

Within recent years, a number of new Pentecostal/Charismatic churches and revival groups, most of which place a good deal of emphasis on prosperity, have popped up all over Iringa. Their proclaimed aim is to reach out for all those mainline Christians, Muslims and pagans who are not born-again. However, in reality, the number of Pentecostals/Charismatics does not grow fast enough to fill new churches with new converts, which means that many newer churches mainly manage to gain a foothold and establish themselves on the religious market through ruthless 'sheep-stealing' from older Pentecostal/Charismatic churches. Some of the new churches in Iringa have been founded after schisms within existing churches or groups. In such cases, the size of the original church or revival group can be reduced significantly, as members who decide to leave and found a new ministry usually make sure that a substantial part of their old congregation will follow them. Other new churches are founded as local branches of national or international denominations (for instance, the Vineyard Church). Some of these churches are strategically and visibly located in big buildings close to the city centre and make extensive use of the radio to assert their presence and advertise their services.

During my latest visit to Iringa in December 2011 and January 2012, I spoke to several members of older prosperity ministries whose membership was declining. Many of them lamented that nowadays initiating and running a prosperity ministry had become too much of a business venture. They placed a good deal of blame on the unscrupulous preachers who, being called by their stomach and not by God, make too hasty promises of material blessings in order to persuade people to come to church and make generous donations. But their criticism also centred on Christians who seek a Pentecostal/Charismatic ministry in order to become rich, but who show little interest in the message of salvation and who are therefore easily attracted to whatever ministry guarantees prosperity and has a convenient location. In the old days (10–15 years ago), I was told, Pentecostals/Charismatics were known as the serious Christians, unlike mainline Protestants and Catholics. But several informants felt that the picture was now a less pretty one, as too much laxity and materialism have entered many, especially newer, Pentecostal/Charismatic denominations.

The perception of a partially corrupted Faith Gospel was clearly articulated in rumours, told to me by both Pentecostals/Charismatics from prosperity ministries and others, that some preachers now use witchcraft to enhance their charisma and persuasiveness. Though processes of routinization and institutionalization are an important part of the history of African Pentecostal/ Charismatic Christianity, many churches and movements are charismatic in the (Weberian) sense that they are centred around particular leaders who (supposedly) function as channels of extraordinary divine powers. Many people in Iringa – Pentecostals/Charismatics and others – have a strong admiration for nationally famous prosperity preachers such as Christopher Mwakasege, who operates within established denominations (see Hasu 2006, Lindhardt forthcoming) and international Pentecostal superstars such as the German Reinhard Bonnke. The visit of Mwakasege to Iringa every two or three years is an event that people look forward to and his rallies attract large crowds of people, many of whom show up hoping that his presence will result in some extraordinary blessing. I have heard no rumours linking Mwakasege to witchcraft, but people commented that other well-known Pentecostal/Charismatic preachers, such as Zakaria Kakobe,

Archbishop of the Full Gospel Bible Fellowship in Dar es Salaam, and several not-so-well-known ones who aspire for greatness and wealth, use witchcraft to produce charismatic effects that people falsely interpret as manifestations of the Holy Spirit. As transmitters of extraordinary divine powers, some preachers can make others fall to the ground (which usually indicates that a person is slain in the Holy Spirit), simply by touching them or breathing on them. But, so many people told me, what sometimes makes a person fall to the ground is in fact some medicine or witchcraft substance that the preacher has placed in his own mouth or on his hands. The witchcraft that is used to imitate the manifestations of the Holy Spirit must be exceptionally powerful and cannot be provided by ordinary local healers and/or witches. As mentioned, Tanga and Sumbawanga are seen as national witchcraft centres, but within a wider African context, Tanzanians consider their own country to be a spiritual province. Someone in search of extraordinary occult powers should go to Nigeria, and this is the place that some Pentecostal/Charismatic preachers are rumoured to visit from time to time.[6]

Conclusion

In contemporary Tanzania, different factors such as the liberalization of the mass media, a widespread assumption that this worldly prosperity is, in part, dependent upon successful management of spiritual forces, and a widely shared experience that the ingredients in a conventional recipe for prosperity – hard work, skills, self-confidence and entrepreneurial initiative – are indeed insufficient to

---

[6]   Why Nigeria of all places? I suspect there are different reasons for this. The country has an international reputation, justified or not, of being a haven of corruption, fraud and tricksters. Besides, many Tanzanians see Nigeria as something of an African superpower, due to the size of the country and its population and to its natural resources that generate excessive wealth for a lucky few. Perceptions of the country as a continental centre of political and economic powers and of fraud are easily projected into the spiritual sphere. But more importantly, due to the influence of the mass media, people in Tanzania are more informed about spiritual powers in Nigeria than in, say, Cameroon, Angola, or even in neighbouring countries such as Mozambique or Uganda. Within recent years, a growing number of Nigerian video movies have become available in Tanzania. Many of these movies explore occult themes such as witchcraft, curses and spiritual warfare. Though such movies are fictional, people consider them to be highly realistic representations of the kinds of spiritual powers that can be found in Nigeria. In addition, people who have access to a television and a sufficiently powerful antenna can watch foreign Evangelical television channels that often show Nigerian revival meetings where intense spiritual battles are fought and testimonies about witchcraft-related problems are told.

produce the desired results, all combine to provide new spaces for spiritual/ medical entrepreneurship. As described, the burgeoning post-liberalization market of occult, spiritual services and products provides consumers with a range of options. But it also inspires an increased scepticism and an awareness of the necessity of distinguishing between genuine healers or prosperity preachers and frauds.

The distrust many people feel towards healers and to some extent towards prosperity preachers is not new and is in part generated by the difficulty of gaining certain knowledge about their powers. There is always a certain measure of uncertainty involved in dealing with an invisible world, whose workings and forces cannot be adequately grasped by the senses or understood through ordinary research and inquiries (see Lindhardt 2012). As explained, healers are ambiguous figures whose opaque relationship with the world of witchcraft is a source of awe and anxiety. Being well aware that the generation of wealth through alliances with the spiritual world can be morally suspicious, Pentecostals/Charismatics have several ritual strategies for emphasizing the transparency and legitimacy of their exchange relationship with invisible forces (God). It nevertheless remains difficult to convincingly authorize wealth as derived from God (see also Meyer 2007: 18), and both wealthy lay members of Pentecostal/Charismatic ministries who ascribe their own prosperity to divine blessings, and pastors whose charisma and persuasiveness enable them to collect large donations, are sometimes accused of witchcraft.[7]

In other words, the seeking of spiritual assistance in material affairs always implies a certain calculated risk of being deceived, as it is difficult to know exactly which kind of invisible power a given spiritual entrepreneur uses to produce material effects. But the widespread suspicion that fraud is rampant in both Pentecostal ministries and among traditional healers has been intensified by the increased marketing of spiritual services and products. In the scholarly literature, one often encounters the argument that both Pentecostal/Charismatic Christianity and up-to-date traditional healing are responding to the needs of Africans in a neoliberal era where individual entrepreneurship is valued and where a privatized rather than a communal sense of prosperity tends to prevail (Hasu 2006, Comaroff and Comaroff 1999, Lindhardt 2009). But when the provision of spiritual services itself becomes too enmeshed in the neoliberal logics of the market, the moral reputation of providers can easily begin to suffer.

---

[7]   See Lindhardt (forthcoming) for an elaborate description of an incident in which a wealthy businesswoman, who was also a prominent lay preacher of a charismatic ministry in Iringa, was accused of witchcraft.

Whether religious pluralism and competition, the commercialization of religious and medical services, and a growing understanding of spiritual entrepreneurship as a potentially profitable career option inevitably foster suspicions of fraud and dishonesty is a question that I shall refrain from attempting to answer in a chapter that is based on a single case study. But in the case of Tanzania, or at least of Iringa, where new ministries constantly pop up, where visiting healers from other parts of the country regularly arrive to advertise their services, where claims to spiritual power are always likely to evoke a certain awe, and where promises of prosperity, made by healers and preachers, often fail to materialize, it seems relatively safe to assert that things are moving in that direction.

Field trips for this article were funded by the Nordic Africa Institute in Upsala, Sweden and the Danish Research Council for Culture and Communication.

Bibliography

Comaroff, J. and J. Comaroff (1999). 'Occult Economies and the Violence of Abstraction: Notes from the South African Postcolony', *American Ethnologist*, 26(2): 279–303.

Finke, R. and R. Stark (1988). 'Religious Economies and Sacred Canopies: Religious Mobilization in American Cities, 1906', *American Sociological Review*, 53(1): 41–9.

Geschiere, P. (1997). *The Modernity of Witchcraft: Politics and the Occult in Postcolonial Africa*. Charlottesville: University Press of Virginia.

Gifford, P. (2011). 'The Ritual Uses of the Bible in African Pentecostalism', in *Practicing the Faith. The Ritual Life of Pentecostal-Charismatic Christians*, ed. Martin Lindhardt. New York: Berghahn Books.

Green, M. and Simeon M. (2005). 'The Birth of the "Salon": Poverty, "Modernization" and Dealing with Witchcraft in Southern Tanzania', *American Ethnologist*, 32(3): 371–88.

Hasu, P. (2006). 'World Bank and Heavenly Bank in Poverty and Prosperity. The Case of the Tanzanian Faith Gospel', *Review of African Political Economy*, 110: 679–92.

Iannaccone, L.R. (1992). 'Religious Markets and the Economics of Religion', *Social Compass*, 39: 123.

Lindhardt, M. (2009). 'More Than Just Money. The Faith Gospel and Occult Economies in Contemporary Tanzania', *Nova Religio. The Journal of Alternative and Emergent Religions*, 13(1): 41–67.

— (2012). 'Who Bewitched the Pastor and Why Did He Survive the Witchcraft Attack? Micropolitics and the Creativity of Indeterminacy in Tanzanian Discourses on Witchcraft', *Canadian Journal for African Studies*, 46(2): 215–32.

— (forthcoming). 'What is the Matter with that Money? Materiality, Mediation and Spiritual Warfare in Tanzanian Charismatic Christianity'. in *The Anthropology of Global Pentecostalism and Evangelism*, eds S. Coleman and R.I.J. Hackett. New York: New York University Press.

Mauss, M. (1954 [first English-language edn]). *The Gift: Forms and Functions of Exchange in Archaic Societies*. London: Routledge.

Meyer, B. (2007). 'Pentecostalism and Neo-Liberal Capitalism: Faith, Prosperity and Vision in African Pentecostal-Charismatic Churches', *Journal for the Study of Religion*, 20(2): 5–28.

Sanders, T. (1999). 'Modernity, Wealth and Witchcraft in Tanzania', *Research in Economic Anthropology*, 20: 117–31.

Smith, D.J. (2001). '"The Arrow of God": Pentecostalism, Inequality and the Supernatural in South-Eastern Nigeria', *Africa*, 71(4): 587–613.

Tripp, A.-M. (1997). *Changing the Rules. The Politics of Liberalization and the Urban Informal Economy in Tanzania*. Berkeley: University of California Press.

West, H.G. and T.J. Luedke (2006). 'Introduction. Healing Divides: Therapeutic Border Work in Southeast Africa, in *Borders and Healers. Brokering Therapeutic Resources in Southeast Africa*, eds T.J. Luedke and H.G. West. Bloomington and Indianapolis: Indiana University Press.

Chapter 9

When Fraud is Part of a Spiritual Path: A Tibetan Lama's Plays on Reality and Illusion

Marion Dapsance

There have been many complaints recently about the Tibetan lama Sogyal Rinpoche, both in the UK and in France. After a first charge brought against him in 1994 in California for 'physical, psychological and sexual abuse' by a female disciple known as 'Janice Doe' – a case which was settled out of court and covered by the media in various Western countries, a second sex scandal broke out in the French press in late 2011. In a left-wing weekly magazine, a young attractive French woman explained how she spent several years at Sogyal Rinpoche's 'service', in every sense of the term. The words used are crude and express a painful personal experience. This article was followed by many commentaries on several blogs and discussed a few days later on a national radio programme. A Canadian television documentary, in a series about scandals in religions, also made allegations about Sogyal Rinpoche having a pattern of bullying and sexually using female disciples.[1] The Wikipedia page dedicated to Sogyal Rinpoche now includes (as of 17 March 2014) a 'Controversy' section, briefly relating both cases. This section appeared around 2008, when the French woman mentioned above started making herself known to journalists and ex-disciples. It mentions the 1994 $10 million civil lawsuit filed against Sogyal Rinpoche and states that:

> ... it was alleged that he used his position as a spiritual leader to induce one of his female students to have sexual relations with him. The complaint included accusations of infliction of emotional distress, breach of fiduciary duty, as well as assault and battery. The lawsuit was settled out of court.

---

[1] I have listed relevant articles, blogs and other media at the end of this chapter.

The section also mentions the 2011 Canadian documentary. Links to the online articles are also provided. French and English new religious movements and 'cults' information centres (Miviludes and ADFI in Paris, Inform in London) have been asked by concerned families to clarify the issue. The main allegations have long been in the public domain; they had already been discussed in western Buddhist circles for more than twenty years. When analysing the narratives of ex-members of Rigpa, and the media discussing these cases, it becomes clear that 'fraud' is considered to be a selfish abuse of authority, the distorted use of a venerable Buddhist tradition in order for the teacher to indulge in his own materialistic and sensual pleasures, at the expense of naïve and trusting disciples.

However, all attempts to discredit the lama failed, and his organization is more influential than ever. This can be explained by sociological, legal and cultural reasons. First, it is certainly the case that Sogyal Rinpoche's supporters have significantly more material and symbolic resources than their opponents, in terms of public relations, advocates, finances and prestige. Secondly, legally, it is very difficult for these young women to prove that abuse was committed by Sogyal Rinpoche. They often realize months or years later that they had been 'abused'; it is materially nearly impossible to establish that a physical or moral violence was actually inflicted on them and that they were thrown into a relationship based on unequal and unclear premises. Thus the defendant can – and does – argue that their relationship was, at the time, based on consent. When asked to testify, Rigpa members suggest that these women were in fact actively seeking to get closer to their teacher and took great pride in being selected by him. In the end, it is their word against his, and, because of unequal resources, these women usually give up their claims to damages. Whatever the nature of their intimate relationship with Sogyal Rinpoche, they generally choose to forget. Thus, apart from the 1994 American lawsuit, there was no official recognition of any kind of abuse or fraud on the part of Sogyal Rinpoche. Third, as several authors have shown (Bishop 1993, Lopez 1999, Dodin and Rather 2001), Tibetan lamas are surrounded by an aura of moral perfection, making the case of an abusive lama almost inconceivable and rarely taken seriously.

Another kind of explanation may be given to the apparent difficulties in de-legitimizing Sogyal Rinpoche's reputation. It has to do with the teaching methods used in his dharma centres, which aim at leading the students to the contemplation of 'reality' beyond 'illusion' – said to bring about enlightenment – and induce the students to view everything their teacher does or says as 'enlightened and compassionate activity'. After a brief presentation of Sogyal Rinpoche's organization, Rigpa, I will describe the teachings he gives on stage, once or twice a year in his Parisian centre. These teachings are representative of Sogyal Rinpoche's own pedagogical style, as they are given along the same lines throughout his whole organization. This study is based on extensive participation in the activities offered by the Paris Rigpa centre (2009–11), and on formal and informal interviews with current and former members, which I have conducted for my PhD thesis in Anthropology.[2]

A New Tibetan Buddhist Organization Created for Westerners: Rigpa

Rigpa is an international Buddhist organization which was founded by Sogyal Rinpoche in 1978.[3] Sogyal Rinpoche belongs to the second generation of lamas who came to teach in Europe and the United States in the late 1970s and early 1980s, after a first generation of pioneers came in the 1960s. Born in Kham (Eastern Tibet) in 1947, he was recognized as a *tulku* (heir of a lineage of reincarnated lamas) by his uncle and spiritual master Jamyang Khyentse Chokyi Lodro, who oversaw the beginning of his religious training. This training was interrupted by the arrival of the Chinese in Kham in the early 1950s. Sogyal Rinpoche, still a child, followed his master into exile in India. There, he received a western education, attending a Catholic high school and a Catholic college in Kalimpong. A few years later, he was granted a scholarship by Trinity College, Cambridge, where he came to study comparative religions in 1971. Along with this western education, Sogyal Rinpoche continued to train in the Tibetan Buddhist traditions with the great masters of the previous generation of exiled lamas, notably Dilgo Khyentse Rinpoche and Dudjom Rinpoche. He served as an interpreter and assistant to Dudjom Rinpoche and helped him organize the Dalai Lama's first visits to the West. Dudjom Rinpoche distanced himself from Sogyal Rinpoche in the late 1970s, for reasons his then students attribute to his promiscuity with female disciples, of which Dudjom Rinpoche didn't approve.[4] In 1978, Sogyal Rinpoche created his own 'Dharma Centre' in Paris and called it 'Rigpa'. A year later, he established another Rigpa centre in London. The Tibetan word *rigpa* comes from the Dzogchen tradition, meaning 'the innermost nature of the mind'. Because of his knowledge of both Tibetan and western cultures, Sogyal Rinpoche is often presented as a mediator, creating a special connection between Tibet and the West. As such, he distinguishes himself from the first

---

[2] My thesis, '"Ceci n'est pas une religion". L'apprentissage du *dharma* selon Rigpa' ('"This is not a religion". Learning *dharma* within Rigpa'), was defended in December 2013; to be published.

[3] See www.rigpa.org.

[4] Interviews with ex-disciples, including the English journalist Mary Finnigan.

generation of lamas who came to the West in the 1960s and 1970s. Except for a few exceptions, these only spoke Tibetan and knew almost nothing about western culture. Sogyal Rinpoche is also the author of *The Tibetan Book of Living and Dying* (1992), a bestseller that brought him international fame. The success of this work gave considerable impetus to Rigpa in the 1990s.

The organization consists of numerous urban 'study and practice centres' and a few rural 'retreat centres'. It is present in 41 countries worldwide, mainly in western Europe, the United States, Canada and Australia. Its mission is to make 'the Buddha's teachings' available to the largest number of people. Its training is thus presented as a 'Tibetan Buddhism adapted to the modern world', a tradition that is both 'authentic and modern'. Buddhism is described as a 'spirituality', a 'wisdom', or a 'science of the mind', whereas the term 'religion' is briskly rejected. In fact, within Rigpa, Buddhism is mostly defined by what it supposedly is not: 'This is not a religion.' To discover what it is, one must 'experience it'. This view is based on a western construction of the diverse traditions inspired by the Buddha, which sees them as a unique, transnational, intellectual and individualistic 'Buddhism' that transcends cultural boundaries and doctrinal variety. Western construction of Buddhism emerged in the 1870s–90s, as a result of cooperation between the native religious and political elite of Ceylon and the Theosophical Society (Masuzawa 2005, Lopez 2002, Sharf 1995), more specifically through the work of Henry Steel Olcott (Prothero 1996). According to this representation, meditation is described as a non-conceptual practice, aiming at rediscovering the Buddha's primary experience of enlightenment. Thus understood, meditation has nothing to do with rituals – despite them being essential in most Asian Buddhist traditions. Parted from its ritual context, meditation is then also disconnected from its cultural and doctrinal basis: reduced to an individual, universal and transformative spiritual experience, whether psychotherapeutic, cognitive, or mystical, it can be practised anywhere, by anyone. Sogyal Rinpoche and all Rigpa members generally speak about Buddhism and meditation in the same way.

To mass audiences, Rigpa offers services that their brochures and websites describe as 'meditation'; to a minority of members, the organization also includes the equivalent of a monastic university, called *shedra*. Sogyal Rinpoche reportedly also offers a modernized version of *dzogchen* to the most advanced of his students. *Dzogchen* is a Tibetan mystical tradition traditionally directed to an elite group of ascetics, specialists in tantric rituals. Their practices are still not well known, but Tibetologists indicate that they involve physical exercises (such as breathing or pressing the eyes), which have physiological effects (notably apparition of lights). *Dzogchen* is based on the Indian philosophical doctrine

Cittamatra ('mind only'), according to which all phenomena, including the self, are projections of the mind. Similar to dreams, these illusions should be identified as such, allowing the practitioner to 'wake'. As Cittamatra-based Tibetan texts describe, this awakening from the apparent solidity of all phenomena leads to the sudden recognition of the eternal basis of the mind, called *rigpa*. This 'innermost nature of the mind' is described as pure and always accessible to any living being, though it is generally concealed by the innumerable projections the mind produces because it fails to recognize its 'true nature'. The goal of *dzogchen* practice is thus to 'recognize' it. In Tibetan *dzogchen* communities, this 'recognition' actually designates the moment, in the ritual, when the master grants to his students a formal authorization to practise rituals, thus acknowledging their new status as 'master' themselves. An important part of the teachings delivered by Sogyal Rinpoche relates to this objective, although the methods used are radically different: they do not involve canonical rituals nor physiological practices. Sogyal Rinpoche claims that the *dzogchen* tradition he transmits is 'authentic', while at the same time 'universal and modern'.

All visitors who wish to become Rigpa members must register as 'students' and follow weekly sessions called 'What meditation really is'. This course is a prerequisite for the participation in Sogyal Rinpoche's retreats and so needs to be described here.

Introductory Sessions: Learning to 'Sit with Rinpoche'

The weekly course entitled 'What meditation really is' is aimed at people who want to learn meditation in the Tibetan tradition. The sessions take place in the main hall of the Rigpa centres. This room is called 'the shrine-room' and looks like a chapel. The walls are covered with silk paintings depicting Tibetan deities (*thangka*), photographs of Tibetan lamas are suspended from the roof and, at the end of the room stands a Tibetan altar with its usual components (one cup of drinking water, one cup of lustral water, flowers, incense, butter lamps, scented water, food, conch shell). Behind the altar is a throne, on which rests a picture of Sogyal Rinpoche, whom the newcomer has often already learned to recognize – either by visiting Rigpa websites or by reading *The Tibetan Book of Living and Dying*. Above this portrait hangs a photograph of a statue of Padmasambhava, the Indian who introduced Buddhism to Tibet, and, at his side, pictures of Dudjom Rinpoche and Dilgo Khyentse, Sogyal Rinpoche's two main teachers. Behind the altar, in front of a dark blue panel, stands a large statue of a sitting Buddha, covered with gold leaves. This is a reproduction of a statue located in Bodhgaya, the Indian village where Siddhartha Gautama attained enlightenment. This original disposition of pictures constitutes a simplified equivalent of Tibetan 'refuge trees', representing the lineages to which disciples belong. Students are thus implicitly told that their own lineage is composed of the Buddha, Padmasambhava, two deceased Tibetan lamas and Sogyal Rinpoche.

This composite altar also includes different technological objects: projectors, sound amplifiers, and a large television screen. At first glance, the situation the newcomer enters is part of a rational, western-style learning programme. Indeed, the individual is registered with the association as a 'student', pays for its annual curriculum (classes are held once a week throughout the year except during school holidays) and receives a course manual, which summarizes the topics addressed throughout the year. Courses are taught by former students of Rigpa called 'instructors'; in front of them sit between four and fifteen people. The course begins with an introduction of all participants, including the instructors. The latter highlight the relationship which unites them to Sogyal Rinpoche, a relationship which the newcomers do not yet know. The relationship to the master is described as both desirable and painful. The explanations given by the instructors on the lama and his teaching is formulated in a specific language, close to a sacred or secret language (Van Gennep 1914). This language, which replaces liturgical Tibetan, is characterized by a dichotomy between 'us', the students, and 'they', 'the masters', the most important of them being Sogyal Rinpoche. The former are characterized by 'illusions', 'obstacles', 'blockages' and 'ego', the latter by an 'incredible love', 'omniscience', 'spontaneity', 'wisdom', 'fullness', 'peace', 'harmony' and 'perfection'. This worldview opposes the vast majority of beings, whose life is led by illusion, to a tiny minority of enlightened masters, no longer prisoners of the dreamlike quality of all phenomena because of their recognition of *rigpa*. Here, an implicit behavioural norm is suggested: devotion. The student learns that, in order to attract blessings and reach enlightenment, they must connect with the master through devotional feelings and behaviours. To justify the need for devotion, which was not supposed to be, at the beginning of the course, part of the 'rational spirituality' Buddhism supposedly is, the instructors translate these devotional standards of conduct into the language of science. Indeed, they use neuroscientific theories related to 'mirror neurons' and apply them to the spiritual encounter between master and disciples: when two people physically meet, their respective neurons adjust to one other, so when they are confronted with Sogyal Rinpoche's presence, students' neurons 'resonate' with his, allowing them to 'absorb' his 'atmosphere', to merge his mind with his. Here appears a new form of *guru yoga*, a tantric ritual that includes prayers invoking the master's powers and visualizations of the student becoming one with him.

The television screen thus leaves its usual speech-transmitting function to become a liturgical instrument, aimed at establishing a devotional relationship with the master. The device becomes a *mediator* between the students who watch and pray with the lama – considered as a supernatural being (all-knowing, pure love, able to manifest in various forms) – and the latter, who sends his 'blessings' through modern technologies. Used in this way, the television screen can be seen as a modernized form of the ancient Asian tantric icon, through which deities are first contemplated as a two-dimensional image, before being 'animated' in various rituals and liturgies, that include codified formulas, visualizations and gestures (Strickmann 1996). In Rigpa, as we shall see, the same evolution happens to the master's image throughout the student's path: introduced to the students as the centre of their practices – and so assimilated to a deity – Sogyal Rinpoche's televised image is the object of contemplation and prayers before being replaced by the physical manifestation of the lama on stage. Because of this continuity with the tantric model, I will call Sogyal Rinpoche's image on the screen an 'icon' and will describe the ways in which the progressive animation of this icon gives rise to various interpretations of the master's deeds, including the accusation of 'fraud'.

During the first lessons, the instructors give some brief information about Buddhism and meditation, preferably called 'sitting'. The term 'to sit' acquires a technical sense, referring to codified attitudes. Three types of injunctions frame the practice of 'sitting'. It is a physical posture (spine straight, legs crossed, hands lying on the knees, shoulders clear, head and chin slightly bent forward, the tip of the tongue touching the palate), a state of mind (watching thoughts and emotions without seizing them), both produced by a prescribed gaze (looking on the tip of one's nose or in the space in front of oneself). The instructors give specific instructions in this regard, the transgression of which is systematically pointed out. After having given these instructions and practiced 'sitting meditation' in silence during a few minutes with the students, the instructors announce that they will watch videos of Sogyal Rinpoche. They instruct students not only to listen to his words and try to understand their meaning, but, more importantly, to try and 'receive' the master 'as fully as possible', through hearing, sight, physical and emotional sensations the master generates by his 'atmosphere'. The particularity of Sogyal Rinpoche, the instructors explain, is that he teaches through his 'being' more than with his words. Sitting in front of him while focusing on his eyes is presented as an 'extraordinary' practice which accelerates the awakening process, because it puts the student's deluded mind in contact with the master's *rigpa*. It is always possible to 'sit' in front of a wall or an 'inspiring picture', but 'sitting with Rinpoche' is a more effective practice. That is why the largest part of the session involves watching the audiovisual image of the master. Introductory courses are thus built around this central moment of visualizing the master, materialized as an animated icon. Unlike other western places of acculturation to Buddhism, which offer teachings based on tantric rituals, on the study of texts, the recitation of mantras, a focus on the breath, visualization exercises, or pilgrimages to Asian sacred places, Rigpa proposes a special focus on Sogyal Rinpoche – a master whose most common mode of presence is the animated picture.

The 'Crazy Wisdom' Theatre

We have just seen that what was advertised by the organization as 'meditation' was in fact a contemplation of the master's animated icon – a practice called 'sitting with Rinpoche'. This practice takes other forms, especially when the master comes and gives teaching retreats in the flesh, in his various centres. What differentiates 'sitting with Rinpoche' within the introductory sessions and 'sitting with Rinpoche' at events where he is physically present on stage? How does the initial materialization as an animated picture give way to another, more physical presence? What devices are used to make the master appear, and what is at stake in this new apparition?

Teachings by Sogyal Rinpoche during weekends at Rigpa urban centres are called 'retreats', although the participants are not residents but simply attend the event during daytime. The retreats take place in the same shrine-room, refitted for the occasion. Huge bunches of flowers are placed on and around the altar, incense smoke saturates the atmosphere, the television screen displays a picture of a Padmasambhava statue and Sogyal Rinpoche's photograph is removed from the throne. There is a festive atmosphere, made of excitement and nervousness. All participants, especially the organizers, await the master's arrival with visible impatience. Some are dressed in party clothes, many women wear silver jewellery and heavy make-up. The organizers (the centre's managers) make an inspiring speech about Sogyal Rinpoche, emphasizing his greatness, but also stressing the confusing nature of his personality. At the beginning of each retreat, they say: 'You mustn't be surprised and draw the wrong conclusions about the way Rinpoche manifests, but rather remain open and always accept what comes with an open mind.' The way the master behaves on stage, they explain, must be 'viewed as a mere appearance', that is to say as an illusion created by the audience's mind.[5] Everything Sogyal Rinpoche says or does, the organizers announce, is charged with meaning that lies *beyond* his physical manifestation. This hidden meaning must be associated with Sogyal Rinpoche's awakened nature: what he does on stage must be 'seen' as an 'expression of his compassion', an example of his 'unconventional way' to teach. The shrine-room, previously used as a classroom, thus becomes a place invested with a ritual dimension, to which instructors immediately attract the audience's attention (Smith 1982, Bell 1992): what appears therein is not reality but a mere projection of the mind. The viewer's duty is then to realize that what they see and hear is but an illusion, the yoke of which they must free themselves from, by seeing beyond the limitations of their own vision.

In the heat of the final preparations, the organizers announce several times the master's arrival, before he finally comes, at a point where he is no longer expected. The room, until then happily buzzing, is now suddenly silent. Sogyal Rinpoche's entrance is thus dramatized in the same way as for celebrities: the instructors are no longer teachers, but presenters, who repeatedly announce the master's imminent arrival, highlight the extraordinary nature of the event, indefinitely repeating and commenting on his greatness and originality.

Once Sogyal Rinpoche is finally on stage (after long minutes or hours of waiting), the organizers stop talking and return to their seats at the forefront of the assembly. The lama is then at the centre of the audience's attention. The teachings will begin. Their theme has already been advertised weeks before: they usually focus on a topic linking Buddhism to daily life, such as 'how to find peace in a hectic world', or 'harmonizing relationships'. While the audience expects him to get into the heart of the subject, as they have seen him do on the videos they watched during the introductory sessions, Sogyal Rinpoche begins to have personal conversations with the people sitting in the first row. These conversations, where he talks more than they reply to him, last for at least 15 minutes. He asks them a number of questions regarding the course of the retreat, the lessons he must deliver today, about a tiny detail of the organization of a past event, or any other matter related to the functioning of Rigpa, matters that totally elude the audience. The latter often feel that they are facing an entrepreneur briefing his employees. People sitting at the forefront receive instructions to perform material tasks (typing teachings, calling someone, cleaning or reorganizing the shrine-room, and so on). They are very strongly criticized, even ridiculed in public. Verbal abuse is not uncommon. Now, the audience may well wonder

---

5   The instructors' quotations here come from the notes I took during several retreats.

whether this so-called 'authentic and modern master' is not, in fact, a 'cult guru'.[6] After this intriguing introduction, the lama finally begins his teachings on the announced topic. His English is fluent, but rambling. He often interrupts his speech to make further personal remarks to one of his close disciples, speaking to them like a father, sometimes tenderly, but mostly in an authoritarian manner. Aware that this behaviour may disconcert the audience, Sogyal Rinpoche sometimes stops to give explanations to the entire assembly. He then tries to clarify his behaviour toward his close disciples. He says that he is giving them 'instructions', the *apparent* nature of which is practical, the *reality* of which is 'spiritual'. As such, these remarks, orders and scolding also concern the general audience, if they know how to look beyond appearances. When criticizing people sitting at the forefront, Sogyal Rinpoche is staging himself as the master in a close relationship with his disciples, to the attention of the novices, whose duty is to discover the 'reality' of this relationship. To do this, they should not approach this relationship ordinarily, by exercising common sense, but should rather consider it as an illusion created by their own mind: what seems to be a guru's behaviour is actually no such thing; what looks like the relationship of a business leader with his employees has nothing to do with reality. This show resembles a ritual theatre but, unlike ancient theatrical performances, it does not confront gods and demons, but instead, as always in Rigpa, the person of the master, in his multiple forms. The mental plays put on stage are thus the new meaning given to the expression 'sitting with Rinpoche'. However, the key to these plays, previously given by the organizers ('seeing everything the lama does as an illusion'), has generally been forgotten by the audience, carried away by Sogyal Rinpoche's entertaining show. In this original form of theatre, the anthropologist might recognize a ritual innovation, based on the personal staging, by Sogyal Rinpoche, of the Cittamatra doctrine – in other words, a new *dzogchen* practice related to the vision of reality. The organizers do not reiterate this interpretation and, therefore, doubts often arise in the mind of the participants: who exactly *is* that famous 'authentic' master who acts so strangely?

Securing the legitimate meaning of this paradoxical, ambiguous and polysemic representation of the master-disciple relationship is the object of 'beginners' sessions', organized by the instructors. Tea breaks are organized when Sogyal Rinpoche unexpectedly leaves the stage and, during this free time, the instructors take the novices apart to a room upstairs and expose them again to the representation's exegesis: what the audience has just witnessed on stage is nothing

---

6   Quotations based on the notes taken during my participation at several retreats, and on personal conversations with students.

else than a 'crazy wisdom master', that is to say, a teacher who uses unconventional and shocking pedagogical methods. 'Crazy wisdom' is a term coined by Sogyal Rinpoche's main inspiration model, Chögyam Trungpa, an iconoclast Tibetan lama who came to teach Buddhism to young Americans in the 1970s (Trungpa 1991). These explanations are supported by new videos of Sogyal Rinpoche, which the instructors analyse. The master thus reappears in his usual form: the televised icon. But, unlike what they do during the introductory classes, the instructors are now focusing their comments exclusively on 'Rinpoche's unconventional behaviour'. Indeed, the video clips are specifically selected to allow such an exegetical development: they show a severe and humiliating Sogyal Rinpoche, whose words and actions are identified by the instructors as 'crazy wisdom' or 'spontaneity'. 'Crazy wisdom' is described as a 'skilful means' intended to awaken the students. A 'skilful means' (*upaya* in Sanskrit) is a term referring to any Mahayana method a master might use as an aid to communicate the dharma to individuals. 'Crazy wisdom' and 'spontaneity' displayed on stage by Sogyal Rinpoche are depicted, not as his *real* petulance or aggressiveness, but as an *artificial trick*, a gimmick he is wisely using to awaken his audience. At all times during the show, wisdom and compassion must be assumed and, as often as possible, publicly asserted. After commenting repetitively on the video clips, the instructors initiate group discussions with a question they ask to everyone (all participants first introduce themselves and then answer the question): 'and you, what did you feel while seeing Rinpoche?' The answers are formulated in the language used within Rigpa, elaborating on the binary worldview students received during the introductory sessions ('us the unenlightened/they the great compassionate masters'). One is expected to speak of the necessity to 'let go of the conceptual mind', to leave the thoughts or emotions provoked by Sogyal Rinpoche's manifestation 'untouched' and 'unelaborated' (as one does with thoughts and emotions emerging in the initial practice of 'sitting meditation'), recognize and regret one's 'resistances' to the master's paradoxical behaviour. One should also conclude on a positive note, such as 'Rinpoche is so impressive', 'I felt so much peace inside when I saw him', 'he's so free', 'Rinpoche has an incredible love for us ... '. In case of a failure or refusal to adopt these linguistic patterns, the participant is stigmatized by the group: the other participants demonstrate animosity against them, the instructors put an end to emerging arguments with a decree of 'no karmic connection with Rinpoche'. If they think the teachings are not 'authentic', such participants silently leave the group. Rarely do they publicly denounce them as a 'fraud': they might have wasted a few hundred euros for the retreat, but they generally do not feel they have been personally deceived; they do not portray themselves as 'victims' and so have no interest in launching a public crusade against Sogyal Rinpoche. Anyway, most participants accept the 'crazy wisdom' theatrical plays as pedagogical devices.[7]

These 'beginners' sessions' are thus intended for the transmission of codified ways of saying – rather than ways of doing. What counts in the master-disciples' relationship, the instructors teach to the novices, is not an actual behaviour – for the lama, most of the time, is physically absent – but a compulsory expression of feelings (Mauss 1921). Rigpa members must acquire these linguistic patterns to be able to recognize a master through the paradoxical experience of a comedy which says: 'This is not an authentic and modern master, you must look beyond these surprising appearances; it is precisely because he *deceives* you that he is *in fact undeceiving* you.' At this stage, there is only one way to relate to the master and this is a linguistic one. There is no other, direct interaction between master and disciples. The closest relationship most Rigpa members can have with their lama is constructed through Sogyal Rinpoche's staging of 'crazy wisdom' and, most importantly, through the inculcation, by elder students, of a special language and of a compulsory way to express devotion.

Interpreting the Lama's Deeds Outside the Ritual Place: Women and the 'Secret Mandala'

The closer, intimate relationships that reportedly happened behind the stage between Sogyal Rinpoche and some of his female disciples are surrounded with secrecy and have given rise to numerous interpretations and rumours. Although he openly claims, in an attempt to defend himself against accusations of promiscuity, to be a non-monastic lama, Sogyal Rinpoche is not clear about his actual personal situation. He does not have a wife or official concubine, but rather seems to enjoy the company of several young women who constitute a group called 'the secret mandala' and are known only by a tiny minority. I discovered the existence of the 'secret mandala' when I talked to Rigpa members who either have (or had) high responsibilities within the group or who were part, as women, of the 'secret mandala' itself.[8] These women are often identified as '*dakinis*', 'sky travellers', a Tibetan term describing female deities or actual practitioners'

---

[7]   This estimation comes from my participation in Rigpa's events for more than two years and from my talking to many members and ex-members over the course of six years.

[8]   Personal interviews with French Rigpa officials (Olivier Raurich, Philippe Cornu), ex-members with high responsibilities (G. Durand, M. Lecomte, P. Delanoë, F. Calmès, S. Boucher), former disciples (Mary Finnigan, Dominique Cowell, Jack Taghioff) and former '*dakinis*' ('Mimi', 'Ny', Victoria Barlow).

consorts, who help visionary lamas to discover Treasure texts or objects (*terma*), through their physical manifestations or via sexual intercourse. During teaching retreats in Rigpa centres, one can usually notice four or five, rather pretty, young women, sitting next to the throne, sometimes pouring tea for Sogyal Rinpoche and disappearing behind the curtain separating the shrine-room and the lama's private apartments, and reappearing later to bring food, drinks, or papers. Their apparitions are neither commented on, nor even mentioned, although they do contribute to the master's theatrical show, emphasizing yet another image: that of a feudal lord being served by servants and surrounded by a female entourage. Neither Sogyal Rinpoche (while on stage), nor the instructors (during the beginners' sessions), comment on the *dakinis*' apparition, as they do for every other aspects of Sogyal Rinpoche's behaviour. Because it is being excluded from the set of acts identified as carrying a hidden, critical meaning in the spatio-temporal frame of the 'retreat' (Smith 1982), the presence of female servants becomes the only staged item that does not belong to Sogyal Rinpoche's 'crazy wisdom', and thus needs to be interpreted by the audience as 'real', that is to say, as *real* female servants *really* serving a *really* powerful and authoritarian master. What does the *dakinis*' exclusion both from Sogyal Rinpoche's theatrical show and from the instructors' exegesis imply?

When asked about the issue, the high-ranking Rigpa members said that the women involved were students selected for their spiritual capacities and special devotion to the lama. Their intimate relationship with the master, though kept within the sphere of 'higher, secret teachings', is also said to result from their formal consent, so that the relationships in question can be identified as 'romantic relationships' between adults. Either as 'higher teachings' or 'love affairs', relationships between Sogyal Rinpoche and selected women are mostly understood within Rigpa as 'great luck', the 'result of a good karma'. As for the women involved, they seem to accept – during several months or years – the various and contradictory meanings attributed to their relationship with Sogyal Rinpoche. They view the polysemy and contradictions of their position (are they mere girlfriends, special tantric consorts, simple servants, elected students ... ? If he is pure compassion, why is he behaving violently?)[9] as the same expression of 'crazy wisdom' they first got used to while attending Sogyal Rinpoche's theatrical shows. Following the instructors' and the master's prescriptions, they view the numerous tasks the lama asks them to perform (from house cleaning to sexual

---

[9]   The expression 'violent behaviour' is used by Mimi in her account of her experience within Rigpa and by other ex-Rigpa members. See the media references at the end of this chapter.

services) as 'apparently chores', but 'ultimately teachings'. If the service ordered is too humiliating, it is seen as 'a devotional test'. *'Dakinis'* apply the prescribed exegesis to their own conduct until a series of incidents happen (for example, they discover they are not the only *'dakini'*, they feel disgust towards the sexual services demanded, they meet another man outside of the group, their husband asks for a divorce, they get a sexually transmitted disease, they experience depression ...),[10] which makes them lose their faith in the pedagogical dimension of their personal relationship with Sogyal Rinpoche. The very few women who started talking about their experience to friends, relatives, lawyers and journalists, identifying their relationship to Sogyal Rinpoche as 'fraudulent', are women who could not reduce this relationship to one defined situation (either a love affair or a master-consort relationship), and who could no longer, at the same time, accept the 'crazy wisdom' exegesis, because their relationship with the lama went far beyond the usual intellectual play on words, as it dealt with their private, daily life and sexuality. Moreover, what was presented to them as 'a teaching' was not, unlike other 'personal instructions', publicly displayed on stage. In other words, their relationship to the lama, as women invested with domestic and sexual functions, was the only one not to be ritualized and to be kept away from the novices' eyes. Confronted with a situation that receives no convincing identification, either realistic ('I was just one of his mistresses'), or dogmatic ('all appearances must be seen as spiritual teachings'), these women seem compelled to identify themselves as victims of a betrayal. They then reinterpret their whole learning path within Rigpa – which was at first enthusiastically embraced – as a 'mental manipulation', from the contemplation of the animated icons to the 'crazy wisdom' theatrical plays to their own work as *'dakinis'*. They then conclude they have been fooled from the very beginning, and that the practices taught within Rigpa were nothing else than a 'cultish personality cult'. The tantric model on which Sogyal Rinpoche elaborated his new teaching methods is then completely denied/rejected by these women and their supporters.

A new term thus appears at the margins of Rigpa, which was never before part of the language taught and used by the group: 'fraud', with synonyms common to this context – 'mental manipulation', 'cultish behaviour', 'personality cult', 'guru attitude'. These replace the positively connoted 'crazy wisdom', 'spontaneity', 'skilful means', 'wrathful appearances'. Leaving apart the possible damages the relationships may produce on the women involved (the harmfulness or illegality of which can only be decided through psychotherapeutic and judicial means),

---

[10]   Personal interviews with Mimi and other ex-*'dakinis'* who wish for their testimony to remain confidential. Also see the media material referenced at the end of this chapter.

the apparition of 'fraud' to describe Sogyal Rinpoche's behaviour towards his students can be explained by the breach of an implicit norm, rather than by a 'breach of trust' – since the key value to relate to Sogyal Rinpoche was never 'trust', 'confidence', 'transparence', or 'sincerity' but precisely *ritualized and institutionalized trickery*. The implicit norm breached here has little to do with the much-commented-upon illusion/reality duality, but rather deals with very practical open/secret type of activities: to be deemed 'teachings' by the group, the lama's words and deeds need to be identified as such through codified linguistic patterns before and after their materialization, by Sogyal Rinpoche himself, in front of an audience. Because they do not follow these implicit rules and happen outside the ritualized space and time of the 'teaching retreats', the intimate relationships between the master and his female disciples are logically bound to be labelled 'fraudulent'. Had they been openly put on stage and discussed within Rigpa's linguistic frameworks, these relationships would have had a clear status: 'appearances hiding a transcendent truth', a paradoxical expression of 'Rinpoche's love and compassion', a pedagogical tool. But in the absence of such ritualization, their nature is not clear, neither for the women, nor for those who happen to learn about their existence. According to Rigpa's ideological and ritual rules, they are not 'teachings', but 'reality as it seems at first sight': female students acting as domestic and sexual servants. The ultimate paradox of this situation is that the 'fraudulent' (that is, secret) status of these relationships is also the reason why the accusations of deviancy are not taken seriously, both within and outside Rigpa. Because they happen in secret, with no other witness than the two parties involved, they can only be treated as 'rumours' and 'private issues'.

References

Allegations about Sogyal Rinpoche's Misconduct

Brown, M. (1995). 'The Precious One', *Telegraph Magazine* (UK), 2 February, pp. 20–29.
Emery, E. (2011). 'Pas si zen, ces bouddhistes … ', *Marianne*, 15–21 octobre http://dialogueireland.wordpress.com/2011/11/15/sogyal-feature-in-marianne-in-both-english-and-french-rigpa (accessed 17 March 2014).
Finnigan, M. (1995). 'Sexual Healing', *Guardian*, 10 January.

Goodwin, D. (2011). 'In the Name of Enlightenment', Vision TV, a Canadian TV documentary http://www.youtube.com/watch?v=yWhIivvmMnk (accessed 17 March 2014).

Lattin, D. (1994). 'Best-selling Buddhist author accused of sexual abuse', *San Francisco Free Press*, 10 November.

'Service Public – Soyons Zen' (2011), France Inter, 7 november, a French radio programme http://www.franceinter.fr/emission-service-public-soyons-zen (accessed 17 March 2014).

The Sunday Programme (1995). A 1995 BBC Radio 4 programme featuring the English journalist Mary Finnigan, the American Tibetologist Donald Lopez and the English Buddhist writer Stephen Batchelor.

Other Publications

Bell, Catherine (1992). *Ritual Theory, Ritual Practice*. New York: Oxford University Press, 1992.

Bishop, P. (1993). *Dreams of Power. Tibetan Buddhism and the Western Imagination*. London: Athlone Press.

Dodin, T. and H. Rather (eds) (1993). *Imagining Tibet. Perceptions, Projections and Fantasies*. Chicago, IL: Wisdom Publications Inc.

Lopez, D. (1999). *Prisoners of Shangrila: Tibetan Buddhism and the West*. Chicago. IL: University of Chicago Press.

— (ed.) (2002). Introduction, in *A Modern Buddhist Bible, Essential Readings from East and West*. Boston, MA: Beacon Press.

Masuzawa, T. (2005). *The Invention of World Religions: Or How European Universalism Was Preserved In The Language Of Pluralism*. Chicago, IL: University of Chicago Press.

Mauss, M. (1921). 'L'expression obligatoire des sentiments (rituels oraux funéraires australiens)', *Journal de Psychologie*, 18: 425–34.

Prothero, S.R. (1996). *The White Buddhist: The Asian Odyssey of Henry Steel Olcott*. Bloomington: Indiana University Press.

Sharf, R. (1995). 'Buddhist Modernism and the Rhetoric of Meditative Experience', *Numen*, 42(3) (October): 228–83.

Smith, J.Z. (1982). *Imagining Religions, From Babylon to Jonestown*. Chicago, IL: University of Chicago Press.

Strickmann, M. (1996). *Mantras et mandarins, Le bouddhisme tantrique en Chine*. Paris: Gallimard.

Trungpa, C. (1991). *Crazy Wisdom*. Boston, MA: Shambhala Publications.

Van Gennep, A. (1914). *Les rites de passages*. Paris.

Chapter 10
Faith Lends Substance?
Trickery and Deception within Religious and Spiritual Movements

Michael Coffey

This chapter is a brief examination of the ways in which certain deceptive practices, commonly associated with magic (magic as entertainment, as opposed to occult practice), stage illusion and stage mind-reading, can be and have been employed by various religious, spiritual groups and organizations, and the intention behind their uses.

> They say this town is full of cozenage,
> As, nimble jugglers that deceive the eye,
> Dark-working sorcerers that change the mind,
> Soul-killing witches that deform the body,
> Disguised cheaters, prating mountebanks,
> And many such-like liberties of sin
>
> William Shakespeare, *The Comedy of Errors*, 1.II.97–102

When people ask me what I do for a living, I tend to wince slightly. On occasion, I've even been known to lie. It's not that a little knowledge is necessarily all that dangerous, but when it's applied to conjuring, it can become difficult for a professional magician to answer any questions about their work with any degree of honesty. The public's perception of what magic actually is, as a performance art, tends to be in varying degrees of contrast to the reality. If anyone goes on to enquire exactly what branch of magic I specialize in, I usually start looking for the nearest exit. Once you've told someone you are a mind-reader, the next question is usually the only thing you can predict with absolute certainty. It's a profession which for some appears to be synonymous with hypnotist, psychologist, neurologist, occultist, spiritualist, in fact pretty much any vaguely esoteric or recondite speciality, with the notable exception, interestingly enough, of magician. You can introduce yourself as a magician or conjuror, it can say as much on your business card and website, but once you've confessed to also performing mind-reading, or mentalism, you might just as well have hypnotized the person you are talking to into forgetting your previous statements. Which is more than a little ironic, as mind-reading is magic, not plain, certainly, but reasonably simple. The principles it employs are those of card magic, coin magic, parlour magic, stage illusion, even comedy magic. The psychology employed is the same, many of the methods are identical, the only real difference is the presentation.

None of which is to detract one jot from the skill set that goes into successful stage mind-reading. There is a tremendous amount of psychology and showmanship that goes into any performance art, be it acting, close-up magic, comedy, or indeed mentalism. To understand the needs of an audience in general, to read the requirements of a particular audience on a given night, to gain their respect, to work them subtly and control their responses, to deal with unforeseen mishaps, all these take a great deal of study and require a lot of experience to master. One of the clearest distinctions between the amateur magician and the professional is that the professional understands that neither an exceptional technical ability nor a remarkable effect are enough, in most instances, to guarantee the interest of a spectator or of a crowd. Of far greater import is the degree to which the magician engages the audience. At its simplest level, if the spectators like the performer then their experience of the performance will be favourable. The more they like the performer, the more they will enjoy, and subsequently favourably embellish, the performance they witness. Quite a few magicians have had the experience of having one of their own tricks or performances recounted to them by an enthusiastic spectator, but with crucial elements either forgotten or exaggerated, so that the memory becomes something no magician, outside a work of science fiction, fantasy, or possibly religion, could ever hope to recreate. To be sure, being likeable isn't the only way in which to engage an audience, and some performers employ a more mysterious or authoritarian approach, but it is by far the most reliable.

Another example of this operant psychology would be the role of the compère (not infrequently a magician or comedian) at a cabaret or variety night. Most of the acts at such nights will only be on stage for ten minutes, nowhere near enough time to build up a genuine relationship with their audience, especially if the act is more skill-based (say, juggling) than interactive. It is the compère's job to do so. He or she engages the audience, gets to know them, gets them to know him/her, gets them to practice clapping, whooping, cheering, all of which sets the tone for the evening, subtly tells the audience how to behave, ultimately informing them that 'this is going to be a fun night and you will be enjoying yourselves.' And more often than not they do. It is here that the true deception begins to take place, one that magicians, psychics, priests, preachers and shamans have known for centuries, and that cognitive science has only recently discovered. Our emotions colour our thinking and our perceptions far more than our rational mind does.

> Emotions change the way we see the world and how we interpret the actions of others. We do not seek to challenge why we are feeling a particular emotion; instead we seek to confirm it. We evaluate what is happening in a way that is consistent with the emotion we are feeling, thus justifying and maintaining the emotion (Ekman 2003).

It's not what actually takes place, but what is perceived, on an emotional level, to have taken place, that makes the effect and makes the difference. When it comes to magic, whether it's a thought plucked from the mind of a willing volunteer, or a card of one suit transformed into a card of another, it is the presentation of the effect and the degree to which the spectator has invested in the conjuror, and as a result in the effect itself, that determines how much of a miracle the spectator will witness.

The presentational conceit of my current show is that of spiritualism. I begin by stating that all of my effects stem directly from the deceits and ruses used by the fraudulent mediums during the course of their séances. I make it clear that I am not attempting to discredit mediumship or any belief in the supernatural. I even go so far as to state that I'm not passing some sort of blanket judgement on the alleged abilities of the mediums and spiritualists that I reference during my show, even though some of them (notably Eusapia Palladino 1854–1918) were prepared to admit to occasional cheating, with a variety of colourful justifications for this. I simply point out that, using the evidence available to us in the twenty-first century, and even in some instances by their own admission (Eusapia Palladino, and the Fox Sisters being prime examples of this, with Uri Geller doing much the same around a century later), it seems clear that at certain points in their careers the mediums I discuss used deception and trickery in a number of their séances, to convince those present that they were witnessing 'spirit phenomena'. The Davenport brothers, creators of the 'Spirit Cabinet', were exposed by numerous magicians, most famously by John N. Maskelyne in 1865; Florence Cook was exposed by the lawyer William Volckman at a séance held in Hackney in 1873; Daniel Dunglas Home by F. Merrifield who wrote up his account in the *Journal of Psychical Research*. I make it clear that I do not claim to be in touch with spirits, possess telepathic abilities, or use various coercive technologies to bend my audience to my well-intentioned will.

Following on from these caveats, I then go out of my way to be as even-handed and as honest as the requirements of my job allow me to be. But these requirements are such that I cannot, for the sake of my audience's enjoyment alone, reveal my methods or state outright that I'm using nothing more than disguised magic tricks to produce my mind-reading effects. I justify what I do by telling myself that I'm there to tell a story, to entertain and engage the people who have given their time and money to see me, and my job is primarily to ensure that they enjoy their evening. I have made my influences clear and in addition have stated that I will not be using hypnosis, or 'the science of coercion'. But I cannot tell them the truth about the way in which I do what I do, and I know full well that a sizable number of those attending will leave after the show convinced that I have powers of influence and suggestion, that I can accurately read an individual's body language and use associated deductive skills to uncover certain facts about them. I cannot relate Derren Brown's comment to a journalist and say that 'The reason why magicians are so precious about secrets is not because there are wonderful secrets, but more often than not because there is nothing there, just rubbish cheating' (Moir 2005). Indeed no less an authority than Harlan Tarbell, whose *Course in Magic* volumes inspired and influenced the formative years of many professional magicians, states clearly, when discussing 'mental magic', that 'If presented as mere tricks, the act would not command anywhere near the same interest and spellbound attention – if indeed, it didn't fall flat' (1989: 81).

It is one of the US's most prolific contemporary mind-readers, Bob Cassidy, who best sums up the conundrum: 'The question, then, is not whether a performer should misrepresent the nature of his work, but rather to what extent he must do so in order to entertainingly create the illusion of mind reading' (2002: 59). Obviously that is never going to be what the audience wants to hear.

The debt modern mind-reading owes to spiritualism cannot be understated. Indeed, it would be fair to say that had it not been for the mediumistic circles of the mid-nineteenth century, and the ruses and tricks the fraudulent spiritualists employed to dupe the public into believing they had either psychic powers themselves, or had access to spirits who could demonstrate such powers, modern mind-reading would not exist. Eusapia Palladino, Daniel Dunglas Home, Andrew Jackson Davies, Kate and Margaret Fox, these are the individuals whose practices and deceptions gave us the techniques magicians, mentalists and fraudulent psychics use today. Again, it is Cassidy who makes this point:

Fundamental methodologies, however, such as nailwriting [the practice of using a small piece of pencil lead, typically placed under a finger nail, to write information down, unobserved by an audience], billet switching, and cold reading, remained those devised by the mediums and seers. (Ibid.: 13).

It was primarily in seeking to expose the fact that certain spiritualists used trickery to obtain their results that magicians uncovered the methods used, went on to demonstrate said methods, and ended up appropriating them for their own purposes, John Maskelyn and the Davenport brothers being a particular case in point. A watch-maker by trade, Maskelyn witnessed a demonstration held by the Davenport brothers, and deduced the workings of the 'Spirit Cabinet', which was essentially a large box in which the brothers would be seated, tied to their chairs with rope and then the box would be closed; instruments which had been placed in the box beforehand would then start to play and at times be thrown around. When the box was opened the brothers would be seen to be restrained in the same manner as before. Maskelyn exposed their methods and went on to become a successful magician in his own right (Hansen 2001: 121).

Spiritualism, as a movement, came about in the mid-nineteenth Century. Its primary belief is that the spirits of the dead can and do communicate with the living, most commonly by speaking to or through a trance medium. These mediums would hold gatherings known as séances, which would typically take place around a table, during which they would profess to commune with the spirits, answer questions put to them by anyone present and either answer on behalf of the spirits or allow the spirits to use them as a vessel and speak through them. Belief in the existence of spirits or non-corporeal entities of one kind or another, as well as in the abilities of certain persons to effect communication with them, is as old as humanity. The Witch of Endor who reputedly summoned the ghost of the prophet Samuel on behalf of King Saul makes a good, though not unique, example (1 Samuel 28:3–25). One of the earliest extant books dealing with the exposure of supposedly magical feats, *The Discoverie of Witchcraft* by Reginald Scot, first published in 1584, includes seven chapters on the Witch of Endor and offers a number of possible methods with which she could have tricked King Saul and fooled him into believing the spirit of the dead prophet was present. In exposing so many of the ruses employed by the alleged witches, and in this pre-empting the magicians' exposés of the spiritualists by three hundred years, Scot finds himself having to apologize to the jugglers (magicians) of his time, for giving away many of their own methods in doing so and thus contributing 'to the hinderance of such poore men as live thereby'. Scot's solution to the question of presentation was the one thing that makes it clear that while he may have been a skilled amateur 'juggler' himself, he was not a professional, as

> When these experiments growe to superstition or impietie, they are either to be forsaken as vaine, or denied as false. Howbeit, if these things be done for mirth and recreation, and not to the hurt of our neighbour, not to the abusing or prophaning of Gods name, in mine opinion they are neither impious nor altogether unlawfull: though herein or hereby a naturall thing be made to seeme supernaturall. (1972: 174)

As hopefully made clear above, when presenting mind-reading, the audience want more than 'it's just a trick.'

Scot was not unique in his rational approach to these matters. In his online article 'Prestigious Demons 3', Erik Davis writes about Johann Weyer, author of *De praestigiis deamonum* published in 1563 and a considerable influence on Scot's work. Weyer argued that witches, far from being agents of the supernatural, were suffering from mental delusions and should be treated accordingly. In addition to the psychological component of alleged witchcraft, he also discusses some areas of trickery, in particular:

> ... the ejection of enormous objects from the mouth – iron nails, strips of course cloth, needles, bones, underwear, 'and other still more ridiculous oddities.' These corporeal apparitions anticipate the ectoplasm and *apports* of later Spiritualists, and like the skeptics who also dogged the Spiritualists, Weyer reaches for prestidigitation as an answer. But in the peculiar way of early modern thought, even the hand behind this sleight of hand required 'the imperceptible subtlety and speed of a demon'. (Davis 2011)

All modern magicians would agree that speed has nothing to do with sleight of hand, and that it is strong misdirection which enables the tricks to be executed. In my own experience, even the misdirection becomes less of a factor after a short while, as once the audience are on your side and engaged with the performance, they aren't interested in trying to catch you out at all. In psychology as well as method, magic finds itself in perfect sync with spiritualism. In the words of Joseph Dunniger, an American mind-reader from the last century, 'For those who believe, no explanation is necessary; for those who do not believe, no explanation will suffice.' Dunniger also is quoted as saying 'There is one primary rule in the fakery of spirit mediumship. That is to concentrate upon persons who have suffered a bereavement' (Kalush and Sloman 2007: 544). It is nigh on axiomatic that those who have suffered some sort of bereavement and are looking for comfort or support from a spiritualist are in no way interested in uncovering a sleight of hand-style trick or ruse. The desperate and overpowering need to believe blinds them to all but the very crudest of executions and even then, if their attachment to the medium is strong enough and their emotions powerful enough, the deception, if uncovered, can easily be rationalized, forgiven and finally forgotten. The majority of people who attend a mind-reading show already have pre-existing notions about hypnosis, influence, suggestion, which they wish to have confirmed. Their expectations colour and shape their belief, which goes on in turn to determine what they perceive.

Spiritualism is somewhat distinct from earlier belief systems in human/ spirit communication, as rather than turning its back on science in an attempt to keep its tenets and claims out of science's harsh and unforgiving gaze, it made use of the then current scientific vocabulary and the scientific method to add weight to its claims. Many of the more successful mediums would even request the presence of respected scientists (and at times even magicians) to their séances, inviting both scepticism and testing, on the proviso that if no method of deception was discovered, the scientist would publicly say as much. There was no Internet in the 1800s and any poor reviews would end up, quite literally, as tomorrow's chip paper, while the more favourable ones would immediately become part of the official press release. Scientists, then as now, are not experts in the art of deception, and magicians have no more trouble fooling a scientist than any other member of the public. The support Howard Thurston (1869–1936), possibly the most famous stage magician of his time, gave to Eusapia Palladino, warrants far more attention. In his own words:

> I do not believe that ever before in the history of the world had a magician and a sceptic been privileged to behold what I then looked upon. I saw Eusapia replace her hands on that table I had examined so carefully. I saw it lift up and float, unsupported in the air; and while it remained there I got down on my knees and crawled around it, seeking in vain for some natural explanation. There was none. No wires, no body supports, no iron shoes, nothing – but some occult power I could not fathom ... I demanded more proof, and with bewildering willingness the strange old lady agreed. Mrs. [Grace] Thurston held her feet, I held her arms. And even then, thus guarded and a prisoner, the table rose again!

> When it finally crashed back to the floor again before my very eyes I was a defeated sceptic. Palladino had convinced me! There was no fake in what she had showed me ... If after reading what I have said of this adventure into the realm where my

> magic cannot penetrate, the reader doubts, not my word, but my observation,
> let me say this: My career has been devoted consistently to magic and illusions.
> I believe I understand the principles governing every known trick ... In all my
> seance examinations I train all my faculties against the Medium, watching for the
> slightest evidence of trickery. I am willing to stake my reputation as a magician
> that what this Medium showed me was genuine. I do insist that woman showed
> genuine levitation, not by trickery but by some baffling, intangible, invisible force
> that radiated through her body and over which she exercised a temporary and
> thoroughly exhausting control. (1910: 2)

It isn't that magicians, especially stage magicians like Thurston, have a more
analytical mind than your average scientist, or that there is a catalogue of
ruses and deceits to which only magicians and spiritualists are privy. At some
risk of coming across as fanciful, deception and misdirection are a language.
Magicians recognize when there is an off note, know when their attention is
being manipulated, when someone has done one thing, often a small thing, that
was in no way necessary to the effect and thereby contains the key to the effect.
It can be as simple as handing out a deck of cards to be shuffled and then taking
the cards back, touching them for the briefest of moments, and in doing so
carrying out whatever move was required to achieve the effect. It can be asking
for something to be written down on a pad of paper, leaving the paper with
the volunteer but taking the pad back, and in doing so surreptitiously gleaning
the written information. These seemingly unimportant moments are glaringly
obvious to all conjurors, and so for Thurston to have been fooled is no small
thing. But then he did believe in Spiritualism, had faith in it, and that makes
a tremendous difference to perception. Carrying on from Eckman earlier, if
we fit the situation around our emotions, we almost inevitably end up fitting
our perceptions to our beliefs. Our beliefs are not separate to us, they are us.
They define us, quite literally give our sense of self its definition. To challenge
someone's beliefs is to directly challenge them. To challenge our own takes a
rather robust psychological constitution.

Recently the idea of cognitive bias has become popular. This is loosely defined
as 'a pattern of deviation in judgment that occurs in particular situations'. Again,
the idea is far from new. Francis Bacon (1561–1626), commonly credited as
the father of the scientific method, wrote of the four idols: of the Tribe (which
are common to the race), of the Den (which are particular to the individual), of
the Marketplace (which come about as a misuse of language) and of the Theatre
(which result from an abuse of authority). He writes that

... if we have any love for natural truths; any aversion to darkness, any desire of purifying the understanding, we must destroy these idols, which have led experience captive, and childishly triumphed over the works of God; and now at length condescend, with due submission and veneration, to approach and peruse the volume of the creation; dwell some time upon it, and bringing to the work a mind well purged of opinions, idols, and false notions, converse familiarly therein. (2012: 5)

These idols are simply the various ways all people have to convince themselves of the rightness of their actions and to ensure that they are and remain the hero of their own story. While there are many such cognitive biases, the ones which seem most pertinent in this instance are Bias Blind Spot – the tendency to see oneself as less biased than other people – and Confirmation Bias – the tendency to search for or interpret information in a way that confirms one's preconceptions. The degree to which these biases affect everything we perceive cannot be understated, with any additional support, here conjuring tricks and deceits, strengthening the perception and so the belief.

That magicians deceive is usually taken for granted. By engaging the emotions of an audience, the magician can bypass the rational mind and effect powerful responses. In the cold light of day, few if any of the spectators will profess to actually believing that the selected card changed into a rose, or that the borrowed ring actually floated, but at the time, assuming the performer did their job well enough, they will have been affected emotionally in much the same way as they would have been had it happened 'for real'. But when it comes to mind-reading, it is less that the emotions are engaged and, unfortunately, more that the performer claims to have abilities, which they do not possess, which they then go on to demonstrate to the audience. Where once the spiritualist would claim to speak to the spirits and obtain information from them, the mentalist of today typically invokes the names of body language, of statistical probability, of pop psychology, even of cybernetics, all the while using the same methods as their shadow-lit predecessor. Is the mentalist behaving in an unscrupulous fashion? Perhaps. When it comes to magic and performance in general, I personally am more concerned with presentation and delivery than I am the illustration of some moral point. I think it is artistically crude to claim to have special powers of one sort or another, and believe there is more that can be done with mind-reading than just, well, pretending to read minds. But what of the people that come to a show absolutely certain that they will witness displays of subtle influence and masterful persuasion, carried out by a Svengali-like character who has plumbed the depths of the human mind and can tell them the secrets of their very own heart? Does the performer disabuse them of their beliefs and turn from entertaining to educating? Or does the performer indulge them, basking in the misplaced praise and attention?

Spiritualists are far from being the only spiritual or religious group to have used dishonest practice to add substance to their claims and beliefs. Anthropological literature is filled with examples of shamanic practitioners using conjuring effects to simulate real magic. In 1755, the Russian botanist Stepan Petrovich Krasheninnikov related witnessing a shamanic rite in Eastern Siberia in which the shaman

> ... pierced his abdomen with a knife and drank the blood which gushed out; but he did this so clumsily that one would have to be blinded by superstition as these people are not to see through such gross deceit ... I couldn't keep from laughing for he performed his trick so crudely that he would have a hard time in our country being accepted by our apprentice thimbleriggers. (Krasheninnikov 2001: 29–31).

In his book '*The Trickster and the Paranormal*, George Hansen recounts that while he began to put together instances of deceptive practices within shamanism, he soon had to give up because 'the task quickly became overwhelming' (2001: 89). The book deals with the nature of deception within spiritual practice and goes a long way to showing that clear divisions between the two are neither possible nor desirable. His chapter on shamanism is titled 'Shamanism and its Sham', and makes clear that deception is an almost integral part of shamanic practice. Citing the two customary reasons given for the use of deception in shamanism as either to facilitate the placebo effect or to demonstrate occult power for personal gain, both of which Hansen agrees can have considerable validity, he goes on to state that there is often more to the issue than a simple dichotomy. Referencing Richard Warner's article 'Deception and self-deception in shamanism and psychiatry' (Warner was the medical director of a medical health centre), Hansen writes:

> Warner admitted that many forms of modern psychotherapy have little innate healing capacity, and the benefits have more to do with the therapist than the mode of treatment. This has been demonstrated by a large number of scientific studies, to the chagrin of various types of psychotherapy (Ibid).

This is not to say that psychiatry and psychotherapy do not have benefits or that they are unable to live up to their claims, only that the grounds upon which their credibility rests are not quite as solid as some of their practitioners might like or assume. A precise definition of consciousness is still very much a work in progress. Even the exact mechanisms with which so blunt a force as clinical anaesthesia affect and influence it are, at present, poorly understood. If pragmatism is the evaluation of any assertion by its practical consequences, it is difficult to see how disciplines such as shamanism, and by extension psychiatry and psychotherapy, can be entirely castigated, if they do result in subjective benefits for subjective ailments. The scientific method is and always will be an exceptional tool for the evolution of human understanding and knowledge. The degree to which the study of consciousness falls within the strict remit of science is, however, still very much up for debate.

Shamanism (using the term in its broadest and no doubt least technical sense) also makes the claim that it can have both a beneficial and a negative effect on a person's health, healing an illness or cursing an individual. Here sceptics tend to, as Hansen points out, cite the placebo effect, and claim that all the ritual and deception merely assists the patients' own healing abilities and bolsters their belief that they will recover. This may or may not be the case, but is in and of itself surely no small thing. Ben Goldacre, in his book *Bad Science*, dedicates a chapter to the placebo effect, detailing a number of instances in which western doctors, utilizing the kind of mummery one would normally associate with less-than-scrupulous psychic healers, have effected exceptional recovery in their patients. As well as citing numerous instances of the power of the placebo, in scientific tests as well as anecdotally, Goldacre also writes about a native Canadian called Quesalid:

> Quesalid was a sceptic: he thought shamanism was bunk, that it only worked through belief, and he went undercover to investigate this idea. He found a shaman who was willing to take him on, and learnt all the tricks of the trade, including the classic performance piece where the healer hides a tuft of down in his mouth, and then, sucking and heaving, right at the peak of his healing ritual, brings it up, covered in blood from where he has discreetly bitten his lip, and solemnly presents it to the onlookers as a pathological specimen, extracted from the body of the afflicted patient.

> Quesalid had proof of the fakery, he knew the trick as an insider, and was all set to expose those who carried it out; but as part of his training he had to do a bit of clinical work, and he was summoned by a family 'who had dreamed of him as their saviour' to see a patient in distress. He did the trick with the tuft, and was appalled, humbled and amazed to find that his patient got better.

> Although he continued to maintain a healthy scepticism about most of his colleagues, Quesalid, to his own surprise perhaps, went on to have a long and productive career as a healer and a shaman (2008: 77).

Again, the literature is replete with examples like this, in which the shaman is either engaging in dishonest practice for their own social or commercial interests, deceiving the patient (and at times audience) in the belief that the deception will aid the patient's healing process, or in some instances is fully aware of the potential for and use of deception, and goes on to shun it outright:

> On my travels I have sometimes been present at a séance among the saltwater-dwellers, for instance among the coast people at Utkuhigjalik. These angatkut (shaman) never seemed trustworthy to me. It always appeared to me that these saltwater angatkut attached more weight to tricks that would astonish the audience, when they jumped about the floor and lisped all sorts of absurdities and lies in their so-called spirit language; to me all this seemed only amusing and as something that would impress the ignorant. A real shaman does not jump about on the floor and do tricks, not does he seek the aid of darkness, by putting out the lamps, to make the minds of his neighbours uneasy. (This comment is made by a shaman called Igjugarjuk, and recorded by Rasmussen in Krasheninnikov 2001: 81–3).

As an aside, it is interesting to note that the medium Daniel Dunglas Home went to great lengths to ensure that people knew that he carried out his séances in well-lit conditions, in contrast to all the other mediums whose meetings took place in near-darkness.

I suspect that here we are close to encountering, if not embracing, what Francis Bacon would have referred to as an Idol of the Marketplace. One shaman is not all shamans and the techniques of one are by no means the techniques of the rest. Even the term 'shaman' itself is somewhat misleading, used as it is to describe a wide variety of psychopomps and healers, spiritual or otherwise, all over the globe.

Ben Goldacre has also recently caused no little controversy within the medical and pharmaceutical establishment with his new book, *Bad Pharma*, in which he extensively details the ways in which large pharmaceutical companies test and market their drugs:

> Drugs are tested by the people who manufacture them, in poorly designed trials, on hopelessly small numbers of weird, unrepresentative patients, and analysed

using techniques that are flawed by design, in such a way that they exaggerate the benefits of treatments. Unsurprisingly, these trials tend to produce results that favour the manufacturer. When trials throw up results that companies don't like, they are perfectly entitled to hide them from doctors and patients, so we only ever see a distorted picture of any drug's true effects. (2012: X).

If contemporary science, based around Francis Bacon's scientific method, uses and abuses statistics to justify its claims, it is difficult to see all that much difference between the 'thimble-rigging' of the suspect shaman and this number-juggling and surprisingly crude misdirection. Faith in science and the medical establishment is all well and good, but is it there because logic and good reasoning have been used to instil it, taking all the factors, both for and against, into account? Or does it stem from an unquestioning submission to a dominant paradigm? I very much doubt that there is anyone who would dismiss the value and worth of the scientific method, but again those Marketplace Idols raise their heads and demand our attention. Just because pharmaceutical companies claim to be employing the scientific method to manufacture their products, doesn't mean that is actually what they are doing.

I have written of deception within the field of magic and mind-reading. That is my profession and the subject I know best. Here, tricks are used to entertain. There is unquestionably a grey area, most notably in mind-reading, where the claims made by some practitioners do not quite tie in with the objective truth of the situation, but by and large no lasting harm is done. In areas such as spiritualism, witchcraft, shamanism and faith-healing, it could be argued that to use such deceits would be unconscionable and immoral, preying on the desperate need of suffering people, abusing their ignorance for the practitioner's own benefit. I believe that to be an overly simplistic approach, once again an example of the Idol of the Marketplace. Glib answers which do not take into account the vagaries of the human condition, internal and external, given by individuals who fail to not only appreciate but actively ignore facts that can and do contradict their own world views, should largely be discarded. There are no experts or authorities here, the field is simply too vast.

To dismiss deception outright is to take an amusingly presumptuous perspective on the notion of objective truth. I am thankful that my chosen career allows me to have a more ambivalent approach to such matters. There are and always have been individuals who have sought out psychics and spiritualists and done their best to discredit them. Individuals who have seen that particular form of deception as a thing abhorrent to their own sense of self, and actively worked to bring it to an end. They seem to labour under the impression that they are doing good. I do not doubt their intentions, but do feel that they are somewhat misplaced.

Belief and truth are abused every second of every day, politically, socially and personally. Advertisers warping our very sense of self, politicians using atrocities to further ill-defined and suspect agendas, economies propped up on less than substantial concepts, individuals acting out their own lives unaware of the biases and idols they unwillingly adhere to, of the origins of their own drives and impulses – these to me are the issues upon which any would-be firebrand seeking to shine the light of their own righteous truth on to a world of darkness and ignorance should focus.

But then they might be faced with the fact that true education is not something to be imposed from without, but sought for by the individual him or herself. The Greek aphorism, 'Know Thyself', inscribed at Apollo's Temple in Delphi, sums this up best. To struggle against the myriad of ways in which we delude ourselves on a daily basis entails a lifetime of concentrated work. To then attempt to counteract, or at least mitigate, any social and conceptual deception that takes place, that one encounters or witnesses, would also be the most demanding of tasks. Going after the fake psychic and spiritualists seems to be more than a little like shooting fish in a barrel. Trying to ascertain exactly why it is that as humans we are so very eager to hand over our spiritual, social and individual freedoms to persons and groups who do not have our best interests at heart, why we so readily believe in the form without thinking about the content and so effortlessly take style over substance, strikes me as a much more worthy endeavour.

References

Bacon, F. R. Ellis and W. Rawley (2012). *The Philosophical Works of Francis Bacon*. Great Britain: Ulan Press.

Cassidy, R. (2002). *The Art of Mentalism*. McAllen, TX: Collectors Workshop.

Davis, E. (2011). *Prestigious Demons 3* http://www.techgnosis.com/chunks.php?cat=phantasy&sec=articles&file=chunkfrom-2011-05-01-1549-0.txt (accessed 13 March 2013).

Ekman, P. (2003). *Emotions Revealed*. London: Phoenix.

Goldacre, B. (2008). *Bad Science*. London: Fourth Estate.

— (2012). *Bad Pharma*. London: Fourth Estate.

Hansen, G.P. (2001). *The Trickster and the Paranormal*. Philadelphia, PA: Xlibris.

Kalush, W. and L. Sloman (2007). *The Secret Life of Houdini: The Making of America's First Superhero*. New York: Atria Books.

Krasheninnikov, S. (2001). 'Blinded by Superstition', in *Shamans throughout Time: 500 Years on the Path to Knowledge*, eds J. Narby and F. Huxley. London: Thames & Hudson, pp. 29–31.

Moir, J. (2005). 'Oh yes, I'm hugely nerdy', *Telegraph* (UK) http://www.telegraph.co.uk/culture/theatre/3638015/Oh-yes-Im-hugely-nerdy.html (accessed 17 March 2014).

Rasmussen, I. and K. Rasmussen (2001). 'Seeking Knowledge in the Solitude of Nature', in *Shamans throughout Time: 500 Years on the Path to Knowledge*, eds J. Narby and F. Huxley. London: Thames & Hudson, pp. 81–3.

Scot, R. (1972). *The Discoverie of Witchcraft*. New York : Dover Books.

Tarbell, H. (1989). *The Tarbell Course in Magic*, Volume IV. New York: D. Robbins & Co.

Thurston, H. (1910). 'Believes in Palladino: Magician Thurston Offers $1,000 If It Be Shown She Depends On Fraud', *New York Times*, 14 May.

Chapter 11
The Zen Master and Dharma Transmission: A Seductive Mythology

Stuart Lachs

This chapter examines Zen Buddhism's legitimating story, which is an expression of its self-definition. It looks at the ritual of Dharma transmission that imputes enormous power and prestige to the living Zen master/roshi and shines light on some of those imputed qualities. It also examines the construction of the legitimating story and discusses its deceptive nature as well as problems and consequences arising from those deceptions. Deception, however, is a complex issue when viewing Zen, as Zen's mythology is a Chinese creation dating back over a thousand years. Deception implies intentionality, which is not a straightforward issue in a cross-cultural context. Neither are unfulfilled expectations a straightforward issue, hence we need to investigate the basis of such expectations. In this chapter, the term 'deception' is used for an intentional misrepresentation intended to mislead the addressees with the result of gain for oneself. In this view, omissions are part of deceptions, too.

Innocent Beginnings

Zen Buddhism[1] has become widely accepted in the West during the past fifty years. At the head of Zen institutions sits the Zen master/roshi.[2] Zen Buddhism derives its legitimacy and considerable authority from the notion that this Zen

---

[1]   Throughout this chapter, I will use the term 'Zen', the Japanese pronunciation of the Chinese character pronounced as Chan (meditation) in Chinese. In Korean, Zen is known as 'Son' Buddhism. Zen started in China but became widely known in the West after the Second World War through Japan and Japanese teachers. Hence the term 'Zen' is better known than Chan or Son.

[2]   Again, 'roshi' is a Japanese term widely used for the title 'Zen master' in the West. This chapter will use both terms as both are generally used in the West.

master is enlightened.[3] The enlightened roshi is presented in the West as a person with superhuman qualities, a Buddha-like figure supposedly beyond the understanding of ordinary folk.[4] According to the orthodox Zen view, the ritual of Dharma transmission publicly confirms these superhuman qualities in a Zen master and is considered the 'authentic transmission of the Dharma, which is the Law of the universe and the teaching of Sakyamuni'.[5]

Dharma transmission in Zen is a ritual signalling that a student is recognized by a Zen master as having attained the 'Buddha mind', which supposedly is the enlightened mind that the historical Buddha Sakyamuni realized roughly 2,500 years ago in India.[6] This scheme resembles a line of candles, each one being lit by the candle before it going back to Sakyamuni and beyond. In this way, the same enlightened Buddha mind is transmitted from Zen master to student in an unbroken chain. Thus the newly transmitted Zen master inherits the supposed unbroken lineage of his teacher.[7] The last in the line, the living Zen master, therefore embodies all the authority of the entire Zen lineage and of the historical Buddha. The gap between now and back-then is overcome in what is presented as perfect connections. In the early formulation of Zen in China, the Zen master was even presented as a living Buddha,[8] meant to replace the historical Buddha's presence and power.

---

[3]   Though the idea of enlightenment is important in Zen, what it actually means is rarely examined. Throughout Zen history up to the present, there have been different understandings of enlightenment: whether enlightenment was lodged in the canonical texts versus direct experience, and whether enlightenment occurred suddenly or gradually, being two such issues. Though most Zen adherents subscribe to sudden enlightenment, there are, however, differing views of what this means. There are also different understandings about the need for cultivation following enlightenment. In actual practice, it is not necessary to have experienced enlightenment, however defined, to become a Zen master.

[4]   This notion that a Zen master is 'beyond the understanding of ordinary people' is standard Zen rhetoric. According to this notion, the master has realized the mind of the Buddha, which ordinary folk have not. I heard, for example, the modern-day Taiwanese Zen master Shifu Sheng-yen proclaim this to his students.

[5]   Morinaga 1988: 20. Morinaga Roshi was head of Hanazono University, the main Rinzai sect university in Japan and abbot of Daishu-in temple in Kyoto.

[6]   Schlutter 2008: 59. This is repeated in many places in Zen writing and in talks.

[7]   I choose to use the masculine pronoun 'his' because most roshi are male; however, there are in fact a fair number of female roshi in the West.

[8]   To highlight the idea of a Chinese Buddha, in particular a Zen sect Buddha, 'The Platform Sutra of the Sixth Patriarch, Huineng' was written. A sutra is by definition the words of a Buddha. In this manner, the Zen sect moved the centre of Buddhism away from India to China. In so doing, it moved the central focus of Buddhism away from Sakyamuni

This orthodox Zen self-representation fulfils all criteria of Bourdieu's basic model of religious authority (see Bourdieu 1991: 117–26). Alan Cole's presentation of Bourdieu argues that the standard set-up for religious authority requires three mutually reliant zones:

1. A deep origin of truth or perfection in the form of a past sage, saint, deity, or Being;
2. A means for bringing that truth-perfection forward in time; and
3. A contemporary spokesperson for that primordial truth-perfection who is sanctioned to represent it in the present, and distribute it to the believing public, which delegates to him just this power and legitimacy.

Bourdieu sees religious authority always involved in a to-ing and fro-ing, shuttling back and forth between its deep origins and its application in the present. Put differently, in any moment of religious authority, there is always an audience focused on the singular priest-figure, who is expected to funnel the totality of truth and being from the past into the present group. (This concise interpretation of Bourdieu's model of religious authority is from Cole 2006: 13.)

In Zen, the past sage is the historical Buddha. The means for bringing truth-perfection forward in time is Dharma transmission and the lineage based on it, while the contemporary spokesperson for that primordial truth-perfection, the priest-figure, is the Dharma-transmitted Zen master. In light of Bourdieu's ideas, it is not surprising that around Zen centres the focus is on the ritual of Dharma transmission and on the question of who does and does not have it. Hence, when digging into questions of fraud and deception, not only the idea of the quasi-divine nature of the modern Zen master needs to be investigated. We also need to look at the Zen institution, especially at the ritual of Dharma transmission, to see its effects and what it means, and what Zen students today believe it to mean.

The orthodox presentation, mostly idealistic, is meant to establish, maintain and enhance the authority of the Zen master. It is also meant to legitimate the Zen institutions with their hierarchical structures. This presentation has been widely and uncritically accepted in the West among Zen practitioners. Even more importantly, it is the source of a variety of problems in western Zen. These problems have included sexual and psychological manipulation of both male and female students by teachers, though the large majority of cases resulting in

---

Buddha, the historical Buddha, to the Zen Patriarchs and later to the newly constructed Zen lineage and Chinese masters.

sexual abuse are by male teachers of female students. Other problems include questionable financial dealings, alcoholism and a very basic undermining of trust. A number of women have described their sexual relationship with their Zen master as being like incest. As one concrete example of these problems, the scandals around Eido Shimano Roshi started in 1964 in Hawaii and have continued with regularity to this day, close to fifty years. Another example is Gempo Dennis Merzil Roshi who in the 1980s had a few affairs secretly with female students while being married with children, only to repeat his scandalous behaviour 25 years later, with a different wife and in a different location. The latest and perhaps most disturbing scandal involves Sasaki Roshi, abbot and roshi of the Mount Baldy Zen Center in California, who has been sexually abusing women students for fifty years.[9] Not to think this is a strictly American problem, there is the case of Dr Klaus Zernickow (also known as Sotetsu Yuzen) in Berlin. The list is long (see below, fn. 32).

How does it Really Work?

Norman Solomon writes that 'any propagandist understands that the essence of propaganda is repetition.'[10] The idealistic yet orthodox presentation of Zen is exactly what we find in the sectarian and popular literature on Zen. It also is what we find coming from the mouths of Zen masters up to the present. This is not surprising, as Zen masters are the main representatives of the institution. Here, repetition is in fact an important factor in making this idealistic view appear true. The texts considered to be classical Zen texts[11] and hence read, studied,

---

9   For documentation on the Sasaki case, see the Sasaki Archive at www.sasakiarchive. com, for documentation on the Shimano case see www.shimanoarchive.com (accessed 1 April 2013).

10   See Solomon 1999. Though Solomon is concerned with political issues, it also applies to Zen, since Zen and politics are much more tied together than generally recognized. This is true in Zen's early formative phase, and continued into the twentieth century with Zen's connection to Japanese imperialism and the Second World War (see Victoria 1997). Zen in Taiwan today is also connected to politics.

11   Zen history is often presented in the form of encounters between Zen masters with monks or, less frequently, with laypeople. These are collected in koan collections. A koan is a story, dialogue, question, or statement meant to provoke doubt in the student. It is often used as a focus of meditation and is used to test a student's progress. Koan literally means a 'public case'. The best-known collections in the West are the *Gateles Gate* (Shibayama 1974), *The Blue Cliff Record* (Cleary and Cleary 1977) and the *Book of Serenity* (Cleary 1990). Also popular are *Transmission of the Lamp* (Ch. *denglu*) texts and 'recorded sayings' (Ch. *yu-lu*,

and, importantly, commented on by living Zen masters, in one way or another repeat the mythology.

To take these reflections out of the abstract realm, let us look at just one of many examples of how a famous modern-day Zen master talked about himself. In his introduction to *Zen Mind, Beginners Mind,* the best-selling English-language book on Zen, author Richard Baker inserted the description of his teacher Suzuki roshi quoted immediately below. At this time, Richard Baker was still only a disciple. However, Suzuki had already informed him that he would be made his Dharma heir, that is, a roshi. Hence, Baker was not only describing Suzuki, but also describing himself in idealistic terms as a future roshi:

> A roshi is a person who has actualized that perfect freedom which is the potentiality for all human beings. He exists freely in the fullness of his whole being. The flow of his consciousness is not the fixed repetitive patterns of our usual self-centered consciousness, but rather arises spontaneously and naturally from the actual circumstances of the present. The results of this in terms of the quality of his life are extraordinary buoyancy, vigor, straightforwardness, simplicity, humility, security, joyousness, uncanny perspicacity and unfathomable compassion. His whole being testifies to what it means to live in the reality of the present. Without anything said or done, just the impact of meeting a personality so developed can be enough to change another's whole way of life. But in the end it is not the extraordinariness of the teacher that perplexes, intrigues, and deepens the student, it is the teacher's utter ordinariness.[12]

This is likely the most idealistic presentation of a roshi in the English language. Though this was meant to be a description of Shunryu Suzuki roshi by his prime disciple and later Dharma heir, Richard Baker roshi, it is written as applying to all roshi. In reality, it is questionable whether this description applies to even one roshi. It certainly does not apply to *all* roshis, as Baker surely knew.

Jp. *goruku*) collections such as the *Recorded Sayings of Joshu* (Green 1998). The Sōtō sect pays great attention to its founder, Zen Master Eihei Dogen's *Shobogenzo*, Treasure of the True Dharma Eye (Okamura 2010).

[12] Suzuki 1970: 19. *Zen Mind, Beginner's Mind* has sold well over a million copies. The paragraph quoted here was written by Trudy Dixon, the editor of the book and a student of Suzuki. It is part of the introduction to the book written by Richard Baker, later to be known as Baker Roshi. When Baker wrote the introduction quoting Dixon's idealistic description of a roshi, he had already been told by Suzuki that he would be his successor. Hence, by including this most idealistic description of a roshi, Baker was describing his future self as a roshi without saying so. Suzuki Roshi read English and supposedly read the book to see how his students understood his teaching.

Another modern instance indirectly confirms the idealistic presentation of Zen masters by Zen masters. In a sense, this indirect confirmation is even stronger, as it lets the student fill in the blanks with their imagination.

In *Dropping Ashes on the Buddha* (1976: 99), one of his more popular books, Zen master Seung Sahn (d. 2004), who was the most famous Korean Zen master in the West, related the following exchange of letters that indicates his view of the Zen master. In a letter to the master, someone asked:

> If a Zen master is capable of doing miracles, why doesn't he do them? ... Why doesn't Soen Sunim [that is, Seung Sahn] do as Jesus did – make the blind see, or touch a crazy person and make him sane? Wouldn't even such a showy miracle as walking on water make people believe in Zen so that they would begin to practice ... ?

The Master [Seung Sahn] replied: 'Many people want miracles, and if they witness miracles they become attached to them. But miracles are only a technique. They are not the true way. If a Zen Master used miracles often, people would become much attached to this technique of his, and they wouldn't learn the true way ... .'

Zen master Seung Sahn not only indirectly confirms that Zen masters in general are capable of performing a range of miracles, but implies that he too could perform miracles similar to the ones attributed to the biblical Jesus. His only concern keeping him from doing so, was that by performing miracles, he would be giving the wrong lesson to people and not the 'true way' that only the master holds. In other words, he is saying that Jesus used miracles to attract people, whereas Zen masters are purer and above such a technique. Again, this is not an extremist claim: from earliest Zen history, Zen masters were considered miracle workers, being centres of spiritual power (Welter 2006: 26).

How to Make a Master

Zen mythology has it that its lineage is unbroken and began with the silent mind-to-mind transmission that occurred between Sakyamuni Buddha and his disciple Mahakasyapa: the Buddha held up a flower before a large assembly and only Mahakasyapa smiled silently indicating his understanding. The Buddha then commented that Mahakasyapa has inherited his true Dharma eye.[13]

---

[13] Welter 2000: 97. The constructed story has the Buddha saying that Mahakasyapa has inherited 'the marvelous mind of Nirvana, the true form of the formless, the subtle dharma gate that does not rest on words or letters, but is a special transmission outside of scriptures'.

The transmission supposedly continued in a unitary lineage through 28 Indian Patriarchs and six Chinese Patriarchs before becoming multi-branched. It is, supposedly, always based on spiritual attainment and became institutionalized through the ritual of Dharma transmission.[14] Though the story seems simple and straightforward, it conceals a complex development and history.

Since the Zen Dharma-transmission mythology begins with and is hence completely dependent upon the wordless transmission between the historical Buddha Sakyamuni and his disciple Mahakasyapa, let us take a closer look at the presentation. It has been shown through detailed textual analysis how this foundation story developed over centuries,[15] which illustrates how the Zen lineage myth has been constructed over hundreds of years. A version of the story in a Zen text dated 801 CE does not include the Buddha holding a flower or Mahakasyapa's smile; instead, the true teaching of the Buddha was presented as the collection of sutras preached by the Buddha and recited by Ananda. At this early stage in the creation of the myth, the Buddha's teaching was presented as 'formless and subtle' (Welter 2000: 96), as with the canonical tradition as recited by Ananda, and was still identified as verbal. Even the later, important, Song Dynasty (960–1280) Zen 'Transmission of the Lamp' record of 1004 CE did not mention the flower and the smile. The flower and Mahakasyapa's smile is first mentioned in a Zen record of transmission in 1036 CE, in a text that also, interestingly, emphasized an interpretation of Zen as a tradition independent of Buddhist scriptural teaching. The first version of the story that explicitly emphasizes the wordless holding-up a flower and the smile transmission and the idea of 'a special transmission outside the teaching', occurs in an apocryphal text in 1077. There is no evidence that this 'scripture' existed prior to the Song Dynasty. This text connects the Mahakasyapa myth with the idea of 'a special transmission outside the teaching', an idea propagated by the Linji (Japanese – Rinzai) sect of Zen rising in power at that time with the Song court. Subsequently, this version of the story began to appear in Zen transmission records. It reached its full popularity only later in the unique Song Dynasty literary form, the collections of kung-an (koan) case studies, such as the

---

[14]   Zen is considered the most prominent form of Chinese Buddhism because it is the most Confucian. Its most eminent clerics and their patrons were from the literati class. They were all familiar with Confucian rituals, 'especially those connected to ancestor worship and its corollary, genealogy'. Zen's 'pseudo-history was stated in terms of genealogy', that is, Dharma transmission and unbroken lineage, when the study of genealogy in China was at its peak. For an in-depth look at the Chan/Confucian connection in the T'ang dynasty, see Jorgensen 1987: 89–134.

[15]   For the full study, see Welter 2000: 75–10.

Gateless Gate (*Wu-men kuan*), compiled in 1228 (Welter 2000: 98). Today, it is accepted as Zen history.

We see here how the myth, the literary creation of the first Zen transmission, developed over hundreds of years. Its acceptance as orthodox was closely connected to the rising power of the Linji Zen sect, in competition with other Zen factions with a differing view. The Linji understanding represented an iconoclastic, anti-canonical and anti-ritualistic understanding of Zen, independent of the tradition in the earlier Tang Dynasty. This new view was favoured by famous literati as well as the imperial court who wanted a freer, less classical form of writing (Welter 2006: 115–60).

Now that we have looked at the historical development of Zen's idealized legitimating myth, let us in contrast, look at the actual application of the Dharma-transmission ritual. Although Dharma transmission is understood as a Zen master recognizing that their student understands the wordless teaching passed from Sakyamuni to Mahakasyapa and then through the whole Zen lineage, it is in fact a more ambiguous and flexible concept than the mythology and Zen teaching would have us believe. Historically, it has been given for many reasons besides spiritual insight: for raising money to sustain a monastery, to establish and expand social connections, to spread a lineage, to enhance the teacher's prestige by having more and perhaps foreign Dharma heirs, to maintain the continuity of the lineage, to enhance the authority of a missionary, to acknowledge managerial skill, even as a favour for a friend, and so on.[16] These motivations are to a large measure in operation today. What is more, though Zen, both in the East and the West, in general makes superhuman claims for the master based on their spiritual attainment, in Sōtō Zen, the largest Zen sect in Japan, enlightenment is not at all a prerequisite for receiving Dharma transmission. Rather, only personal initiation between a master and disciple is required. Zen's mythology notwithstanding, in practice Dharma transmission is an institutional sanctioning of a teacher bestowing membership in a teaching lineage and may be no more than, as Buddhist scholar Holmes Welch said

---

[16]   There is much written on the many ways Dharma transmission has been understood. For the surprising uses of Dharma transmission, see Faure 1991: 14, 17, 221, 225. For transmission given to someone without ever having met or knowing if he would accept it, see Welch 1967: 315. For Dharma transmission being only dependent on the ritual of personal initiation, rather than whether the disciple realized enlightenment or not, see Bodiford 1993: 215. See also Lachs 1999: 14–18. See Downing 2001: 69 for Suzuki Roshi giving Dharma transmission as a favour to a friend, jokingly referred to as 'telephone transmission'.

'[getting] a Flash Gordon pin'.[17] There is no uniform understanding among Zen sects or even teachers within a sect as to what Dharma transmission is or implies.[18] Dharma transmission tells us therefore nothing of spiritual attainment or character or teaching skill, and it was designed that way from the beginning. However, the whole edifice of Zen is built on the notion of Dharma transmission. All the claims of an unbroken lineage of masters going back to the historical Buddha that are a prominent feature of Zen are based on Dharma transmission; so too, is the distorted understanding of the Zen master.

While modern-day masters are imputed to possess the outstanding qualities mentioned above, this mythology is not nurtured by the roshi alone. Frequently, the interests of the institution,[19] the Zen master and the students overlap. Arguably, both teachers and students internalize the Zen rhetoric of enlightened Zen master, Dharma transmission, and of the unbroken lineage going back to the historical Buddha and perhaps beyond.[20] The students expect the real teacher to be an ideal teacher and look forward to having such an ideal teacher lead and instruct them (Chang 1997: 209). The students who enter the practice, having read a myth, expect to find this myth as reality, and consequently will not recognize the myth for what it is. However, what they really find, all too often, is another story of ordinary and often flawed human behaviour.

---

[17]   Welch 1963: 93–149. Flash Gordon was a science fiction comic strip hero first drawn in 1934. It was later made into a film series and television serial. It seems to reincarnate periodically, even into the twenty-first century.

[18]   For instance, in the Sōtō sect in Japan, roughly 95 per cent of monks have Dharma transmission which is required to be abbot of a temple, usually inherited from their father. It is usually obtained after an average two-year-long stay in a monastery. The Rinzai sect requires going through their koan curriculum which at least theoretically requires having some awakening experience. What this experience actually means is entirely up to the individual roshi.

[19]   By the 'institution', I mean the organizations representing teachers in a given lineage or sect such as the Sōtō or Rinzai sects in Japan and America, or the Chogye Order, the largest sect of Korean Zen. These groups can be quite large. For instance, the White Plum Asanga, an association of roshi in the direct lineage of Maezumi Roshi, has over 110 roshi. The Sanbokyodan sect, popular in the West and started by Yasutani Roshi, has even more roshi as members.

[20]   The historical Buddha was Sakyamuni. His predecessor supposedly was Dipankara Buddha. The coming Buddha is to be Maitreya. Zen sometimes refers to the previous Buddhas as the six Buddhas preceding Sakyamuni. Other sects of Buddhism talk of 27 Buddhas preceding Sakyamuni. See Snyder 2006: 496.

Is this a Set Up?

Students, for their part, develop a desire for the master's recognition and approval. They learn to kow-tow to his authority and legitimacy. Further, they quickly learn that their advancement up the institutional ladder is completely dependent upon the master's good graces. Because the Dharma-transmitting Zen master acts not in his own name and authority, but rather as the only full delegate of the institution, with all the authority and power that entails, he also monopolizes the means to salvation. He has the sole, unquestioned authority to promote and sanction someone as a Zen master and to promote people to positions of power and respect within the group. On the other hand, he can marginalize at his will any student in his group.

Clearly, there might be multiple motives for 'not seeing' the master as he really is,[21] even if there is evidence for an absence of compassion or wisdom, or the presence of sexual improprieties, or self-serving behaviour, or a need for adoration or alcoholism, or questionable financial activities as could be witnessed over fifty years in western Zen. Instances of this will be discussed below. This 'not seeing' is supported by the Zen notion that all the words and actions of the Zen master are teachings, if only the student could get it.

Another aspect of the standard Zen story that colours social functioning at Zen centres is the belief that the master embodies the enlightened Buddha mind. This is a constant theme repeated in Zen teaching and biography, though at times stated in a slightly disguised fashion.[22] The Zen master, supposedly, is beyond the understanding of ordinary people because he always acts from the enlightened mind.[23] Once this view is accepted, all problems with a student's practice, with a master's questionable behaviour, or with the Zen centre are the result of the student's shortcomings. In particular, if they are troubled by a master's behaviour, the problem is solely with their perception.

---

[21] As mentioned earier in fn. 7, there are female roshi; however, I know of no sexual or financial abuse committed by them.

[22] The late Morinaga Roshi (d. 1995) repeats this idealization:, ' ... from master to master we trace our Zen lineage back to Sakyamuni Buddha, Inka is the seal of authentic transmission of Dharma, which is the Law of the universe and the teaching of Sakyamuni' (Morinaga 1988: 20).

[23] See Downing 2001: 254, 256, where if someone was confused or worried about something Baker did, the most senior students fell back on the mystery of Transmission. Baker had Transmission, which to them meant that Suzuki Roshi 'somehow had mystically invested his spirit in him'. Numerous scholars have discussed the many aspects and meanings of the construction of Chan history, including A. Cole, B. Faure, G. Foulk, J. McCrae, M. Schlutter, and A. Welter.

Since the mind of the Zen master is beyond the understanding of ordinary people, pointing out the shortcomings of the master is often interpreted as immaturity on the part of the student. This is exactly what happened at the San Francisco Zen Center (SFZC) in the early 1980s, as Baker Roshi's behaviour became more obviously self-serving and new students questioned his actions to older students. The older students assured the questioners that Baker had received Dharma transmission from Suzuki roshi and that the new students were just too immature to understand what they were seeing.[24] This dynamic was not limited to the SFZC.

While a Zen master in fact might possess admirable personal qualities, a multitude of insights, and the ability to both correct his students' practice and inspire them to practice diligently, the image held up in the standard model of Zen rather describes Zen mythology and ideology than the way a real person can, and does, actually live. The problem here is that the idealistic description of a Zen master/roshi is not of a long dead saint to be venerated for their supposed holiness and perfection, but rather, of a living person acting as teacher, guide and role model. The Zen master as the living legitimate representative of the Zen lineage and hence, the enlightened mind, is the definer and final arbiter of reality.[25] Having received Dharma transmission, he is thought to carry all the qualities inscribed in the social definition of the role (Bourdieu 1991: 121).

Hence, not getting it is, by definition, always a shortcoming of the student.[26]

---

[24]   Downing 2001: 255. *Shoes Outside the Door* gives the story of the Baker scandal and the trouble at the San Francisco Zen Center through eighty interviews of people directly involved. Baker was forced to resign when a scandal erupted in 1983 when it was discovered that he was having an affair with his best friend's wife. This opened the door to other long-simmering complaints such as his high living while having his students live at subsistence levels, his affairs with other students, bullying, betraying trust, and so on. The San Francisco Zen Center was the largest Zen Center in the US at the time.

[25]   Berger (1967: 32) writes: 'Religion legitimates so effectively because it relates the precarious reality constructions of empirical societies with ultimate reality.' The Zen master is the living embodiment of the historical Buddha and hence the enlightened mind that knows ultimate reality.

[26]   When Baker Roshi of the San Francisco Zen Center was told by a senior student at the last Board meeting that he did not listen well, his reply was 'If I have a problem listening, it is because you haven't taught me.' Another senior student added, 'Even that was our fault.' See Downing 2001: 49.

Selflessness?

Let us also look at one of the main tenets of the Zen master, that is, his supposed lack of self-interest, usually spoken of as his 'selflessness'. Whether actually stated or merely implied, every student of Zen is made to understand that the Zen master has no self-interest, only an interest in saving all sentient beings. That is to say, at a minimum, he is assumed to have only the best interest of the student at heart. This is not to say the master actually has no self-interests, only that they can easily be disguised beneath the Zen ideals of enlightened mind, compassion, selflessness and purity imputed to the Zen master.[27]

This claim of a lack of self-interest is not unique to Zen. Pierre Bourdieu writes that to talk of interests has a 'radically disruptive function: it destroys the ideology of disinterest, which is the ideology of clerics of every kind' (Bourdieu 1991: 215). One can see however, that this ideology is instrumental in separating the cleric from the flock, creating an absolute divide, whereas, in reality, there are continuous shades of grey. The cleric who lacks self-interest is viewed as being more capable of judging what is best for his flock, and consequently is more readily obeyed.

In Zen, selflessness is a quality consistently attributed to Zen masters from its earliest history to the present. This is not surprising, as in China the sage was distinguished from common people who were viewed as 'not being trusted, because by nature their actions are driven by self interest' (Barbalet 2012). It is, on the other hand, common to read of Zen masters receiving a purple robe from the emperor or a high-ranking official. Such a purple robe was the highest imperial honour awarded to Buddhist monks, as well as an honoured title such as 'Truly Enlightened, Great Master' or 'Buddha-Eye Chan Master'. It is also common to read that 'though he accepted these honors, it was as if he had not. Even though he wore the robe, it was as if he had not' (Welter 2006: 94). Similarly, into the present, we find the same claim to selflessness. The recently deceased Taiwanese Zen master Sheng Yen in his auto-hagiography presents himself as rising from humble beginnings, reaching a position as a world-famous, yet selfless Zen

---

[27] Eido Shimano Roshi, who had been implicated in numerous sexual scandals with his female students beginning in Hawaii in 1965 and continuing at least until 2010, said at a Board of Directors meeting, 'If I did not accept the sexual advances of female students, I would be creating worse karma than if I agreed to their advances.' This was reported by Shimano's Dharma heir Genjo Marinello who, after years of defending Shimano, realized that his teacher Eido Shimano Roshi was a sexual predator who must be banned from the Center's grounds and buildings http://www.zenforuminternational.org/viewtopic.php?f=7 3&t=3584&start=1600#p112310 (accessed 28 August 2012).

master, proclaiming 'I have met with world leaders and given a keynote address in the general assembly hall at the United Nations. My disciples include high-level officials in Taiwan. I was received as a VIP in motorcades in mainland China and Thailand. I am venerated by my followers' (Sheng Yen 2008: 171). Evidently, being selfless does not keep him from announcing his accomplishments to the world, both in the religious and secular arenas. Rather, it is by presenting his accomplishments under the persona of a Dharma-transmitted selfless Zen master that he can inform people of his worldly accomplishments, yet dismiss it as meaning nothing to him and still be taken at face value.

In contrast, an ordinary person without the stamp of authority of an orthodox Zen master, when enumerating his worldly accomplishments and international fame, but then immediately adding 'it doesn't make any difference to me', would be looked at as being self-congratulatory, duplicitous, or phoney. Indeed, this attribution of selflessness to the Zen master by the institutional mythology thus becomes impossible to refute (Bourdieu 1991: 124).

On the other end of the scale, it is common for Zen students to hear from their master: 'You have too much ego; you are too concerned about yourself.' A student's anger is understood as a problem of ego. Ego or sense of self, also referred to as 'ignorance' in Zen, is often seen as the internal enemy that is to be overcome or seen through by intense meditation. Are the master's words always spoken in the best interest of the student? Or are they sometimes spoken, whether consciously or unconsciously, to keep the student off-guard, pliable, or non-questioning? The master, however, sanctioned by the ritual of Dharma transmission is always allowed to express anger without being branded as having too much ego. The Zen master by definition is always teaching. Therefore, his anger too is a teaching and is understood by disciples as exactly what the student needs at that moment. This is a common understanding around Zen centres. The master's inducing a mind of self-criticism in the individual student often serves as a means of self-defence against the student's questioning of the institution, of the master's decisions, or his activities or views (ibid.: 219).

Zen Retreat: A Novel Situation

These mindsets are especially at work in interpersonal relations between the students with the master, which are heightened during the intensive week or longer meditation retreats (Jap. *sesshin*) and through private interviews (Jap.

sanzen/dokusan) with the master during these retreats.[28] This is especially so in the Rinzai or Sanbokyodan sects of Zen which emphasize koan[29] practice. This type of relationship with its inherent quality of domination is referred to by Pierre Bourdieu as being 'concealed beneath the veil of an enchanted relation'.[30]

During week-long meditation retreats, there is commonly nine or ten hours or more of seated meditation daily. Often students stay up later at night to meditate even more. There are up to five private interviews daily with the master in relation to the student's meditation practice and progress. Often there is much pressure put on students to have an awakening experience during the retreat. The private interview is especially important. It is considered by many students as the marrow or heart of Zen practice, especially for people doing koan practice. Some interview times are mandatory while for others, the students have the choice to attend or not. After waiting for her turn, the student enters the interview room, makes small bows and then deep bows to the floor and finally sits in front of the master. Incense is burning, while the master sits silently and solidly waiting. The student recites her koan if that is their practice, then presents her understanding. The master can choose to engage the student with a question or a word, or quickly dismiss the student with a quick ring of his bell. The master can harangue the student or even hit the student. He can encourage the student. He can dismiss her answer in a second with his bell, or even ring his bell and dismiss the student before she has had a chance to sit down. He can engage the student in dialogue or discuss the case. The master can move the student along to the next case in the curriculum,[31] or congratulate her insight. Everything is at the master's discretion. The student, after hours and days of meditation, after many private

---

[28]   One cannot overemphasize the importance of private interviews with the master, especially so during intensive meditation retreats.

[29]   A koan (Jp. from the Ch. *gong an*) is a story, statement, question, or interaction used as a subject of meditation or to test a student's progress. Koans defy rational solutions. Literally, the word means a public case, taken from Chinese law.

[30]   Bourdieu 1991: 24: 'The enchanted relationship is a form of symbolic violence, in contrast to overt violence; it is gentle, invisible violence ... chosen as much as undergone.' See also pp. 51–2, where Bourdieu importantly points out that symbolic violence can only be exerted on a person predisposed to feel it. It is dependent on the social conditions that produce the intimidator and the intimidated. Symbolic violence is violence wielded with tacit complicity between its victims and its agents, in so far as both remain unconscious of submitting to or wielding it. See Bourdieu 1996: 17.

[31]   For Zen groups affiliated with the Japanese tradition, aside from the Sōtō sect, there is an actual curriculum, a course of koans to go through. What 'go through' or pass means is another story, as there is a process of moving the student along that is not discussed and is fully at the master's discretion.

interviews, many quick rejections, repeatedly looking for the master to approve their insight, to approve their entire understanding of Zen, really of life itself, becomes desperate for the master's approval. All the student's years of meditation and numerous retreats are condensed into this short private interview with the master. The master is viewed as Buddha-like, judging the student from on high. For the students, everything – from moving along through the koan course to being recognized as senior students looking to become Zen masters – entirely depends on the master's decision. Her entire Zen career and chance to become a master depends solely on the master's discretion. The master's bell, which the students waiting their turn to enter the interview room also hear, becomes a symbol of the master's unquestioned authority and power. When the master rings his bell, the interview is over, period!

A System that Induces Problems

The idealized image of the Zen master is accepted by most western Zen practitioners. This belief in the ideal may serve the purpose of motivating the student to practice. However, imputing qualities and attainments to people that do not really possess them also has negative consequences. These consequences, including psychological, financial and sexual exploitation, are especially pronounced in the highly hierarchical setting of Zen.[32] These troubling consequences are not limited just to students. It also makes the master into a disingenuous role player, alienated in Peter L. Berger's sense.[33] The Zen master/roshi is viewed and treated as an idealized being, while in his mind he knows that the usual attractions, dislikes and upsets of life are still in operation. He

---

[32]   Because I have a number of papers available on the Internet, I have received many emails from people who feel they were deceived and hurt by Zen teachers. These people, sometimes in extreme distress, often feel confused because they cannot understand how there could be a Zen master and Zen social context that so misled and disempowered them. The list of major Zen centres involved in scandals is long, including but not limited to the Zen Studies Society in New York City, the San Francisco Zen Center, Moonspring Hermitage in Surrey, Maine, the Los Angeles Zen Center, the Rinzai–Ji Zen Center in Los Angeles, the Minneapolis Zen Center, the Kwan Um Zen Center in Providence, Rhode Island, the Order of Buddhist Contemplatives (OBC), in Mt. Shasta, California, the Toronto Zen Center, the Kanzeon Zen Center in Bar Harbor, Maine and 25 years later, a near-repeat performance in its new home in Salt Lake City, Utah, and the Mumon Kai Zen Center in Berlin.

[33]   Berger 1967: 81–101. The section 'Religion and Alienation' describes this process well. Berger points out that alienation may become a great source of power as it removes doubts and uncertainties that may cause problems and hesitancy in a non-alienated person.

may then view his students with disdain for viewing him as an idealized being while he knows he is much closer to ordinary with the usual assortment of human foibles.

The Dharma-transmitted masters' understanding of themselves and the behaviour they feel obliged to now adopt must conform to the role. This sanctifying by the institution marks a crossing of a line that induces a separation between the master and the flock. This line separates the master from the vast majority of Zen students, as well as from the general populace who will never receive Dharma transmission and hence, never be sanctified as Zen masters. It is easy to see how this socially induced discontinuity, made to appear objective by the ritual of Dharma transmission, can lead to delusional thinking in the Dharma-transmitted master. It is also easy to see how some Zen masters will demand and receive complete authority over their disciples with the concomitant abusive behaviour. I maintain that this is what we find all too often with Zen roshi.[34]

The ritual of Dharma transmission thus produces dramatic effects. It actually changes the transmitted people: first, it transforms the understanding others have of them and importantly, the behaviour they adopt towards them. They are now addressed as roshi, a title of great respect. Secondly, the ritual of Dharma transmission simultaneously appears to change the understanding the transmitted people have of themselves and the behaviour they perhaps feel obliged to adopt in order to conform to their new role.[35]

When analysing how this Zen dynamic plays out in the US, one must keep in mind that no living Zen master ever needs to make claims for their own attainment. Rather, this is done by holding up the great attainment of their teacher and their teacher's hallowed line of ancestors going back to the Buddha. Hence, it is never necessary for any particular Zen master to make claims concerning their own level of perfection. The Zen institution does it for the master by repeating the claim in the form of stories, transmission histories, koans, rituals, and so on. An environment is created that predisposes both students and masters to act in certain ways. In the end, both fall prey to these fantasies.

---

[34]   Master Hua, founder and leader of the City of Ten Thousand Buddhas in northern California, said to the author, 'I only speak the truth, if others can not take it, then that is their problem.' See also Gopfert 1999: 342, fn. 62. With regard to the six teachers in her study, Gopfert states, 'There is no evidence, however, that the teachers in these stories learned anything ... For the most part, these particular teachers continued harming other students.'

[35]   Bourdieu 1991: 117–26. See especially p. 119, where Bourdieu discusses the 'process of investiture'.

How did we get this Story: Is it Deception?

Through looking at the Zen system of legitimization and orthodoxy, I showed how the Zen institution presents itself to its followers in the West. I also referred to the history of this narrative, and the consequences of the unquestioning acceptance of this narrative.

But is Zen from its inception in early China presenting a fraudulent view of itself? The modern West has one view of biography and historiography, demanding historical and factual accuracy. However, in the Song dynasty (960–1280), when Zen history based on biography was written, fictionalization was often seen not as the falsification of events but as the verification of truth. These Chinese authors were not interested in the facts of the events, but rather, in the truth they wanted to convey. Their literary imagination was always ready to intervene to enhance the story (Welter 2008: 162–3). One can see this in the changing use of language and emphasis in different versions of the *Recorded Sayings of Linzi*,[36] or in the changes from the early versions of the *Platform Sutra* to the orthodox version written hundreds of years later in the Song dynasty,[37] or in the first Dharma-transmission story of Mahakasyapa discussed earlier. The compelling dramas we read in Zen texts are essentially literary creations that are far from accurate portrayals of the episodes depicted. As a kind of historical fiction, they appeal to the literary imagination to seduce the reader in the guise of historical episodes, dramatically retold (Welter 2006: 214). Song-era texts were also meant to strengthen the faith of followers. I do not think we can call this fraudulent, as it was written with a different understanding of how biography is to be used.[38]

---

[36]   Welter 2008: 133. 'The true man of no rank' is central to Linji's teaching. Yet, the variance with which it is presented in different sources, suggests a four-stage development, that is, it developed over time.

[37]   Schlutter 2007: 401–8. The orthodox version of the Platform Sutra, written some time between 1183 and 1225, not only contains new elements but also changes the focus of the earlier Dunhuang version. The Dunhuang version focuses on Huineng's authority as the Sixth Patriarch and the Platform Sutra as the epitome of his teaching, while in the later orthodox Song version lineage ideas are played out and Huineng's disciples are viewed as fully enlightened equals to Huineng. In the earlier versions, Huineng's disciples have little prestige or power.

[38]   Cole 2009. Cole discusses how literary tropes and lineage connections were borrowed from competing groups and from 'the dustbin of history', among other insightful ideas. Cole looks at early Zen from a critical textual analysis view rather than reading them for 'historical claims to owning truth'. There was, however, from its earliest history a strong

Another question is whether this depiction of Zen was maintained by the missionaries who brought Zen to the West, in order to intentionally deceive the converts – and if so, why. Did they just believe the mythology themselves as no doubt many did?

At the same time, some must have seen how westerners bought the mythology wholeheartedly, which also empowered the missionary who was delivering the story.

The ideas western Zen followers have about Zen and its main representative, the Zen master, were not created out of nothing, but reflect what has been presented to them by Zen missionaries, mostly coming from Japan after the Second World War. These Japanese missionaries, who brought the story to the West, did not change the essential story that was written in Song-dynasty China, nor did later Zen missionaries from Taiwan, Korea and Vietnam. In addition, westerners who went to Japan and then returned brought back the same story.[39]

The Great Promise

The Zen story presented to westerners is an enticing mythology: it offers a history and view of itself as concerned only with enlightenment, as opposed to western religions so often seen as self-serving, connected to and serving state powers, at least partially for their own gain and power. The Zen story, on the other hand, presented a picture of enlightened beings, Zen masters as being free-wheeling, iconoclastic, anti-ritualistic, anti-canonical, and being independent of governmental influence.

This mythology was fully embraced when Zen took hold in the US and the West in the late 1960s. It was a time of rising revolt against the war in Vietnam and the rising force for racial equality. Western society was in revolt on many fronts, especially among young people. The cities were burning and college campuses were being occupied. At the same time, the psychedelic drug

---

element of deception in Zen between Zen factions and their competing lineage claims, along with accompanying narratives.

[39] D.T. Suzuki was the most influential person bringing Zen to the West from Japan. Suzuki, being a scholar, most likely knew that Zen history was not as simple and straightforward as he presented it. Later, Shunryu Suzuki Roshi of the San Francisco Zen Center was the most influential Japanese missionary. Alan Watts and later Philip Kapleau with his book *Three Pillars of Zen* (1980) were extremely influential in the acceptance of Zen in the West. Later Zen missionaries came from China, Taiwan, Korea and Vietnam, but the story remained largely the same.

culture with its promise of expanding consciousness offering a radical break with establishment views and styles of living was readily available, of course with some serious side effects – for example, the 'bad trip'. Into this setting of cultural upheaval and calls for radical change came Zen and other eastern religions, offering time-tested alternatives.

Zen promised westerners instantaneous enlightenment often accompanied by the belief that this enlightenment would solve all problems. It also promised experienced living Zen masters as teachers, along with a powerful tool with a long-tested history for individual transformation: seated meditation. This combination of factors promised a safe and complete transformation in the midst of turmoil and uncharted territory. The Zen story as presented seemed an enticing programme, a perfect match for the times. The story was accepted mostly at face value, by academics, leading cultural figures, and other seekers.

It is safe to say that D.T. Suzuki and other early missionaries were good salesmen.

Who is Deceiving Whom?

The ritual of Dharma transmission was and is felt to be important to guard against fraud. It is understood to be the recognition of an enlightened person by another enlightened person, whereas, according to the tradition, an 'ordinary person' lacks this ability. Around Zen Centres, Dharma transmission is viewed almost as magic – instantly sanctifying and transforming the new master into an enlightened being. Along with the ritual of Dharma transmission, a newly recognized master receives a Dharma-transmission certificate, proving the master's orthodoxy and importantly, their lineage affiliation which is written on the certificate.[40] However, receiving Dharma transmission is a coveted goal for some Zen practitioners which can set in motion strange and competitive relationships among students. It can also engender a fawning and pandering

---

[40]   Bodiford 2008: 261–79. Bodiford discusses a medieval Japanese ritual of Dharma transmission and its most powerful symbol, the genealogical table [lineage chart] known as the 'blood lineage' chart. In this ritual, the blood comes by cutting the tongue. The blood lineage chart is still used in Dharma transmission rituals, though in a less esoteric and simpler form; at the least, the tongue is not cut. But like the past, lineages today are not chiselled in stone. In 2012, Ryutaku-ji monastery in Japan would not put in writing whether the scandal-coloured Eido Shimano Roshi was in their lineage or not. This was conveyed to me on 22 December 2010 in a private conversation with Kobutsu Malone, full priest, formerly associated with Eido Shimano.

attitude on the student's part directed towards the master, so that the student should be viewed in a 'good' light. This can induce cultivation of personality aspects and behaviours that the master favours. The student may seem more diligent but in fact is really less sincere. Some of these supposedly 'selfless' masters dangled advancement and perks in front of their students for their own advantage.[41] After all, the master is the sole unquestioned judge who determines whom among their students will get the coveted prize, that is, Dharma transmission or advance to positions of respect and privilege.

Thus Dharma transmission is not a measure against deception, but often encourages it.

What about Abuse?

Another question raised is whether this presentation of Zen, a folkloristic story in Far Eastern disguise, along with the structures of power it engenders, is conducive to abuse. As long as the story is presented as it is, with enlightened Zen masters beyond the understanding of ordinary people, completely selfless as orthodox Zen claims, then abuse is waiting to happen – and this is exactly what we find with the short history of Zen in North America and in Europe[42] to the present day. I even argue that it is a system that makes abusive behaviour virtually inevitable. Having Master Sheng Yen (d. 2009), a highly respected and orthodox Zen master, describe Zen masters in the following way is begging for trouble: ' … it should be remembered that the mind of the master is ever pure … and even if the master tells lies, steals, and chases women … he is still to be considered a [Zen] master as long as he scolds his disciples for their transgressions.'[43]

Sheng Yen informs us, at least implicitly, that the Zen master is beyond conventional morality and understanding.[44] Such a view of a respected Zen master makes it impossible for a student to distinguish abusive or even mentally

---

[41]   See Downing 2001 to see how Baker Roshi used his students' desire for advancement and perks to manipulate them and keep them in their place. He also marginalized one woman who questioned him by announcing that she was mentally disturbed.

[42]   See Hamacher 2012. He describes two cases of scandalous Zen masters, one in New York City (Eido Shimano) and one in Berlin (Dr Klaus Zernickow, also known as Sotetsu Yuzen). See also Lachs 2002 for a look at the Baker Roshi case.

[43]   Sheng Yen stated this in a public talk at his centre in Queens, NY. It was also printed in his centre's magazine, *Ch'an Newsletter*, 38 (1984): 1–2.

[44]   Sheng Yen was considered a conservative and well-educated Zen master, having received a PhD in Buddhist studies in Japan, though coming from Taiwan and supposedly living as a celibate Chinese monk.

disturbed behaviour from helpful and supportive behaviour or teaching. While it is completely disempowering of students, it is, however, an invitation to charlatans and sociopaths.

This is evidenced by the fact that often self-serving behaviour by Zen masters is explained away as 'crazy wisdom': according to this notion, the abusive behaviour of supposedly highly enlightened beings only seems self-serving because ordinary folk cannot understand such highly evolved people. The interpretation of 'crazy wisdom' thus justifies all manner of abusive and self-serving behaviour. An extreme example of such a reinterpretation of abusive behaviour as 'crazy wisdom' is the following remark by a student of Shimano roshi in 2012 in connection to the ongoing Eido Shimano scandal: 'Let me say, I do not consider myself worthy of examining the behaviour of a living Buddha ... These alleged affairs, should they be true, most probably are a Zen teaching.'[45]

Here we see the most idealistic elements of Zen mythology internalized by this student. Interestingly, virtually all of this supposed behaviour labelled 'crazy wisdom' seems to bring pleasure to and to serve the needs of the 'wise one' acting so, often to the detriment of others and themselves. Similar behaviour displayed by other people would be called self-serving, a weakness, or an addiction of some sort.[46]

An Alternate Reality

The strong element of hierarchy created by the idea of Dharma transmission along with Zen's legitimating story and its constant repetition often creates an alternative reality at Zen centres. There is delusion on the parts of both the master and the students. The Zen master starts to believe the constantly repeated Zen mythology encouraged by having scores of adoring and reverential followers. Having so much power changes people and as we have witnessed, abuse of one form or another is waiting to happen. The master's followers look to preserve their years of investment in the practice and perhaps their advancement, to maintain the wish of having such a highly evolved teacher, to keep the illusion of being separate and beyond the understanding of the rest of society, among

---

[45] This remark was part of an open letter to the Rubin Museum of Art in New York City, dated 30 August 2012 in relation to the scandal surrounding Eido Shimano Roshi. See Hamacher 2012: 32.

[46] The degree of delusion is difficult to imagine – for good examples, see Hamacher's paper, 'Zen has No Morals' (2012), or Michael Downing's book, *Shoes Outside the Door* (2001), both mentioned earlier in this chapter.

other reasons. The student may just be afraid to be on their own, after years of a connection to a group with an all-wise leader and perhaps holding a position with prestige and privilege within the organization. Some, after years of being part of a large group, feel they cannot or are unprepared to function well in society at large. Some may feel other Zen groups are too inferior to even consider a switch, while others may embrace the idea of an all-wise master as a way of avoiding being responsible for their own lives.[47] A manifestation that hints at this is the answer, 'roshi says ... ' heard around Zen centres when asking a student a question.

Western Zen Roshi

Even though at some Zen centres today we see less emphasis on the all-wise Zen roshi, the basic underlying legitimating story is still there, waiting for the next charismatic or delusional leader to use it to their own advantage. In a sense, Zen is trapped in its own creation mythology waiting for the next case of abuse.

Another question in this context is what one may ask of modern western Zen roshi, seeing that a large corpus of writing in western languages has been available for roughly twenty years, showing the constructed nature of Zen history and hence, Zen biography, especially so of its iconic figures. This constructed story created in Song-dynasty China, that matched the political and religious needs of that time and place, is still repeated today as if it really happened. It is certainly dishonest and deceptive for western teachers to continue in this fashion, as it is widely known to be a fiction. That is, it is accepted as a fiction by virtually every modern western scholar of Zen. Western roshi claiming ignorance that Zen's legitimating story is mythology must possess an intention not to know. That these stories are fictions does not mean they are unimportant. It is, however, problematic to present them as if they really happened.

The Zen stories that have attracted westerners, though seemingly descriptive, are in fact prescriptions for how a Zen master should sound and behave. Hence, it is only the Zen master, as the authorized representative of the institution, sanctioned through Dharma transmission, who can speak in the recognized Zen fashion. Often what we see at Zen centres closely resembles performance,

---

[47]   For a most interesting example of the dynamics and abuse that can occur at a Zen centre, see www.sasakiarchive.com (accessed 14 March 2014) for a view of the fifty-year history of Sasaki Roshi in the US.

theatre by both the roshi and his disciples.[48] Indeed, as the recognized legitimate representative of the institution, as the authority, the roshi's words may not lose their power just because they were not understood.

On the other hand, roshi can be seen as victims of deception too. When we think of Zen masters, we usually have in mind the literary created images mentioned in Zen texts. As both the fictive literary Zen master and the living master have the same title, we are led to believe they have the same qualities. Hence, much of the authority of the present-day Zen master is the reflected authority of the iconic figures who all bear the title 'Zen master'. This title is constantly mentioned in Zen talks, stories and koans which depict the words and actions of the famous Zen masters of the past. Though we have little idea what the term 'Zen master' actually means in relation to a specific person, in this way, along with services, rituals, meditation, special robes, private meetings with the master, and so on, a set of dispositions is created in both the master and the disciples, which elevate the Zen master to the level of the literary created fictive Zen masters. However, it is also very attractive to the master: the living master always gets the final word. The master gets to comment on and judge the words and actions of all the famous masters of the past, even of the historical Buddha. The master also has tremendous authority over his students along with great prestige. It is a too highly desired position to let go or to not cultivate in the first place. The view of the Zen master as an all-wise enlightened being beyond your understanding is thus an institutionally anchored deception.

References

Barbelet, J. (2012). 'Review of *Philosophy and Religion in Early Medieval China*', *SUNY Series in Chinese Philosophy and Culture* (July), eds A.K.L. Chan and Y.-K. Lo. Albany: State University of New York Press, July http://www.h-net.org/reviews/showrev.php?id=35893 (accessed 14 March 2014).
Berger, P. (1967). *The Sacred Canopy*. New York: Doubleday.
Bodiford, W.M. (1993). *Soto Zen in Medieval Japan*. Honolulu: University of Hawaii Press.

---

[48] See Downing 2001: 234. When it was suggested that a senior student leave for a time, he thought, 'I was horrified at the thought. Leave Zen Center? Leave show business? No.' On ibid., p. 154, another student is quoted as commenting about the Zen Center, 'If you are not walking around wearing a black or brown tablecloth [robe] with no hair, you are not serious. Really it is laughable.'

— (2008). 'Dharma Transmission in Theory and Practice', in *Zen Ritual: Studies of Zen Buddhist Theory in Practice*, eds S. Heine and D.S. Wright. New York: Oxford University Press.

Bourdieu, P. (1991). *Language and Symbolic Power*. Cambridge MA: Harvard University Press.

— (1996). *On Television*. New York: The New Press.

Chang, J. (1997). *Mysticism and Kingship in China*. Cambridge: Cambridge University Press.

Cleary, T. (1990). *Book of Serenity: One Hundred Zen Dialogues*, 3rd edn. Hudson, NY: Lindisfarne Press.

— and J.C. Cleary (1977). *The Blue Cliff Record*. Boston, MA: Shambhala Publications, Inc.

Cole, A. (2006). 'Simplicity for the Sophisticated: Rereading the Daode Jing for the Polemics of Ease and Innocence', *History of Religion*, 46(1): 1–49.

— (2009). *Fathering Your Father: The Zen of Fabrication in Tang Buddhism*. Berkeley, Los Angeles and London: University of California Press.

Downing, M. (2001). *Shoes Outside the Door: Desire, Devotion, and Excess at San Francisco Zen Center*. Washington, DC: Counterpoint.

Faure, B. (1991). *The Rhetoric of Immediacy*. Princeton, NJ: Princeton University Press.

Foulk, G.T. (1993). 'Myth, Ritual, and Monastic Practice in Sung Ch'an Buddhism', in *Religion and Society in T'ang and Sung China*, eds P.B. Buckley and P.N. Gregory. Honolulu: University of Hawaii Press.

Gopfert, C.R. (1999). 'Student Experiences Of Betrayal In The Zen Buddhist Teacher/Student Relationship', PhD dissertation, Institute of Transpersonal Psychology, Palo Alto, California.

Green, J. (1998). *The Recorded Sayings of Zen Master Joshu*. Boston, MA: Shambhala Publications, Inc.

Hamacher, C. (2012). '"Zen Has No Morals": The Latent Potential for Corruption and Abuse, as Exemplified by Two Recent Cases', International Association of Cultic Studies Annual Conference, Montreal, Canada, July http://www.thezensite.com/ZenEssays/CriticalZen/Zen_Has_No_Morals.pdf (accessed 14 March 2014).

Jorgensen, J. (1987). 'The Imperial Lineage of Ch'an Buddhism: The Role of Confucian Ritual and Ancestor Worship in Ch'an's Search for Legitimation in the mid-Tang Dynasty', *Papers in Far Eastern History*, (35) (March): 89–134.

Kapleau, P. (1980). *The Three Pillars of Zen: Teaching, Practice, and Enlightenment*. Garden City, NY: Anchor Press/Doubleday.

Lachs, S. (1999). 'Means of Authorization: Establishing Hierarchy in Chan Buddhism in America', American Academy of Religion Conference, Boston, MA, November, 1999 http://www.h-net.org/~buddhism/aar-bs/1999/lachs.htm#_ftn1 (accessed 21 August 2012).

— (2002). 'Richard Baker and the Myth of the Zen Roshi' http://www.thezensite.com/ZenEssays/CriticalZen/Richard_Baker_and_the_Myth.html (accessed 27 August 2012).

— (2006). 'The Zen Master in America: Dressing the Donkey With Bells and Scarves', American Academy of Religion Conference, Washington, DC, 18 November http://www.hsuyun.org/docs/english/pdf/DressingTheDonkey.pdf (accessed 15 July 2012).

McRae, J.R. (2003). *Seeing Through Zen*. Berkeley and Los Angeles: University of California Press.

Morinaga, S. roshi (1988). 'My Struggles to Become a Zen Monk', in *Tradition and Transmission*, ed. K. Kraft. New York: Grove Press, pp. 13–29.

Okamura, S. (2010). *Realizing Genjokoan: The Key to Dogen's Shobogenzo*. Somerville, MA: Wisdom Publications.

Sahn, S. Zen Master (1976). *Dropping Ashes on the Buddha: The Teachings of Zen Master Seung Sahn*. New York: Grove Press.

Schlutter, M. (2007). 'Transmission and Enlightenment in Chan Buddhism Seen Through the Platform Sutra', *Chung-Hwa Buddhist Journal*, 20: 379–409.

— (2008). *How Zen Became Zen*. Honolulu: University of Hawaii Press.

Sheng Yen (2008). *Footprints in the Snow: The Autobiography of a Chinese Buddhist Monk in New York*. New York: Doubleday.

Shibayama, Z. (1974). *Zen Comments on the Mumonkan*. New York, NY: Harper and Row.

Snyder, D. (2006). *The Complete Book of Buddha's Lists – Explained*. Las Vegas, NV: Vipasanna Foundation.

Solomon, N. (1999). 'Norman Solomon vs. The Propaganda System', *Washington Free Press*, 39 (May/June) http://wafreepress.org/39/propaganda.html (accessed 23 July 2012).

Suzuki, S. (1970). *Zen Mind, Beginners Mind*. New York and Tokyo: Weatherhill.

Victoria, Brian (1997). *Zen At War*. Tokyo: Weatherhill.

Welch, H. (1963). 'Dharma Scrolls and Succession of Abbots in Chinese Monasteries', *T'oung Pao International Journal of Chinese Studies*, 50 (1963): 93–149.

— (1967). *Buddhism in China: 1900–1950*. Cambridge, MA: Harvard University Press.

Welter, A. (2000). 'Mahakasyapa's Smile', in *The Koan*, eds S. Heine and D. Wright. New York: Oxford University Press.

— (2006). *Monks, Rulers, and Literati: The Political Ascendancy of Chan Buddhism*. New York: Oxford University Press.

— (2008). *The Linji lu and the Creation of Chan Orthodoxy*. New York: Oxford University Press.

Yampolsky, P.B. (1967). *The Platform Sutra of the Sixth Patriarch*. New York: Columbia University Press.

Index